DUDLEY PUBLIC LIBRARIES

The loan of this book may be renewed if not required by other readers, by contacting the library from which it was borrowed.

Recent titles in the series

A BRIEF HISTORY OF

ROMAN BRITAIN

JOAN P. ALCOCK

For Maureen Walsh, an encourager to greater efforts

Constable & Robinson Ltd
3 The Lanchesters
162 Fulham Palace Road
London W6 9ER
www.constablerobinson.com

First published in the UK by Robinson,
an imprint of Constable & Robinson, 2011

A copy of the British Library Cataloguing in Publication
Data is available from the British Library

ISBN 978-1-84529-728-2

1 3 5 7 9 10 8 6 4 2

Printed and bound in the UK

CONTENTS

LIST OF ILLUSTRATIONS

CHRONOLOGY

BC

55   First invasion of Britain by Caesar

54   Second invasion by Caesar

51   Gaul made a province from *mare nostrum* to Oceanus

34   Augustus intended to invade Britain, but concentrated on the Rhineland

AD

7   Dubnovellanus and Tincommius sought help from Augustus

16   Roman soldiers wrecked on British coast get help from Britons

39   Cunobelin's son, Adminius, fled to seek help from Emperor Gaius. Gaius made preparations to invade Britain but desisted

40   Death of Cunobelin

43   Verica fled to Rome for help

43   Invasion of Aulus Plautius with Legions II Augusta, IX Hispana, XIV Gemina and XX. Visit of Claudius

47–52   Governorship of Ostorius Scapula

48   Colchester was founded as a *colonia*

49   Romans extracted lead from Mendips

52–8   Governorship of Didius Gallius

51   Caratacus fought the Romans in North Wales, was defeated and fled to the protection of Cartimandua. Betrayed and taken captive to Rome.

55   Exeter founded

57–8	Governorship of Quintus Veranius
58–61	Governorship of Suetonius Paullinus
60	Defeat of the Druids on Anglesey
60–61	Rebellion of Boudicca. Legion XIV given title of Gemina Martia Victrix and Legion XX given title Valeria Victrix
61	Gaius Julius Alpinus Classicianus arrived as procurator
61–3	Governorship of Petronius Turpillius
63–9	Governorship of Trebillius Maximus
67	Legion XIV withdrawn from Britain and replaced by Legion II Adiutrix Pia Fidelis
69	Year of the Four Emperors
69	Problems in the Brigantian territory required help from the army
69–71	Governorship of Vettius Bolanus
71–4	Governorship of Petillius Cerealis
72	Probable date of the fortress at York and the establishment of Aldborough
74–7/8	Governorship of Julius Frontinus. Defeat of the Silures and foundation of Caerleon and Chester forts. Development of Bath as a spa and religious centre
77/8–83/4	Governorship of Gnaeus Julius Agricola
78	Defeat of the Ordovici; policy of Romanization began
79	Verulamium became a *municipium*
81	Forts laid out along Forth–Clyde Isthmus
82	Fort built at Inchtuthil
84	Battle of Mons Graupius
84	Withdrawal of Legion II Adiutrix Pia Fidelis from Britain
90/92	Lincoln founded as a *colonia*
96	Gloucester founded as a *colonia*
107	Last recording of Legion IX in Britain. Probably withdrawn to the east

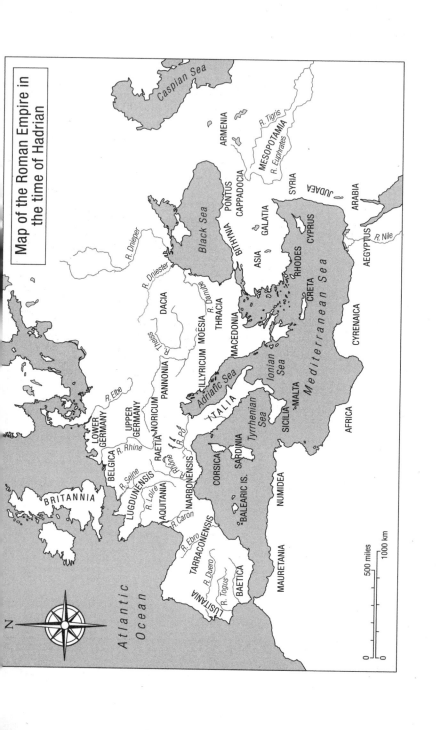

Map of the Roman Empire in the time of Hadrian

Map of the Saxon Shoreforts and the Yorkshire Signal Stations

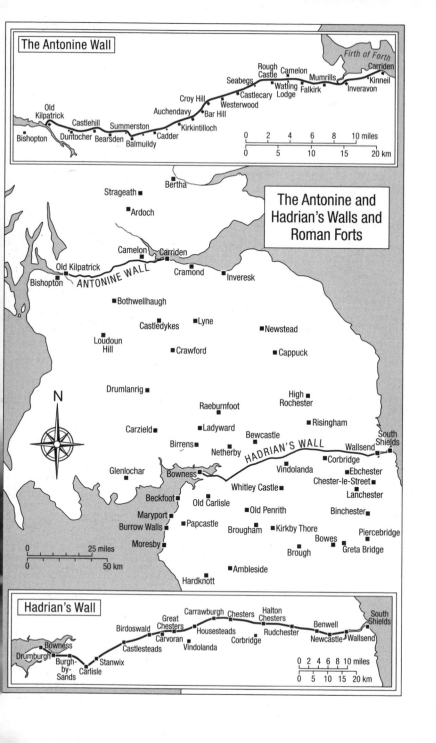

The Antonine Wall

Firth of Forth

Carriden
Kinneil
Rough Castle
Camelon
Mumrills
Seabegs
Watling Lodge
Inveravon
Falkirk
Croy Hill
Castlecary
Westerwood
Auchendavy
Bar Hill
Old Kilpatrick
Castlehill
Summerston
Kirkintilloch
Bishopton
Duntocher
Bearsden
Cadder
Balmuildy

0   2   4   6   8   10 miles
0   5   10   15   20 km

The Antonine and Hadrian's Walls and Roman Forts

Bertha
Strageath
Ardoch
Camelon
Carriden
Old Kilpatrick
Cramond
Bishopton
ANTONINE WALL
Inveresk
Bothwellhaugh
Castledykes
Lyne
Newstead
Loudoun Hill
Crawford
Cappuck
Drumlanrig
High Rochester
Raeburnfoot
Risingham
Carzield
Ladyward
South Shields
Birrens
Bewcastle
Netherby
HADRIAN'S WALL
Wallsend
Corbridge
Vindolanda
Ebchester
Glenlochar
Bowness
Chester-le-Street
Beckfoot
Whitley Castle
Lanchester
Old Carlisle
Maryport
Old Penrith
Binchester
Burrow Walls
Papcastle
Brougham
Kirkby Thore
Moresby
Bowes
Piercebridge
Brough
Greta Bridge
Ambleside
Hardknott

N

0   25 miles
0   50 km

Hadrian's Wall

Carrawburgh
Chesters
Halton Chesters
South Shields
Great Chesters
Birdoswald
Housesteads
Benwell
Carvoran
Rudchester
Bowness
Castlesteads
Vindolanda
Corbridge
Newcastle
Wallsend
Drumburgh
Burgh-by-Sands
Carlisle
Stanwix

0 2 4 6 8 10 miles
0   5   10   15   20 km

Tribes of Britain in the
first century BC

Plan of North Leigh Villa

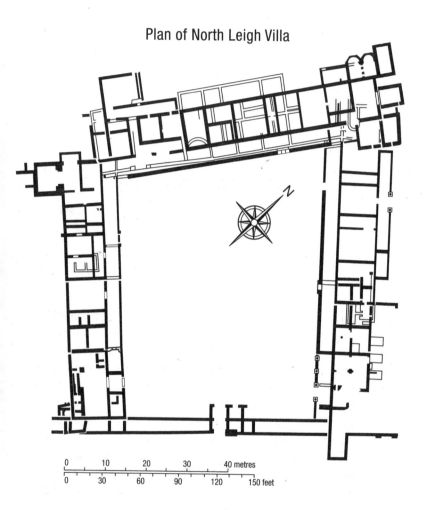

N

0   10   20   30   40 metres
0   30   60   90   120   150 feet

I

PRE-ROMAN BRITAIN

Britain prior to the Roman conquest was a country peopled by Celtic tribes, often at war with each other but following a civilized way of life on their own terms. Much of the evidence for their areas of control comes from the second-century Greek geographer Ptolemy, whose literary data has often been supported by archaeological excavations. The Cantiaci covered the area of modern Kent and part of Sussex as far as the Pevensey district and may even have stretched beyond the Thames as far as the Chiltern Ridge. Caesar mentioned four kings who probably ruled different regions and who were hostile to Rome. The Stour, the Medway and the Darent divided three of these regions; the fourth was probably in the Weald. There were three major *oppida* (or hillforts) in Kent – Bigbury, the precursor of Canterbury, which was almost certainly destroyed by Caesar, Quarry Hill, the precursor of Rochester, and Oldbury, which controlled the Darent Valley. All these hillforts date to the early first century BC.

Most of the area was covered by isolated settlements and farmsteads usually surrounded by enclosures, many lying in the Medway and Stour valleys. The proximity of the area to the English Channel suggests commercial and possible tribal links with Gaul, and Caesar mentioned that the chief of the Suessiones, a tribe in north-east Gaul, had some control in Britain. Coinage found in Kent includes both locally struck and Gallo-Belgic coins indicating commercial contacts. As the Cantiaci were hostile to Caesar this may have affected subsequent relations with Rome. There are few deposits indicating rich imports and only the Aylesbury and Swarling cemeteries have shown any sign of wealthy burials. Towards the end of the first century BC coinage stops, which may have been due to expansion of the Atrebates into the area. Later coins of the Catuvellauni take their place as the area came under the control of that tribe, which also may have deliberately controlled their trading links.

Ptolemy located the tribe of the Regni to the west of the Cantiaci. They were mainly centred on west and east Sussex as far as the Pevensey area. Their most important lands stretched from the edge of the Hampshire uplands to the cliffs of Beachy Head. Although the scarp slopes were uninhabitable they provided pasture for livestock. Settlements varied from large villages to isolated farmsteads, growing mainly wheat and barley and herding cattle, sheep and pigs. By the end of the first century BC much of the land suitable for cultivation had been colonized.

There were some *oppida*, which may have been founded in the Neolithic period, for example the Trundle near to Chichester. Formidable *oppida* in Sussex existed at Selsey, Chanctonbury Rings and Cissbury, but smaller ones were added so that by the first century BC most of the prominent chalk hilltops had some protective structure with ramparts and ditches. These could have been used as tribal groupings for defence against hostile tribes or as stock enclosures. The fertile region attracted immigrants from the continent and there was an almost continual arrival of the tribe of the Belgae from Gaul, probably as a result of Caesar's activities. This increased in the 60s and 50s BC, which links with Caesar's comments that the chieftains of the Bellovaci, a Belgic tribe, fled to Britain to escape his advance into their territory. These incomers seemed to have settled in the area of the Thames Valley. The Belgae soon formed a well-defined group west of the Regni. Their main territory included an *oppidum* near the future town of Winchester and was extended later as far as Calleva. They had political and cultural links with both the Regni and the Atrebates as indicated by finds of pottery and coinage.

Caesar mentioned that Commius, who had helped him on his second reconnaissance of Britain in 54 BC, ruled the tribe of the Atrebates in Gaul. Later Commius supported the Gallic chieftain Vercingetorix, and, when the latter was defeated, Commius fled to Britain together with his tribe. They settled in eastern Berkshire, Hampshire and Wiltshire, making a base at Calleva, the pre-Roman centre of Silchester. A large number of Celtic coins and evidence of settlement was found under the Roman town and also at Winchester. The territory may have extended as far as Dorchester-on-Thames but the Catuvellauni later absorbed this area. Hillforts include Bury Hill (Hampshire) and, in Wiltshire, Boscombe Down and West Yarnbury, which were probably defensive sites in times of trouble.

The Catuvellaunian tribe occupied a large area covering parts of Hertfordshire, Berkshire, Buckinghamshire, Oxfordshire, Cambridgeshire and Northamptonshire, and stretching into the Nene Valley and the Fenlands. Archaeological evidence is ambiguous about their origins, and the distribution of their coinage may represent trade and exchange rather than tribal immigration. Individuals probably drifted into the area before forming tribal communities. Yet their origins may lie in Caesar's comments that a group of the Belgae had raided Britain and settled in the southern area.

Caesar never mentioned the tribe by name but gives details of Cassivellaunus whose power lay north of the Thames and who founded a dynasty that became a major political force in pre-Roman Britain. Caesar implies that Cassivellaunus had been continually at war with other tribes but his influence was such that when the Romans arrived in 54 BC he united the tribes in resistance to a common enemy. He seems therefore to have been a king or a powerful tribal chieftain, who may have had a fortress at Wheathampstead. His power did not last long as nothing more is heard of him after his defeat by Caesar, which probably led to demise in his authority. Later, another leader, Tasciovanus, emerged with a centre at Verulamium but with territory covering Northamptonshire and central and south Berkshire. Roman goods found in cemeteries seem to indicate excellent contacts with Rome, which were continued by Tasciovanus' successor Cunobelin who established a capital at Camulodunum.

Ptolemy placed the tribe of the Trinovantes to the east by the Thames estuary with land stretching from at least Camulodunum to the mouth of the river. Caesar mentioned them, and implied that they were the most powerful tribe in Britain. Immigrants from the continent, who began to exploit the iron ore areas, probably joined native groups, and scattered groups of iron-working people are noted from the seventh to sixth centuries BC at West Harling (Norfolk) and Sheepen (Essex). Sherds of hand-made pottery, based on continental metal prototypes, are common, in styles brought by newcomers from north-west France such as a dark fabric with a burnished exterior. A few hillforts were constructed in south and west Essex – Leighton Camp, Ambresbury Bank and Wallbury Camp – all defended by ramparts and ditches.

In the late second century the Belgae began to move into the area, bringing with them gold coins in the Gallo-Belgic style, but the main wave of immigration did not appear until about 100 BC. In 54 BC Caesar relied on the Trinovantes as his ally as they were the traditional enemy of the Catuvellauni, especially as Cassivellaunus had defeated a Trinovantian king, whose son, Mandubracius, had fled to Caesar for protection.

After Caesar's departure in 55 BC the Trinovantes enjoyed a good relationship with Rome, honouring treaty obligations and establishing trading relations. Graves excavated at Welwyn (Hertfordshire), Welwyn Garden City (Hertfordshire) and Mount Bures have produced amphorae once holding imported wine and other goods imported from Rome. Later the Trinovantes joined the Catuvellauni to form a federation and seemingly established a joint capital at Camulodunum under Cunobelin, which developed into a thriving industrial, religious and cultural site. Much of their wealth came from salt. At least 1,000 saltern sites have been found which operated for different lengths of time between 400 BC and AD 450, most of these being active in about 100 BC.

Although given a tribal name, the Durotriges or the Durotrages appear to have been composed of smaller groupings and their name is found later on inscriptions on Hadrian's Wall where some of the tribe helped in rebuilding the Wall. The tribal area was Dorset and part of Somerset, giving an outlet to the Bristol Channel, but may have stretched as far as the New Forest. Hillforts in Dorset at Maiden Castle, Hod Hill, Hambledon Hill and Badbury Castle contained nucleated settlements of small huts set alongside streets. These also provided defensive places in time of tribal warfare and were to play a major role against the Roman advance along the southern coast.

The tribe seems to have established trading links with Armorica and Brittany and this gave them access to the Atlantic and Mediterranean areas with major trading posts at Hengistbury Head and at Poole Harbour. Imports included large quantities of amphorae from Italy. Exports included iron ore, probably obtained from the Mendips on the border with the Dobunni tribe, copper and tin. Shale, suitable for jewellery and furniture, was obtained from the Kimmeridge area, grain from the Wessex hinterland and salt from the seashore. A pottery industry produced black burnished ware; pottery imports of north-west French cordoned ware were reproduced especially around Poole Harbour. In the second half of the first century BC, however, probably because of Caesar's advances into Armorica, trade declined leading to the collapse of the lucrative Channel trade. As well as trade, farming played a major role. Grain, grown on small farms, and large numbers of animal bones suggest that cattle not only supplied food but also provided excess meat and leather for trade.

The Dobunni, according to Ptolemy, lay to the north of the Durotriges, which would place them in the Worcestershire, North Somerset and Gloucestershire regions, but they seem also to have stretched along the Upper Thames valley, probably making contact with the Atrebates in the west. Atrebatian coins, stamped with their ruling kings, Bodvoc and Comux, are found in their territory and later Catuvellaunian coins appear. The Dobunni began to copy their coins about 35 BC.

Major hillforts were sited at Worlebury (Somerset), Worcester, Bredon Hill (Worcestershire) and Wappenbury (Warwickshire), which may have been important meeting points for the Dobunni and their northern neighbours the Cornovii. Their territory also included the sacred springs at Bath dedicated to the goddess Sul that were later to be exploited by the Romans. This was also an important crossing point on the River Avon. Iron was extracted in the Forest of Dean and there was possibly some rivalry with the Durotriges for control of the lead mines in the Mendips.

The Dumnonii, according to Ptolemy, were situated west of the Durotriges, seemingly in the south-west peninsular of Cornwall and Devon and therefore making them relatively isolated. This isolation possibly kept them from being a menace to neighbouring tribes and there is little evidence of Roman occupation in the region, apart from forts at Nanstallon and St Austell. They developed no coinage of their own and seem to have used those of the Durotriges and the Dobunni. Their main defensive structures were cliff castles and storage took place in *fogous* (underground rooms) similar to those found in Armorica. A cross-Channel and Atlantic trade had been established, mainly based on the export of tin and some lead obtained from trade with the Dumnonii. Isolated settlements in Devon were composed of huts set within multiple ditched enclosures for defence. In Cornwall, courtyard houses were surrounded by massive stonewalls. Some were placed together, as at Chysauster and Carn Euny, to form villages.

Ptolemy placed the tribe of the Coritani (or Corieltauni) throughout Leicestershire and Lincolnshire and probably Rutland and most of Warwickshire. Their principal sites seem to have been in Leicestershire where Iron Age pottery was discovered in large quantities. Other sites with similar pottery included Ancaster and Old Sleaford in Lincolnshire. Old Sleaford was the site of an Iron Age mint where over 3,000 broken clay moulds testified to Coritanian coins being cast there. Large settlements with circular houses and ditched enclosures were the norm, one being excavated at Dragonby near Scunthorpe. Smaller settlements are found throughout the region, most consisting of small huts surrounded by a bank and ditch. One at South Ferriby on the south side of the Humber could have been a trading post as well as commanding this part of the Humber. There also seems to have been a strong cultural connection between the Coritani and the Belgae in the south but this must have been through trade, as there was no hint of invasion.

There are few hillforts, some of the most important being in Leicestershire at Breedon Hill and Burrough Hill. None of the larger sites was surrounded by elaborate defences so it would appear that they did not fear threats from any neighbouring tribes; slight defences were to keep out animals and isolated intruders. Mixed farming took place on the light soils of the river valleys and on the limestone of the Jurassic ridge. Iron-working may have determined the site of some settlements, notably in south-west Lincolnshire, Rutland and Leicestershire, and good quality iron would have had a ready market, especially for exchange with neighbouring tribes.

The tribe of the Cornovii was north of the Dobunni in the Shropshire–Cheshire area. Much of this area, especially in the south-west, was hill country with volcanic intrusions such as the Wrekin and the Clee Hills. The tribe had no distinguishing characteristics and seemingly had no distinctive metalwork or pottery except for that produced by small groups of potters working in the Malvern Hills region. There is little or no evidence of continental connections.

There was a major hillfort on the Wrekin and a group of hill-forts on the Welsh Marches – the Berth, Breiddin, Credenhill and Caer Caradoc being the main ones. Titterstone Clee commanded the Clee Hills and the approach to the Severn Valley from the south-east. In the north there were fewer hill-forts. Old Oswestry (Shropshire) was one of the largest and Maiden Castle, Bickerton (Cheshire), was placed on the ridge of hill dominating the central part of the Cheshire Plain.

There is some evidence of pre-Roman salt extraction in Cheshire and some lead extraction activity at Linley, but, as much of the land was hilly, pastoral activities dominated. Few traces of extensive cultivation have been found, one of the most intensive being on the south of the Long Mynd in Shropshire. There are examples of large enclosures, in which were rectang-ular or circular huts, but no large townships until the Romans occupied the area and moved the tribespeople from the Wrekin. They grouped round the Roman fort of Wroxeter, which later became Viroconium or *civitas Cornoviorum*, thus identifying the name of the tribe.

Parisian culture, in the north-east, is defined by cemeteries of the so-called Arras culture, which began in the mid fifth century BC in the east Yorkshire region. A series of small long barrows, some surrounded by ditches, conceal burials, some with a person buried with a chariot or a cart; sometimes the chariots were upright and some had the wheels removed. These graves, as at Dane's Graves, Eastburn and Wetwang Slack, ceased in the Late Iron Age, but were richly furnished, often having a joint of meat or a pot that had contained drink. At North Grimston, Bugthorpe and Grimthorpe there are single warriors buried with only their weapons, which may indicate a change of fashion, thus cutting down on the ritual. Barrows are scarce elsewhere in the region.

These burial sites are comparable to those found in eastern France, especially Burgundy, and must refer to an influx of people from a tribe called the Parisii in the Paris region. One burial at Cowlam contained bracelets, necklaces and other jewellery in similar style to that found in Burgundy. This suggested immigration on a large scale similar to that of the Atrebates and the Belgae. Gallo-Belgic pottery found at North Ferriby on the north bank of the Humber suggests this was a trading post linked to Romanized Gaul and this might explain why the Parisii did not resist the Roman advance. Farming was mainly arable with evidence of grain being stored in granaries. Pasturing took place on the Wolds, where driveways often led from a central area to funnel into an enclosure where cattle could be kept away from crop-bearing areas. Major dike systems across the Wolds, which are not high enough to form defensive structures, may be ranch boundaries or form land divisions with separate areas for settlements, cemeteries, arable land and pasture. Late Iron Age settlements at Langton and Rudston were gradually replaced by Roman houses, which developed into villas, giving an impression of gradual change.

The most important tribe in the north was almost certainly that of the Brigantes. Ptolemy said that their territory stretched from ocean to ocean. Certainly the Brigantes occupied a large tribal area with a possible southern boundary at the River Mersey, then stretching through the Peak District to beyond the Tyne–Solway line, which meant that later Hadrian's Wall would form a barrier across their territory. Their name is Celtic for 'the high hill dwellers' and the Brigantes probably encompassed smaller groups under different names – the Carvetii in the Eden Valley (who later became a separate *civitas*), the Setantii of the Fylde area, the Textoverdi and Lopocares of Northumberland and the Gabrantovices of east Yorkshire, who would have come into contact with the Parisii. There were probably other similar groupings, all coming together in one large confederation possibly organized by an ancestor of Cartimandua. Tacitus called her *pollens nobilitate* (powerful in lineage). That such smaller groupings were possible is indicated by the physical geography of the area with its mountainous ranges and deep valleys. Their tutelary deity was the goddess Brigantia and dedications to her have been found in the region of Hadrian's Wall, in the west Yorkshire area and especially at Birrens, where a relief has been found depicting the goddess in warrior guise. The tribal roots go back to the Bronze Age with incomers from Hallstatt and La Tène traditions as a result of trading connections.

Surprisingly, given the mountainous area that the tribe covered, there were few hillforts; these were small but with substantial defences. They include Mam Tor (Derbyshire) and, in Yorkshire, Almondbury, which has origins in the Bronze Age, and Ingleborough where the defences surrounded Iron Age hut circles. There was a major promontory fort at Sutton Bank (Yorkshire). Most of these forts were not in use by the

Late Iron Age and Stanwick (Yorkshire), laid out about the time of the Roman conquest, resulted from a matrimonial quarrel between Cartimandua and her husband. This fort also seems to have operated as a centre of tribal power and, judging by the pottery and the metalwork, as a distribution centre for long distance and local trade. On the whole it would seem that the Brigantes were not given to serious tribal warfare but were powerful enough to keep other tribes out of their area.

Settlements ranged from groups of huts to isolated farms, many sited on hill slopes where sheep farming and cattle rearing would be normal practice. Mixed farming took place in lowland and valley areas as indicated by field systems. Sub-rectangular plots at Ledston (Yorkshire), for example, suggest grain cultivation and more evidence of this is provided by beehive querns, hand-powered mills for grinding grain, found throughout the Pennines. Native wealth probably lay in wool and hides with a side industry in keeping pigs. Pottery was produced in isolated settlements and use was made of wooden and leather vessels. Ironworking was carried out and bronze-working produced decorative metalwork for horses, cattle and weapons.

To the west was the area of Wales with three main tribes. The two strongest were the Silures and the Ordovici. The Silures occupied the coastal plain and areas of Glamorgan and Monmouth and the valleys of the Black Mountains. There were a series of hillforts in the east of the territory but mainly the people, like those at Mynydd Bychan (Glamorgan), occupied small ditched settlements of timber circular huts, later replaced by stone ones, set within walled enclosures. Another settlement, excavated at Whitton (Glamorgan), showed round timber houses surrounded by rectangular ditched enclosures. Later, rectangular houses replaced the round houses, either due to a change of ownership or to a change of lifestyle.

The Ordovici, situated to the north of the Silures, covered an area as far as the Cheshire border. They had hillforts but followed a mainly pastoral existence, with settlements consisting of enclosed farmsteads, and traded in lead and some gold. In the far south-west were the Demetae, again living in small enclosed settlements of circular huts. Their defensive structures were cliff castles similar to those found in Amorica. They were possibly the most peaceable of the Welsh tribes as later there was little Roman activity in their area. A smaller tribe, the Gangani, who may possibly have originated in Ireland, occupied the Lleyn Peninsula.

Tribes in Scotland occupied the wildest part of Britain and the Romans never subdued those in the farthest north. The Romans came mainly into contact with the southern tribes, with whom they established reasonable, though somewhat wary, relations, and after the second century they rarely penetrated into the northern regions. The four largest tribes were the Selgovae, the Votadini, the Damnonii and the Novantae; later the Romans contained them to the south of the Antonine Wall. The Selgovae occupied the lowland area with a main hillfort on Eildon Hill North, which was occupied until the first century AD. The Votadini inhabited the eastern coastal region and the lowlands between the Tyne and the Clyde. Their main hillfort was Traprain Law, which continued as a main centre throughout the Roman period. The Damnonii occupied an area along the west coast to the Clyde to the north of the Novantae, who occupied the Galloway and Dumfriesshire area.

There were also smaller tribes like the Epidii and Creones in the north and west and the Vacomagi and Venicones in the east. In the northern centre were the Maeatae and the Caledonii, who were temporarily defeated by Agricola in his last great campaign. Most of these tribes lived in settlements of stone-built houses or within walled enclosures surrounding huts and yards. Later their defences increased with widely spaced ramparts and ditches.

In the Western Isles and the Orkneys and Shetlands numerous small chieftains had built brochs. These were tall stone-built towers, with living accommodation within the broch or set round the walled courtyard surrounding it, providing defensive positions. Later these were replaced by wheelhouses, which were less defensive than domestic. These were circular stone structures, which had radial stonewalls projecting into the interior from the outer wall. These may have supported roofs of wood or turf, thus forming interior rooms. At Clickhimin in Shetland the wheelhouse was inserted into the broch. The Roman fleet penetrated into those areas on reconnaissance, but did not attempt any hostile campaigns.

This was the state of Britain before the arrival of the Romans. The northern areas of Scotland were never to be subjected to Roman rule and in the wilder parts of Wales, the lowlands of Scotland and northern England life probably continued much as before the conquest. In the southern areas the Romans realized that the hierarchy of tribal authority could be directed into their concept of administrative powers.

This was probably because, in Celtic Britain, there was an established society based on systematic control. According to Caesar, in Gaul and most likely in Britain, there were two principal classes, the Druids and the Knights. The Druids represented the professional group of lawyers, judges, historians and priests having control of religion. The Knights, the warrior group, were divided with kings or chieftains having bands of retainers who served them in return for their keep and for prestige. Below these came the craftsmen working in metals and pottery, and at the lowest end of the scale came those who performed the menial tasks. Many of these were slaves working on the land or as servants to the upper groups. This hierarchical division between the ruling warrior class and the others was made clear after death, when the former were buried in graves containing chariots, jewellery, weapons and other personal objects.

After the conquest the Druids were proscribed and hunted down while Celtic religious beliefs became syncretized with Roman deities. The Knights, the tribal leaders, were encouraged to adopt Roman lifestyles and if the older generation did not subscribe to these, as Tacitus indicated, the younger generation embraced the comforts and the concepts of a more civilized life, thus adopting Roman customs. Celtic tribal leaders did not wish to lose their power over their tribesman and control was kept by their acceptance of magisterial positions. This desire for comfort and control extended with the growth of towns and rural establishments such as villas. Almost unconsciously Celtic Britain was subsuming part of Roman belief and lifestyle and this would continue throughout the next three centuries. Yet this subsuming was only in part. A Celtic way of life would continue and reassert itself again in the fifth century AD.

2

RELATIONS WITH ROME:
HOSTILE AND PRACTICAL

Britain is an island. As such it remained an enigma to Rome but Rome also regarded its island people as a menace. Julius Caesar complained that in almost all his campaigns in Gaul the Britons had sent reinforcements to help the Gauls. The Britons may have been attracted by a love of warfare or as mercenaries paid for their services. Quantities of Belgic staters (coins) found in Britain were possibly payments for these services. In 55 BC, when Caesar had convinced himself that he had pacified Gaul, the Veneti rose in revolt, as did their neighbours and men from the British tribes. With some difficulty Caesar regained control, subduing a number of tribes including the Morini and the Menapii and destroying the Venetic fleet. The revolt, however, focused his attention on Britain. He was aware that the Druidic priesthood was a menacing presence, for the Gauls sent men who wanted to make a more profound study of their rites to Britain. As the Druids were one of the most vehement opponents of the Romans this was a disturbing fact.

Above all, Caesar had more definite plans. Caesar was an ambitious politician whose manoeuvrings were directed towards one goal – the enhancement of his reputation. Combining military prowess and administrative resourcefulness with a gift for oratory, he inspired both soldiers and civilians. His military campaigns, committed to writing, show a genius for propaganda devoted to the endorsement of self-interest and boundless ambition allied to ruthlessness to ensure his ends. He had been created Pontifex Maximus in 63 BC and Praetor in the following year. In the teeth of Senatorial opposition he secured a five-year command in Cisalpine and Transalpine Gaul with an extension into Dalmatia and Illyricum. Probably the Senate thought that this would keep him occupied for longer but his command enabled him to defeat an attempted invasion of the Helvetii and to subdue a German invasion in 58 BC. In 57 BC he defeated an uprising of Gallic tribes in north-west Gaul and received the surrender of tribes in Normandy and Brittany. Therefore he had, to his satisfaction, pacified Gaul and was ready to move on to Britain.

There was another reason for going to Britain – the conquest of Oceanus. The Romans had two important water deities. Neptune was the god of the rivers and the sea, but Oceanus, the son of the Sky and the Earth goddess, was the begetter of all water deities. His rule over infinite waters was absolute and it was necessary to invoke his protection when crossing vast areas of water in order to avert disaster. The stretch of water between Britain and Gaul represented Oceanus, which in Roman minds marked the boundary of the known world. If Caesar crossed Oceanus and returned, having defeated the Britons and seemingly conquered the island, he would not only have indicated his mastery of Oceanus but would have ensured a military triumph in Rome, thereby promoting his political ambitions.

Caesar remarked casually that he thought it would be advantageous to visit Britain, have a look at the inhabitants and make himself acquainted with the land, checking out the harbours and the landing sites. He said he had tried to get information about conditions in Britain from traders and merchants but they were reluctant to help him, either because they knew little beyond their trading activities or because they did not want to alienate their commercial connections. Caesar may have known more about Britain than he cared to admit because he wanted his invasion to have the appearance of a venture into an unknown and dangerous land. What presumably he did not know was how the native tribes would receive him and where the best landing places were situated. He therefore sent Gaius Volusenus, a trusted lieutenant, to check on the strength and character of the Britons, their methods of fighting and the places where his ships could successfully land.

This reconnaissance aroused the suspicion of the Britons and probably the merchants, conscious of Caesar's intentions, had also warned them. Some tribes, having information about the strength of the Roman troops and wary of what could happen, offered hostages to Caesar and indicated that they would submit to Roman rule. This suited Caesar who received their overtures gracefully and ordered them to agree to his terms. In addition he sent Commius, King of the Atrebates, a Belgic tribe living in north-west Gaul near Arras which had allied with Caesar, across the Channel. Commius had orders to move round the tribes urging them to accept Roman protection. Presumably Caesar thought that he would be received as an ally of the British tribes. Suspicious, however, of Commius's intentions, the tribes imprisoned him in chains and he was not released until the end of Caesar's campaign.

Volusenus returned five days later and seemingly gave Caesar a favourable report of possible landing places, although he had not been able to land anywhere because of the hostility of the tribes. Caesar commandeered a fleet of 80 transports from the Gallic coastal areas, which could carry 2 legions, Legion VII and Legion X, implying a carrying capacity of 125 to 150 men per boat, together with a number of warships, which he had had built for the expedition against the Veneti. The warships, propelled by oarsmen, housed catapults and could carry archers and slingers who would provide covering fire for the legionaries when they landed. The sight of the ships alone would have been enough to alarm the Britons. What Caesar had not reckoned with was a contrary wind, which held up eighteen transports from joining the rest of the fleet. He had embarked the cavalry on these and their non-arrival was a serious problem for the expedition.

He embarked at midnight on 26 August 55 BC from Portus Itus (Boulogne), probably arriving off the coast of Britain after daybreak on the following morning. He may have been taken aback to see that his welcome was not as he had anticipated. Hostile tribesmen, warned of his coming, were gathered on the cliff-tops prepared to repel any attempt to land. He therefore moved along the coast for seven (Roman) miles before beaching his warships on an evenly sloping beach, probably at Walmer or Deal, but leaving the transports at anchor. Unfortunately the tribesmen kept pace with him, also moving along the coast.

Their aggressive tactics together with their uproarious clamour, part of their tribal warfare tactics, dismayed the Romans. In addition the heavily armed troops were aware that jumping into deep water could cause many casualties not only from drowning but being wounded by the javelins being flung at them. To disconcert the Britons Caesar ran some of the warships on to the beach on the enemy's flank. The Romans could then train their catapults on to the Britons. In doing this Caesar was reasonably successful, but the day was saved when a soldier of Legion X jumped into the water invoking the gods and, according to Caesar, crying, 'Jump down comrades unless you want the enemy to take our eagle. It shall be told that I did my duty to my country and to my general.' This galvanized the Romans into action for the loss of the standard would not only be a disgrace but would bring severe punishment.

Even so the attack of Celtic horsemen and the sheer tenacity of the opposition delayed the Romans making a secure landing. The lack of cavalry also meant that the Romans could not pursue the enemy, and Caesar is careful to explain that this was the one thing that prevented him from achieving his usual success. The cavalry had sailed four days after the rest of the fleet and when they did make headway a violent storm drove some ships back to harbour and scattered the rest. The Romans had no idea of tidal conditions in the English Channel and did not realize that a full moon causes the highest tides. The storm, which was probably a storm surge combined with a high tide and actuated by a deep depression in the North Sea area, also caused damage to the ships beached on the shore and to the transports which dragged their anchors. Many ships lost their anchors and their tackle, so that, as Caesar admitted, this caused the army great consternation. Probably the Romans feared that it was Oceanus's revenge for their temerity at crossing his domain, thus preventing them from returning to Gaul.

Caesar also seemed to have brought no supplies with him, relying on getting provisions from the land. To do this he sent out men to reap corn but the Britons harassed them with chariots swooping down to make short sorties. Caesar had not encountered chariot tactics in Gaul and he found it difficult at first to come to terms with them in Britain. Sheer dogged determination kept the Britons at bay. The Britons, however, were unused to prolonged warfare. Their tribal chieftains had collected their followers for battles but when none occurred they all began to drift away to return to their homesteads. The chieftains were then compelled to approach Caesar to seek terms. He secured the release of Commius and demanded hostages. This was agreed but when he got back to Gaul only two tribes sent hostages.

In spite of the unsuccessful nature of the expedition – the lack of cavalry, the loss of ships and the evasive tactics of the

Britons – Caesar deemed it a success. He had taken two legions across Oceanus and returned, assessed the battle tactics of the British tribes and secured hostages who would provide more information. In addition the Roman Senate granted him a public thanksgiving (*supplicatio*) of twenty days, the largest ever granted to a successful Roman general. Preparations could now be made for a second expedition.

In 54 BC his expedition to Britain was much larger, which indicated that he anticipated a more difficult campaign and that he had conceived an undoubted respect for Celtic fighting tactics. Twenty-eight warships and 600 transports were either ordered to be built or commandeered, and Caesar urged on their construction so that they would be built over the winter months. The transports were lower and broader than those usually constructed in order to carry more cargo and draught animals and to be easily beached on the shore. All the ships were fitted out with oars as well as sails to make them manoeuvre more easily. He gathered the ships at Boulogne where 5 legions (25,000–30,000 men) and 2,000 cavalry could be embarked. Sixty transports did not arrive because of the weather and probably fewer men were transported in each boat, which would allow them to carry more equipment.

Even with these precautions the crossing was not without incident. He set sail at the beginning of July but at about midnight the wind dropped and tidal currents caused the fleet to drift far off course. Luckily, when the tide turned, the oarsmen, a vital addition on the ships, were able to row towards Britain. The fleet landed on a soft and open beach, a place that Caesar had marked out on the previous year. This is thought to have been between Deal and Sandwich. This time the landing was unopposed which puzzled Caesar but he later learned from Britons who had been captured that the tribes had been alarmed by the sight of so many ships and withdrawn inland.

Caesar was therefore able to disembark his legions successfully and make camp. Hating any delay in attacking an enemy, he left 10 cohorts of legionaries and 800 cavalry to guard the camp and moved the rest forward on what was apparently a night mission. Twelve (Roman) miles further he encountered the Britons on high ground overlooking a river, probably the River Stour. They failed to bar his way with their chariots and retreated to what Caesar indicated was a 'well-fortified position of great natural strength', which, it has been suggested, was the hillfort of Bigbury. The Britons sent out raiding parties to stop the Roman advance but to no avail. Soldiers of Legion VII formed a 'tortoise', advanced and captured the fort, but did not pursue the enemy, as Caesar was uncertain of the ground. He was always a cautious general, carefully assessing a situation before deciding on the best strategy.

Instead he fortified his position, and then the next morning sent out cavalry and infantry to seek out the enemy. Unfortunately he received news from a messenger sent by Quintus Atrius, whom he had left in charge of the base camp, that a storm in the night had damaged almost all the ships as many had dragged their anchors and the cables had not held. At least forty ships had been lost and Caesar had to recall his pursuit of the enemy and devote time to ordering repairs to be made. He returned to the beach, noted the damage and sent a message to Labienus, his able general in Gaul to build more ships. He ordered all the ships to be beached and enclosed within a fortification. All this took ten days to complete, and perhaps he might be blamed for this delay; given what had happened in the previous year, he might have anticipated what could occur.

The delay gave the Britons time to regroup. For once they set aside their tribal differences, choosing as their leader Cassivellaunus, chief or king of the Catuvellauni, who inhabited a large area north of the Thames. This was a notable advance in cooperation amongst the tribes because, as Caesar said, Cassivellaunus had repeatedly attacked neighbouring tribes. His tribal forces now followed their own battle tactics using chariots and cavalry to make frequent attacks on the Romans. Even though he had met chariots on his previous visit, Caesar had ignored their effectiveness; the tactics of the charioteers particularly alarmed the Romans. These men skilfully guided the chariots towards the Romans, allowing their warriors to jump down to fight, and then leap back on to dash away. Legionaries could not pursue them in their heavy armour and did not leave their tight formations. The cavalry seemed bewildered by the speed of the chariots. It took time for Caesar to work out a solution to this problem.

The Romans needed to strike a decisive blow and this almost came the next day when the Britons attacked a Roman foraging party. Gaius Trebonius, one of Caesar's generals, with three legions and the whole of the cavalry managed to stop this attack, driving the enemy away and pursuing them so that their flight became a rout. As usual, in the face of determined onslaught, the Britons became disheartened. They slipped away and only Cassivellaunus with his tribe offered resistance. He retreated beyond the Thames but Caesar found a point where the Thames was fordable. (Suggestions for the location have ranged from Brentford to the City of London.) Caesar said that stakes lined the riverbank and were inserted into the riverbed. Bede, in his *Ecclesiastical History of England*, written in the eighth century AD, gave a succinct history of the two invasions and mentioned that the remains of the stakes are still to be seen, but Sheppard Frere suggests these might be remains of the first London Bridge.

The river did not deter the Romans. It was forded, the enemy were overpowered and the Romans advanced north of the Thames causing Cassivellaunus's army to melt away. Only his charioteers kept faith, darting out at the Romans from the dense woodlands. Cassivellaunus knew that the Romans would plunder the country for supplies and therefore he carried out a scorched earth policy to deprive them of provisions. Caesar appeared to have been so worried by this that he determined to bring the Britons to battle.

He was assisted in this by the action of another Celtic tribe. Mandubracius, a prince of the Trinovantes, had previously gone to Gaul to put himself under Caesar's protection, having been alarmed when Cassivellaunus had invaded Trinovantian territory in the Essex region and killed his father. The Trinovantes suddenly sent messages to Caesar promising the surrender of the tribe and assuring Caesar that they would assist him provided that he would protect them against Cassivellaunus and bring back Mandubracius to rule as their king. Caesar demanded forty hostages and large quantities of grain. Both were promptly sent.

Urged on by this, the Cenimagni, Segontiaci, Ancalites, Bibroci and Cassi surrendered to Caesar, probably seeking his protection. They had possibly been at war with Cassivellaunus or been menaced by him, as Caesar said that before his arrival there had been a constant state of war in Britain. Caesar ordered them to provide information about Cassivellaunus's stronghold, protected by forests and marshes, possibly the hillfort of Wheathampstead (Hertfordshire). Meanwhile Cassivellaunus had ordered four kings in the Kentish region, Cingetorix, Carvilius, Taximagulus and Segovax, to attack Caesar's naval camp. This attack was repulsed and Cassivellaunus, realizing that he that he was losing the conflict and aware that his forces could melt away before he could strike a decisive blow, approached Caesar, using Commius as an intermediary, to seek terms of surrender.

Caesar wanted to end the conflict as he wished to return to Gaul, fearing that the Gallic tribes might revolt. Autumn would also bring adverse weather conditions and it was necessary to get all his troops across the Channel safely. He therefore demanded hostages, imposed an annual tribute on the British tribes and ordered Cassivellaunus not to attack the Trinovantes and Mandubracius. Once the hostages had arrived he returned to the camp and satisfied himself that some of the ships were seaworthy. He embarked for Gaul in two trips, cramming into the remaining ships his army, prisoners and hostages. Luckily the sea was calm so that all arrived safely in Gaul.

It is surprising that in spite of intensive investigation nothing has been found of Caesar's visits to Britain. One suggestion has been that a large number of coin hoards in Kent and Essex, dated to this period, may be linked to the alarm caused by Caesar's campaigns. Deposits made by people who had fled from the conflict also might explain those hoards found in Suffolk.

In his account of the invasion of Britain in the *Gallic Wars*, Caesar probably exaggerated his success. He ignored his near disaster in 55 BC but in 54 BC he presumably thought that he had subdued Britain and that the island was ready to submit to Roman rule. He had negotiated a surrender treaty (*deditio*) with Cassivellaunus and with other British tribes and arranged that they would pay a yearly tax (*vectigal*). These are technical terms. A *deditio* implied that the inhabitants of the area would pay the tax to Rome because they were under its domination. The Senate was supposed to follow this up by ratifying Caesar's arrangements, thus beginning the process of turning Britain into a Roman province. The kings and chieftains in Britain would become client rulers of Rome under Roman protection. If Caesar, however, had intended to make another expedition there was no opportunity because the Gallic tribes began to revolt under the leadership of Vercingetorix and Caesar was forced to concentrate on putting down massed rebellion. The Senate lost interest in Britain and when Gaul was made a province in 51 BC it was declared to be from '*mare nostrum*' to Oceanus, thus ignoring Britain. Later, in 31 BC, in a long speech made to his army, Mark Anthony refers to areas that the

Romans had subjugated but pointedly refers to them merely as having 'passed over the sea into Britain'.

Britain was far from Rome. There was no administration that could compel the tribes to pay tribute. Probably Cassivellaunus and Mandubracius would pay, having recent knowledge of what the Romans could do. Strabo implies that the tribute was not paid but, with heavy duties on imports and exports, there was no need to garrison the island. He said that at least one legion and some cavalry would be needed to exact tribute money and that this was not worth the expense. In addition, the Romans now felt that they had little to fear from Britain.

There were other changes. Commius, who had been sent by Caesar to spy out the land, turned against Caesar when Vercingetorix made his last stand, avoided several attempts to kill him and fled with many of his tribe to Britain. They settled in the Hampshire and West Sussex districts, eventually establishing a capital at Calleva (Silchester). Coin evidence suggests that Commius had three sons, Tincommius, Eppillus and Verica. Commius seems to have been succeeded by Tincommius in about 25 to 20 BC. Coins of his reign start to bear the word REX, which suggests either that he was enhancing his position by boasting of a friendship with Rome, or that contact, even perhaps a treaty, with Rome had led to the grant of a title. If so, the treachery of his father Commius had been forgiven or forgotten.

This group of Belgic settlers embedded themselves deeply in the area and became a rival to the Catuvellauni and the Trinovantes. Either Cassivellaunus or his successor Tasciovanus moved his capital from Wheathampstead to Prae Wood, which later was the site of Verulamium on the evidence of coins with a mint-mark VER. Some coins are stamped with a rider on a horse blowing a carnyx, the Celtic war trumpet, which may indicate power or military achievement. In the Essex region Mandubracius ruled over the Trinovantes. Having sought help from Caesar they probably relied on Roman protection or at least the promise of it. In addition there was a natural drift of people into Britain for a variety of reasons. Merchants found a ready market; Druids came to study what was considered to be the purest form of their religion; fugitives sought shelter from Roman domination in Gaul. The tribes in Britain were probably well aware of what was happening in Gaul.

By now Octavius, having become emperor with the title Augustus, was fully occupied with establishing his power in Rome. There seems to have been some unrest in Britain for Dio Cassius said that twice he had moved into Gaul with the intention of invading Britain – in 34 BC in emulation of his father Julius and in 27 to 26 BC. But Augustus was distracted by problems in other parts of the empire, especially those of tribes beyond the Rhine and the Danube, a revolt of the Salassi and hostilities of the Asturians and the Celtiberians. About the same time Horace in one of his Odes implied that Augustus was serious about moving against Britain, once asking the goddess Fortuna to protect Augustus, 'soon to go to Britain, furthest of earth's people'. Frere has suggested that these moves were either to complete what Caesar had begun or because new rulers had not been so amenable in accepting the former treaty terms.

Another king in Essex according to inscribed coins was Addedomaros. He was succeeded by Dubnovellaunus, who probably invaded from south of the Thames. Power shifted again for he was driven out of his capital at Camulodunum either by Tasciovanus or his son Cunobelin, who were extending Catuvellaunian power to the west. Dubnovellaunus seems to have fled to seek help from Augustus, for the *Res Gestae*, the inscription dated to AD 7 set up in Rome by Augustus to record his deeds, mentioned that Dubnovellaunus and Tincommius, kings from Britain, sought help from Augustus as suppliants. If they did, Augustus took no action. The result was that the Catuvellauni had now taken over the Trinovantian area in defiance of, or indifference to, the command of Caesar. But

Caesar had left Britain fifty years previously and the Roman invasion was just a memory. In any case the Roman army had suffered a great defeat in AD 9 when 3 legions, 15,000 strong, were destroyed in the Teutonic forests and, even though this did not mean that Rome intended to give up an interest in the northern areas, Augustus was occupied elsewhere.

Eppillus had now supplanted Tincommius. He and his successor Verica struck coins bearing the title REX, a word employed by rulers who wished to emulate Roman power. As the designs on these coins were derived from those on Roman coins, they might have been the result of Roman craftsmen who had visited Britain. Probably Augustus thought it easier to give these kings recognition as client kings even though this led to the expansion of the kingdom into that of neighbouring territories. British rulers also established tribal centres – Calleva, Camulodunum and Verulamium – thereby setting up seats of political and religious power.

It is therefore possible that Cunobelin and Verica are the kings whom Strabo mentioned as keeping on good terms with Augustus by sending embassies and offering courtesies to Rome, even making offerings on the Capitol. Courtesies were also paid in AD 16 when some Roman soldiers were shipwrecked on the British coast during a storm in the North Sea for they were safely returned to Gaul. Gestures these might have been but they appear to have kept the Romans generally happy about the situation in Britain. By now, according to Strabo, Britain was exporting goods to Rome – corn, silver, gold and iron, together with hunting dogs – and there appears to have been a thriving slave trade. Strabo indicated that occupying Britain would have disadvantages for at least one legion and some cavalry would be needed to exact tribute money from them and this could lead to further dangers.

The Romans remained cautious when Cunobelin extended his kingdom into Kent and moved into the Upper Thames region. This kingdom may have extended further west. Dio Cassius indicated that Cunobelin extended political control over the tribe of the Bodunni, which certainly is the Dobunni. Towards the east Cunobelin's coins are found in Icenian territory and in Cantian territory, indicating that his power extended north and south of the Thames, thus giving him control over river traffic. His actions are entirely compatible with normal Celtic intertribal warfare. Suetonius may have been right in referring to him as *Britannorum rex* (King of the Britons). Epaticcus, another of Tasciovanus's sons, carved out territory for himself from Verica's area and may even have taken over Calleva. The Emperor Tiberius was not willing to interfere in Britain even as Cunobelin seized more and more land, presumably believing that Cunobelin was strong enough to keep his area peaceful and not hostile to Rome.

Cunobelin ruled for over thirty years, thus justifying Tiberius's belief. His strong relations with Rome are indicated by the wealth of rich burials of the aristocracy, many of these containing amphorae that had held imported wine. His coinage became increasingly Romanized. In AD 39, however, there seems to have been some dispute in Cunobelin's household. Cunobelin had several sons which, given the Celtic disposition for violent quarrels, would result in disharmony. One of the sons, Adminius, was driven out and fled across the Channel seeking help from the Emperor Gaius Caligula. Caligula seems to have toyed with the idea of invading Britain but Oceanus still had terrors for the Romans for Dio recounted that Caligula first lined up the legions on the shore facing Britain, then sailed out in a trireme, turned and sailed back again. Instead of embarking the troops he ordered them to pick up seashells.

Caligula had obviously not made any preparations to invade Britain. What he was good at was 'spin'. He claimed that the seashells gave him victory over Oceanus, proclaimed himself Britannicus, and to commemorate his so-called victory built a lighthouse at that place (now Boulogne). The lighthouse survived until 1644 when part of the cliff on which it was standing gave way. Caligula had obviously been faced with something more serious than Oceanus, probably a mutiny on the part of the troops who were still uneasy at having to cross the Channel, especially as they were led by an emperor with so little military experience.

Thus matters stood in Britain until about AD 40 or 41 when Cunobelin died. He had remained on good terms with the Romans but his death led to a shift of control. He was succeeded by two sons, Caratacus and Togidubnus, who had no sense of Roman power nor of its long reach. They divided the kingdom between them and immediately began attacking neighbouring tribes to expand their respective territories. This included an attack on the Atrebates which drove out Verica, who immediately fled to Rome and appealed for help from the new Emperor Claudius. Rome's attention now became firmly fixed on Britain.

3

CONQUEST

Dio Cassius reported Verica's appeal to Claudius but gave the name of Berikos. Whatever the name the situation suited Claudius who had recently been created emperor by the actions of the Praetorian Guard. In describing Claudius's childhood Suetonius said that he was so troubled by illness that he grew up half-witted and with little physical strength. Unprepossessing and with a club foot he was contemptuously despised by his mother as a man whom Mother Nature had begun to work on and cast aside. This was doing Claudius an injustice. He was certainly not a fool and made some astute choices in selecting his generals. Suetonius dismissed Claudius's future campaign as being of no great importance but he does state that the emperor saw attacking Britain, an island which no one had attempted to invade since Caesar's time, as a much needed chance for military glory. Claudius's argument was that Britain was in turmoil as a result of the driving out of Verica, and its refusal to return fugitives from Gaul was provocative and a diplomatic breach. He might also impress the Romans by crossing Oceanus to bring this isolated island into the Roman Empire.

Claudius did not intend to lead the invasion as Caesar had done. He selected Aulus Plautius, whom Dio describes as a senator of distinction. He had been governor of Pannonia, a province probably not unlike Britain in its mountainous areas. A cousin of Claudius's ex-wife Urgulanilla, he was well known to the emperor. Other senior men chosen for the invasion included those tried and trusted in warfare. One of the legionary commanders was extremely competent: he was the future emperor Vespasian. Another was the future emperor Sulpicius Galba. This invasion was obviously to be treated as a serious campaign.

Plautius chose 4 legions, probably about 20,000 men, to accompany him – Legion II Augusta, Legion IX Hispana, Legion XIV Gemina and Legion XX. Three had been brought from the Rhineland; Legion IX had been in Pannonia and therefore was well known to him. In addition, a large number of auxiliary regiments were allocated to the invasion, bringing the force up to about 40,000. This would be a major expense but there would be an advantage if Britain were to prove to be a source of mineral wealth. Above all, it would keep the legions and the auxiliaries occupied and in a position where Claudius could control them.

There was again restlessness on the part of the legionaries who were still reluctant to cross Oceanus, but Plautius in a shrewd move sent a freedman Narcissus, who was on Claudius's staff, to address them. When he started speaking the troops roared 'Io Saturnalia', referring to the winter festival when masters and slaves changed places. The troops were either putting Narcissus in his place or may have resented being addressed by a man of lowly rank. They may also have felt that their courage was being impugned. Whatever the reason they lost their obduracy and preparations for the invasion were swiftly resumed.

Plautius probably sailed from Boulogne and, as in the case of Caesar's invasions, there were problems with the tides and the weather because the ships were driven back on their course. The Romans had yet again failed to understand the tidal system and had miscalculated the winds, as indeed other invading forces were to do in British history. The Romans, with their superstitious nature according to Dio, were encouraged when a flash of light shot across the sky from east to west, pointing in the direction in which they were travelling. This is a curious statement because if they were to land in Kent they would have been travelling north-westwards. The flash of light can be explained as a shooting star. The discrepancy in direction may be explained by the fact that the fleet had been blown very far to the east and therefore was turning back to land in the Richborough area.

Dio said that the fleet had sailed in three divisions, possibly one after the other. It is not certain how many ships were entailed. Frere calculated a fleet of 800 ships. John Peddie in 1977 estimated that 933 ships would be needed to carry the large numbers of troops, cavalry horses, baggage animals, equipments and supplies but if the expedition did sail in three divisions this would mean between 200–300 per group and that not all the fleet might have been driven off course. They could have been strung out along the Channel. The passage might take from ten to twenty hours, implying that they could have been at sea overnight, which the Romans hated to do, especially as the animals would have to be fed and watered.

Dio reported that the landing was unopposed but his comment on three divisions could indicate a dividing of the fleet and that there were several landings. It is uncertain where these might have taken place. Suggestions have ranged from Hampshire to Essex. The time limit would have been feasible to reach any of these areas. One of the complicating factors is that the first tribe that capitulated was named by Dio as the Bodunni. As mentioned, this must be the Dobunni who inhabited the Gloucestershire area and possibly one division landed west of the Solent in the Hampshire region. From there one Roman legion could have moved swiftly north-westwards to secure the submission of the Dobunni.

Modern interpretations, however, have hardened on East Kent with a main landing place either at Dover or in the Wantsum Channel, where the Romans were to establish the fort of Richborough. Excavations there have revealed two parallel ditches dated to the Claudian period, but even more important has been the recent discovery of a shingle harbour buried beneath 1.83 m (6 ft) of soil near Richborough. The fort was situated at the southern end of the Wantsum Channel that separated the Isle of Thanet from the mainland. Over the centuries this channel has silted up but in AD 43 this would have provided a sheltered lagoon and a perfectly safe anchorage for a fleet.

Aerial photograph of Richborough Roman fort, Kent. The outer walls are of the Saxon Shore fort. To the upper left are two short parallel lines of the original Claudian fort ditches. The masonry cross is the foundation of the triumphal arch erected in the 1980s (possibly by Agricola) to commemorate the conquest of Britain and as a gateway to the island. Around this are the banks and ditches of an earth fort intended to protect the monument in the third century AD and to transform it into a lookout post

Dio's account, which is the most detailed though the most problematical, said that the Romans advanced to a river, probably the Medway, where a huge battle took place lasting two days. Eventually the Romans were victorious and crossed the river. They then advanced to the Thames where in another skirmish Togidubnus was killed but this made the Britons even more determined to resist. Dio said that Plautius was worried about the situation, as he was unsure of the numbers of the British tribes and about crossing the Thames. It was more likely that once he realized that the Thames was fordable he hesitated so that he could obey his orders to bring Claudius to Britain and allow him to claim the victory.

Claudius had already sailed from Ostia to Marseilles, almost being shipwrecked by furious north-westerly storms. He marched through Gaul to Boulogne and embarked for Britain, bringing reinforcements and an entourage that included elephants. Their appearance must have startled the Britons. Dio said that Claudius took command although this must have been nominal given the military experience of Plautius. The Romans crossed the Thames – suggestions for the location range along the Thames between the City and Brentford – and advanced to the capital of the Trinovantes at Camulodunum, which was quickly taken.

Claudius stayed only sixteen days in Britain. He returned more leisurely to Rome, probably travelling along the Rhone and crossing the Alps before proceeding south through Italy and taking nearly five months on the journey. During this time no move had been made against his rule and on his return to Rome a compliant Senate granted him the title Britannicus, which was passed to his son, awarded him a triumph and an annual festival to commemorate the event, and ordered the building of two triumphal arches, one in Rome and one in Gaul. All this was what Claudius would have wished. On his triumph he rode in a decorated chariot followed by his wife Messalina and the officers who had ensured his glory. This must imply that some legionary officers had been withdrawn from Britain. In addition, on the Campus Martius he ordered the representation of the storming and sacking of a British town as well as replicating the surrender of British kings.

Suetonius said that Claudius had fought no battles and suffered no casualties, which was probably true as he had left all this to Plautius, but that he had reduced a large part of the island to submission. According to an inscription from the Roman arch dedicated in AD 52, now partly preserved in the courtyard of the Musei Capitolini, Rome, Claudius received the surrender of eleven British kings and 'was the first to bring the barbarian people across the Ocean under the power of the Roman state'. Caesar's exploits were conveniently ignored. Three of these kings must have been Togidubnus, Cogidubnus and an ancestor of Prasutagus, King of the Iceni. Others might have been kings in Kent and those ruling the Dobunni and the Coritani and possibly Cartimandua or her predecessor as ruler of the Brigantes, although it is doubtful that Roman intelligence had reached so far north. Suetonius said that Claudius placed a naval crown on the gable of his palace as well as a civic crown as a 'sign as it were, that he had subdued Oceanus'. Tacitus laconically summed it up: 'tribes were conquered, kings captured and destiny introduced Vespasian to the world'.

Tiberius Claudius Cogidubnus ruled the Chichester area and Tacitus, in the *Agricola*, said that 'he had remained totally loyal down to our own times in accordance with the long-standing policy of making kings even their agents to enslave peoples'. As Tacitus was writing in the AD 90s this implies that Cogidubnus had a long reign. On an inscription found in the area, dedicating a temple to Neptune and Minerva by the guild of smiths, he is called Tiberius Claudius Cogidubnus, which suggests that Tiberius had given Roman citizenship to him. He is also named *Rex* and *Legatus Augusti* in Britain, an astonishing title but which may indicate that Cogidubnus had calculatedly decided to throw in his lot with superior forces and become a suppliant client king. He may also have realized that allying with Rome provided protection against an attack by Catuvellaunian power. The kings of the Cantii and the Iceni may also have realized this, which would account for the ease of Roman conquest in the south. The Romans had long experience in wooing individual tribal leaders by a series of inducements, rewards and threats. Client kings could keep their independence and privileges provided they pledged their loyalty to Rome and ensured that of their followers. This tactic was to succeed in the north. It was in the west of Britain, especially in Wales, where the most hostile tribes might be found.

Before he left Britain Claudius had sensibly given command of the army back to Plautius instructing him to subdue the rest of the island. This Plautius proceeded to do, sending the Legion II Augusta along the southern coast under its commander, the future emperor Vespasian. This legion swept through the country, possibly aided by Cogidubnus's loyalty in providing a base. Suetonius succinctly reports in his life of Vespasian that the future emperor fought thirty battles, subdued two warlike tribes and captured more than twenty *oppida* as well as the Isle of Wight.

The tribes were possibly the Durotriges and either the Belgae or the Dumnonii. Amongst the *oppida* were certainly two in Dorset, Hod Hill and Maiden Castle. Others are probably Hembury (Devon), Spettisbury Rings (Dorset) and the Somerset sites of Worlebury, South Cadbury and Ham Hill. Excavations at Hod Hill revealed that one particular hut seemed to have been bombarded by *ballistae* (weapons for projecting missiles such as bolts). This was assumed to be the chieftain's hut as it was situated on the main street near the most important gate. A Roman fort was established in one corner of Hod Hill thus securing that area. The Britons at Maiden Castle may have

Aerial photograph of the hillfort of Maiden Castle, Dorset

put up equal resistance to the Romans. A vast hoard of sling stones had been prepared to repel any attack and the hillfort's complicated arrangement of ramparts and ditches could have repelled attacks by neighbouring tribes. These defences, however, were useless against the firepower of Roman catapults and an onslaught by disciplined troops. Telling evidence on the uselessness of resistance was the finding of a body of a British victim, buried quickly in a mass grave, with a *ballista* bolt cut into his spine. The hillfort was overrun and eventually the inhabitants were moved into the ordered civilization of the Roman town of Dorchester. A mass grave of over forty-five headless bodies dating to the early first century found recently near Weymouth (Dorset) may also have been the burial place of victims of the invading force. Sweeping aside any resistance it continued into Cornwall, establishing a base at Nanstallon. Later it swung north and centred the headquarters of Legion II Augusta at Exeter in about AD 55.

Vespasian also seems to have laid out a series of bases, which could be used by the fleet. Evidence of Roman occupation was found at Fishbourne, Hamworthy in Poole Harbour (Dorset) and Topsham (Devon) on the estuary of the River Exe. Coastal stations giving wide views were situated at Abbotsbury (Dorset), tacked on to a huge Iron Age fort (presumably another of the captured *oppida*), and High Peak, west of Sidmouth. Military bases were added at Dorchester, Ilchester, Camerton and Sea Mills. These soon attracted people who gathered there for security and thus developed into small towns.

Meanwhile, Plautius proceeded with an advance to the north. The Iceni quickly went over to Rome, possibly as a check to Catuvellaunian advance into their territory and allowing their king to become head of a client state. East Anglia therefore seemed relatively safe. Legion XX established Colchester, a base adjacent to Camulodunum, which was chosen to indicate that Roman power had superseded British power. Colchester could be also used as a port for landing supplies from the Rhineland and Gaul and shipping them along the eastern coast.

Legion IX was sent north to subdue the Catuvellauni and soon established a fort at Longthorpe on the River Nene. Little resistance seems to have been shown and troops pressed on, eventually siting their main base at Lincoln, probably in the AD 50s. A network of garrisons was linked by roads, the most important of these being Ermine Street leading directly north. Possibly a fleet also moved along the coast establishing supply bases. One seems to have been situated at Kirmington and another at Old Winterington on the River Humber. From here it would have been easy to send supplies along the River Trent to camps as far as Newark and Margidunum (Nottinghamshire). Forts were also sited at Leicester, Broxtowe (Nottinghamshire) and Strutt's Park near Derby to control the midland area. Plautius's policy seems to have been to establish camps and forts at important river crossings, on high ground or near to native settlements, so that a watch could be kept to determine opposition. This policy seems to have succeeded and for the next fifteen years there was little sign of trouble.

Legion XIV was sent towards the midland region along a line later developed as Watling Street, although none of the forts on that road date to the early period. It established a base at Alchester (Warwickshire). Detachments moving along the Thames established a fort at Dorchester-on-Thames. The strategy seems to have been a swift movement to convince the Britons that resistance was futile and in this Plautius was successful, for as far as is known there was no considerable show of force.

When Plautius returned to Rome in AD 47 he could faithfully claim that the invasion had created a new province for Rome. For this he was given an *ovatio*, a lesser honour than a triumph but with the additional honour of the Emperor Claudius going out to meet Plautius when he entered the city and walking with him to the Capitol.

The road crossing the midland area from the south-west to Lincoln, the Fosse Way, has been suggested as marking the frontier established by Plautius but this is debatable as such a frontier played no part in Roman strategy at that date and it cut across tribal territories. Although there are forts along this line there is no evidence for any coordinated action between them. The Fosse Way was probably an important strategic route provided with stopping places. Beyond this lay tribes assumed to be hostile and Rome could not be satisfied until they had been subdued. There were also riches to be won. Strabo had mentioned the minerals exported from Britain and Tacitus in his biography of Agricola had spoken of gold, silver and other metals: *pretium victoriae* – the price of victory. These deposits were known to exist in the Mendips, Shropshire and the Welsh areas. For all the Romans knew they could be found in the north. The conquest of Britain therefore had to continue and so quickly did this happen that by AD 49 Roman troops were extracting lead and producing silver from deposits in the Mendips.

The advance continued under the next two governors – P. Ostorius Scapula (AD 47–52) and Aulus Didius Gallus (AD 52–8). Ostorius concentrated on Wales, to where Caratacus had fled from the invading armies of Plautius. His first move was to ensure his rear was secure by disarming the tribes. This was in accordance with the *Lex Julia de vi publica* that forbad conquered people to have weapons except for hunting or to defend oneself on a journey. Bearing weapons, however, was essential to a Celtic warrior and the disarming brought an immediate reaction from the Iceni, hitherto quiescent. The centre of the rebellion is suggested to be Stonea Camp (Cambridgeshire) as this Iron Age settlement was abandoned in AD 47, its ramparts slighted. Ostorius responded quickly and established Prasutagus as an overall tribal client king. Forts were established at Saham Toney (Norfolk) and possibly Caistor-by-Norwich to control trouble but resentment continued and was to break out later in full rebellion.

Ostorius then advanced through the midlands to concentrate on defeating the Deceangli in north-east Wales, devastating their territory and allowing his troops, according to Tacitus, 'to look for and seize booty far and wide', presumably to emphasise the strength of his army and forestall resistance. He was probably also anxious to begin to exploit the mineral deposits in the area. News of this reached the Brigantes, some of whom began to move towards an attack. They were quickly subdued and Ostorius left the problem to Cartimandua, who still seems to have remained loyal to Rome.

Ostorius's prey was Caratacus, who had roused the Silures. He first established military bases in Staffordshire at Wall, Kinvaston and Metchley and an auxiliary base at Wroxeter, which later became a legionary fortress. A line of forts was sited along the Welsh Marches to hold a frontier and another fort at Gloucester probably held some of Legion XX, which had been moved from Colchester, leaving in its place a *colonia* of veterans which would ensure a strong Roman presence in that area. Doing this ensured there would be future trouble, for the new colonists had no compunction in seizing land, probably the best agricultural land, from the Trinovantes.

Aware of the threat to the Silures in south-west Wales in AD 51 Caratacus moved his base to the Ordovici in central Wales. Here he made a stand. The site of this battle has been disputed. Tacitus described it as one where the approaches and the escape routes helped Caratacus and impeded the Romans. On one side there was a precipitous slope and on the other a river of uncertain depth. Two sites in Powys are suggested: Llanymynech and Caersws. In this battle the Roman troops defeated Caratacus's army, who were described as being without the protection of either breastplates or helmets, and captured his wife, daughters and brothers. Caratacus fled north, seeking protection from Cartimandua. Mindful that it was in her interests to keep in with Rome, the queen informed the Roman authorities, who took him captive to Rome.

Tacitus recorded that, as Caratacus's fame had spread far beyond Britain into the adjoining provinces and even as far as Rome, many people wished to see the man who had defied Rome's power. Together with his wife, daughters and brothers, he was in a Roman triumphal procession, but never looked like a dejected captive. He gave a defiant speech saying that had he been as moderate in success as his noble rank and birth were great he would have entered Rome as a friend rather than a captive. If the Romans would spare his life, he would be a memorial to their clemency. In response to this speech, the Emperor Claudius pardoned Caratacus and his family. They seemingly lived out the rest of their lives in Rome, probably being a living example of the emperor's clemency.

Having disposed of Caratacus, Ostorius still had to subdue the Silures but the campaign was bitter and for Ostorius exhausting. A massacre of a camp prefect and several legionary cohorts was narrowly avoided but a foraging party was overwhelmed together with cavalry sent to their assistance. Tacitus reported that Ostorius, frustrated at this resistance, said that the tribe should be totally exterminated or transported to Gaul, words which made tribal resistance even more certain. Worn out by this campaign, Ostorius died in AD 52.

The new governor, Didius Gallus, found things even worse than he had anticipated. The Silures had now defeated a legion, possibly Legion XX, and were on the rampage. Didius contained the tribe by establishing a series of auxiliary forts and a legionary depot at Usk to replace Kingsholm (Gloucestershire), and moving Legion XIV to a new base at Wroxeter to control the northern Marches. He then turned his attention to the Brigantes, where a marital dispute had caused unrest amongst the tribe. Cartimandua was married to Venutius but her betrayal of Caratacus had led to a dispute between them. She had tried to contain the situation by seizing his relations but this led to uproar. Knowing the value of Cartimandua's allegiance, Didius sent a legion to restore order and established forts at Chesterfield and Templebrough (South Yorkshire) on the borders of Brigantian territory.

Claudius was murdered in AD 54 and was succeeded by Nero. Suetonius said that the new emperor considered withdrawing from Britain but refrained because he did not wish to belittle his adoptive father's glory. Too much money and military manpower, however, had probably been committed to Britain to consider a withdrawal and, when Didius's term of office finished in AD 57, Quintus Veranius, who had been involved in mountain warfare in southern Asia Minor, replaced him. It was clear that the Roman government intended him to move into the mountainous regions of Wales and the north of Britain.

Unfortunately Veranius died in his first year of governorship. His successor was Suetonius Paullinus (AD 57–61), who had subdued the tribes of the Atlas Mountains in Mauritania. This experience of mountain warfare certainly stood him in good stead. Tacitus said in the *Agricola* that he enjoyed two seasons of success establishing strong forts and conquering tribes, presumably the Silures and the Ordovici. The remnants of these tribes had taken refuge in Anglesey, but this was not the only reason why Paullinus decided to attack the island. Anglesey was rich in minerals, especially copper. It provided a corn supply for the Ordovici that would be useful for the troops. Above all, it had become a haven for Druidic resistance. The Druids had been outlawed in Gaul by Tiberius and Claudius but had become notorious in Britain for their hostility to Rome. Paullinus determined to put an end to this. He constructed flat-bottomed boats to transport the infantry, probably from Legions XIV and XX, across the Menai Strait and sent the cavalry part wading, part swimming across. These may have been Batavians who were used to this type of action. Other troops crossed by fords, possibly near Bangor where the water is relatively shallow.

At first the Romans were dismayed by their hostile reception. Women dressed in funereal black brandished torches and wailed loudly; Druids poured out curses. Then the Romans moved, urged on by the generals and the threats of the centurions, smashing into the mass awaiting them and burning them with their own torches. The groves, which Tacitus said were devoted to their savage rites, were cut down but the occupation of the island was halted by news from the east of Britain.

Prasutagus had kept the peace amongst the Iceni and been a loyal client king. He had hoped to continue this peace after his death by leaving his kingdom half to the Emperor Nero and half to his daughters in his will. Whether this would have worked is uncertain and it is equally unclear why he did not include his wife Boudicca in his will as women rulers appear to have been acceptable to Celtic tribes. The Romans were having none of this. Suetonius stated that Nero seized 'the whole estates of those who had shown ingratitude by not bequeathing him enough'. The Roman procurator, Decianus Catus, probably on orders from Rome, sent slaves from his office and centurions from the governor's staff, together with troops, into the kingdom to secure it for Rome. Outrages followed. Boudicca was whipped, her daughters raped and the property of the Icenian nobility was seized.

Resentment led to open revolt and the Iceni were joined by the Trinovantes who resented the confiscation of their lands by the veterans in the Colchester *colonia*. They had also been harshly treated, being forced to quarry stones and make tiles for the building of the town and to pay taxes for the upkeep of the Temple of Claudius. To pay these many had taken out loans from moneylenders and other Romans. Amongst these, according to Dio Cassius, was Seneca, Nero's tutor, who had lent 10,000,000 drachmas, a considerable fortune. These debts were now called in 'all at once and in a heavy-handed manner'. This may have been contrary to what many of the Celts believed for so great was their belief that death in this world would result in a new life in the real world that, according to Valerius Maximus, an early first-century AD writer, the Gauls lent money to each other to be repayable in the next world. Decianus, however, also demanded repayment of subsidies, possibly gifts, which Claudius had given to friendly Britons, claiming these were also loans. That the actions of the Romans were unjust was commented on by Tacitus in the *Agricola* when he said that the Britons were willing to be recruited into the army, pay tribute and have other obligations imposed by the government provided that they were not abused for 'they have been broken to obedience but not to slavery'.

Dreadful warnings were noted. The statue of Victory at Colchester fell down for no reason and with its back turned as if fleeing from the enemy. A clamour of strange voices was heard in the Senate House; the theatre resounded with wailing; frenzied woman prophesied destruction. In the Thames estuary an apparition of a *colonia* in ruin appeared while the sea turned blood red and threw up shapes like human corpses. The mention of a Senate House, a theatre and the Temple of Claudius shows that the *colonia* had progressed with its Romanizing policy and was trying to involve the Britons in this.

Even so, there may have been another reason for this revolt – a desire for booty, which had always been a factor in Celtic warrior raids. The attraction of a rich settled town, without much protection, may possibly have revived a latent Celtic craving for a style of life and a yearning for a combatant past before the Romans had taken control. As it was the Iceni and the Trinovantes were ready for rebellion and they found their leader in Boudicca. With many of the tribespeople she swept down on Colchester, destroying the undefended *colonia*, including those who made a last stand in a two-day siege of the temple. She then intercepted Petillius Cerealis, Legate of Legion IX, who was probably hurrying from the Longthorpe fortress, and annihilated his infantry. Petillius was then forced to retreat.

On hearing this news Paullinus immediately moved towards London, but this was 402 km (250 miles) away. Leaving Legion XIV and some auxiliary troops to follow he moved along the line of Watling Street. Needing reinforcements he summoned Legion II Augusta to join him from their base in the south-west but their legionary commander was away and Poenius Postumus, the Praefectus Castrorum, was ridden with uncertainty and refused to give orders to move.

Paullinus decided that London, then, according to Tacitus, an important and busy centre for trade, had to be abandoned. Refusing to listen to the pleas of the inhabitants he moved out together with as many of the citizens who could leave. The rest were left to their fate, which was not long in coming as the

Britons invaded the city. They then moved on to Verulamium where they again exacted revenge. Tacitus gives a figure of 70,000 people killed, as the Britons took no prisoners. Even if this is halved or reduced to a third, this indicates the severe defeat that the Romans had suffered. Excavations at Silchester have revealed extensive burning in parts of the town between AD 60 and 80, which may indicate that some of Boudicca's forces reached this area and exacted their revenge.

Paullinus decided to make one last stand, gathering together troops from Legions XIV and XX and some auxiliaries, probably about 10,000 men. This may have been either near Mancetter or High Cross in Warwickshire. Recent research using computerized generated tactics has suggested that the battle may have been fought farther west. If the Boudiccan forces did destroy Silchester or parts of the town, the possible site of the battle may have lain in the Kennet Valley or near the Goring Gap, near to Silchester, which could also relate to the evidence of burning in the town.

Wherever the battle took place, it was a disaster for the Britons. Boudicca's army was stated to be about 250,000, a number probably exaggerated to give prominence to a Roman victory. This was not two disciplined armies fighting each other, but a well-trained military fighting machine against an ill-disciplined crowd. It was not that the Britons were not brave. Individually Celtic warriors fought as well as any Romans but the emphasis was on individuals. Strabo had said, somewhat contemptuously, that the whole race, which is now called Gallic or Galactic,

> is war-mad, high-spirited and quick to battle . . . when they
> are stirred up they assemble in bands for battle, quite openly
> and without foresight so that they are easily handled by those
> who desire to outwit them. For at any time or place and
> whatever pretext you stir them up, you will have them ready

to face danger, even if they have nothing on their side but strength and courage.

This, as Strabo implied, meant that they ignored tactics and strategy, which were implicit in the Roman army.

Boudicca led her army into battle in a chariot, riding round to harangue each tribe to urge them to victory and avenge their loss of freedom. The chariots swooped down on the Romans, throwing them into confusion. The Romans used archers to shoot at the charioteers, only to be surrounded by chariots and being forced to retreat, before regaining the advantage. Gradually the discipline of the Roman army began to bear down on the Britons. Boudicca had also drawn up women and children and the baggage train behind the fighting men so that when the Romans made a breakthrough and her army began to flee they became entangled with their followers and the baggage train so that the resulting slaughter was appalling.

Tacitus gave the British casualties as 80,000 and the Roman as 400. The first figure is impossible; the second indicates that the Romans encountered some fierce resistance. He said that Boudicca took poison; Dio said that she sickened and died. There was another casualty. Poenius Postumus, realizing the disgrace that had befallen him and that he had cheated his legion of a share in the glory of victory, fell on his sword. For their part in the battle Legion XIV Gemina received the title of Martia Victrix and Legion XX were probably given the title Valeria Victrix.

That the Romans were shaken by this rebellion is indicated by the fact that 2,000 legionaries, most of whom were added to Legion IX, 8 auxiliary cohorts and 1,000 cavalry were sent to Britain. Paullinus intended to take revenge. Several natives sites in the territories of the Iceni and the Trinovantes were laid waste. This included the religious site at Thetford (Norfolk) where the buildings were torn down and the ramparts slighted with the debris filling the ditches; the site was not in use again for 200 years. Forts were refortified and military government was imposed. Evidence of the unrest can be noted in the number of hoards that have been discovered. These included 217 silver denarii at Sutton (Suffolk) and 872 silver Iceni coins dated to AD 60–70 at Fring (Norfolk). Metalwork hoards include at least four around Thetford, a large number of silver cups that had been beaten out of shape to provide scrap metal from Hockwold-cum-Wilton (Norfolk), and others found at Brandon and West Hall in Suffolk, and Saham Tracy and Santon in Norfolk. These were buried either to save them from Boudicca's rebels or from Roman vengeance.

Paullinus may have intended to take further measures but his actions were checked by the arrival of a new Procurator, C. Julius Alpinus Classicianus. Classicianus died in AD 65 and his tombstone (now reconstructed in the British Museum, although not necessarily as it was first erected) reveals further details about him. It was erected by his wife, Julia Pacata, daughter of Julius Indus, a Celtic noble from the area round Trier, who had helped to subdue a revolt in Gaul in AD 21. He had raised a cavalry auxiliary regiment, the *Ala Indiana*, which later served in Britain. Both Classicianus and Julius Indus were from the Celtic areas of the Roman Empire but were Roman citizens in imperial service. Classicianus's background would therefore lead him to be sympathetic to the plight of the Britons.

Classicianus protested to Rome about Paullinus's harsh measures, concerned not only about the destruction taking place but also because he feared that these would lead to a reduction of tax revenues from a battered province. He also had to make certain he secured Nero's share, if not the greater part, of Prasutagus's will. Polyclitus, a freedman of Nero, was sent to ascertain the facts. Tacitus sneered, saying that to the enemy he was an object of derision because they still hungered after liberty and they were amazed that a general and an army engaged in a great war should be so obedient to slaves. Polyclitus, however, reported unfavourably on Paullinus's conduct because soon afterwards he was recalled on a charge that he was responsible for the loss of some ships and their crews. Consequently, P. Petronius Turpilianus (AD 61–3) was sent as governor.

Tacitus, hostile as usual, said that this man was a novice in handling the crimes of an enemy, had no military experience and kept control of the province by easy-going administration. Turpilianus, however, realized that Britain needed a period of recuperation and both he and his successor, M. Trebellius Maximus (AD 63–9), concentrated on restoring the province. They ensured that Legion II Augusta was established at Gloucester to supervise the Silures, probably in preparation for a prolonged campaign. Colchester was provided with adequate defences and London began a rebuilding programme, including a large forum and a major new quay at which ships could dock to unload cargoes from all parts of the empire. Forts were added in East Anglia to keep a watchful eye on the Iceni. Forts in the midlands, including that at Baginton (Warwickshire) guarded the route to the north-west. Baginton is now regarded as a training area for a unit of cavalry preparatory to them moving further north. The rebellion had made the Roman forces even more determined to continue the advance northwards.

4

REBELLION AND CONTROL

In AD 69 there was a crisis in the empire. Nero, because of his bizarre behaviour, was declared a public enemy by the Senate, who supported Galba. Realizing his impossible position Nero decided to commit suicide. The result was a struggle for power with AD 69 becoming known as the Year of the Four Emperors. The legions supported their own candidates and Galba, Otho, Vitellius and Vespasian fought for control of the empire. Little of this seems to have touched Britain. Tacitus reported that the army in Britain was quiescent and that the legions conducted themselves with the greatest integrity, either because Oceanus had cut them off from their colleagues or because they preferred to fight an enemy rather than each other. There was one problem when Roscius Coelius, legate of Legion IX, who had long despised Trebellius, accused him of robbing his legion and reducing them to poverty, seemingly embezzling funds that were meant for the legion. Support gathered so that Trebellius was forced to flee to Vitellius but Britain still remained quiet. Vitellius, however, demanded support from the legions of Britain and contingents were transferred to him.

Trebellius obviously could not return so M. Vettius Bolanus (AD 69–71) was sent in his place. He was accompanied by Legion XIV Gemina, which had supported Otho, thereby compelling Vitellius to send them to a distant province. It stayed only a short time before being recalled to help in the suppression of a revolt of Civilis in the Rhineland and seemingly playing no part in the politics of Britain. The struggle for the empire in AD 69 finally resulted in Vespasian gaining control. He had led Legion II along the southern coast and possibly realized the value of Britain to Rome, provided that the island was made quiescent. He seemingly determined that there should be an advance to the north especially because problems had arisen with the Brigantes.

A poem written by the first-century AD poet Statius to Bolanus's son extolled the glory which a native of Caledonia would extend to the father who dispensed justice, and mentioned a breastplate which he took from a British king. This implied a campaign in Scotland but might easily have been a campaign in any northern area to deal with the Brigantes. Forts sited at Malton (Yorkshire) and elsewhere might have been established to curb the Brigantes in the east and to secure the Vale of York.

The Romans had relied on the client kingdom of Cartimandua to protect their north-western area. But, as mentioned, Cartimandua's betrayal of Caratacus in AD 51 had divided her tribe. Cartimandua had married Venutius, whom she thought was loyal to Rome; he was either her consort or a man with whom she shared power. He soon, however, became the leader of an anti-Roman faction and either because of this factor or because Cartimandua was having an affair with Vollocatus, his standard bearer, she determined to discard him and therefore she divorced him and promptly married Vollocatus. Not unnaturally her action outraged Venutius, for it was not only an insult to his sexual prowess but also to his political standing. Tacitus hinted that this scandalized part of the tribe of the Brigantes, already outraged by her betrayal of Caratacus. Venutius roused these to rebel and also encouraged enemies outside her kingdom to attack.

Alarmed at Venutius's action, Cartimandua sought Roman protection and Bolanus was forced to dispatch a force of auxiliary cavalry and infantry. These succeeded in rescuing the queen and putting down the unrest so that she remained as queen, seemingly with Venutius quiescent, but probably remaining in the tribe simmering with rage. Tacitus said cryptically that, 'Venutius was left with the kingdom, we with the war.' This meant that the north-west area was no longer a friendly client kingdom but one which could become hostile to Rome if Venutius decided to rebel.

In AD 71 Bolanus was recalled and replaced by Petillius Cerealis (AD 71–4), a friend and relative of Vespasian who knew something about Britain because he had been legate of Legion IX, which had been blooded in a fight against Boudicca. This may have spurred him on to control unrest in Britain. He brought with him Legion II Adiutrix, which had been raised from the fleet to replace Legion XIV and was stationed at Lincoln; Legion IX was moved to York, where a new fortress was built. Cerealis seemed to have moved immediately against the Brigantes, which implies that there was further unrest in that tribal area. What happened there is rather vague. Tacitus mentioned numerous battles, some of them bloody, and that large parts of the territory were overrun. Venutius may have moved out to construct the fort of Stanwick (North Yorkshire), lying at a junction of ancient Celtic routes where he could amass a large number of his followers, together with their families and their herds, while protected by dykes and ditches. These were no match for the Romans who constructed temporary forts around them while they gathered their forces.

No mention of this is made in the literature or the histories but archaeological excavations have indicated that the fort was destroyed during Cerealis's campaigns. From now on the

Romans would have to control these areas and this they did by building a series of forts to lock down the tribes. Later the town of Aldborough was established by the Romans to provide a focus of civilization for the Brigantian tribe. It is not certain what happened to Cartimandua, who disappears from history.

In AD 74 Cerealis was recalled and replaced by Julius Frontinus, who is better known in Roman history for being appointed *curator aquarum* in Rome by Nerva in AD 96 and for writing a two-volume study of the Roman water supply and *Strategemata*, four books on military strategy. In Gaul he had gained experience of putting down a rebellion and thus was well able to move against the Silures who had roused themselves to attack Roman camps. Frere suggests that a new generation had grown up who were willing to challenge Roman power. Frontinus quickly put an end to their attacks, establishing new forts along the coast of Wales at Cardiff, Neath and Carmarthen.

A fort at Brecon allowed easy access into both south and north Wales and cut off the Silures from the Ordovici. A network of roads and forts was now beginning to cover the areas and control the Welsh tribes. Frontinus moved Legion II Augusta to a new fortress at Caerleon. These forts would allow troops to move quickly along the valleys into the interior. He may possibly have moved against the Ordovici to make sure that they were subject to Roman authority. To make sure they did not join up with the Brigantes he established a fort at Chester for Legion II Adiutrix.

He was recalled in AD 78 and replaced by Gnaeus Julius Agricola, one of the best-known Roman governors of Britain as he had the good fortune to have as his son-in-law Tacitus, who wrote his biography, which has survived for posterity. Tacitus, remarking that famous men from 'time immemorial had their life stories told, and even our generation, with all its stupid indifference to the present, had not quite abandoned the practice', obviously placed his father-in-law in the best possible light. Nevertheless Tacitus's account provides vivid evidence for the state of Britain in the first century AD. Agricola was a provincial, born at Forum Julii (Fréjus) and an interesting example of how men born in Roman provinces could achieve a career in the *cursus honorum*, the career path leading to high honours. He had had previous experience of Britain through various commands in the legions – he has been called a British specialist – but this was all to the good. He had been a tribune serving under Suetonius Paullinus, experiencing at first hand Boudicca's rebellion, and then passing through the stages of being a quaestor in Asia Minor, and then Tribune of the Plebs and praetor in Rome. He had secured imperial favour by pledging himself immediately to Vespasian in AD 69 and had partaken in more military service as legate of Legion XX in AD 71 under Petillius Cerealis. He had then served for two years as governor of Aquitania, a province already pacified, so he could concentrate on civil government before being elected one of the two Roman consuls in AD 77. It was during his consulship that Tacitus married his daughter.

Given this career no one could accuse Agricola of not having experience for the post of governor of Britain. Aged about thirty-eight he arrived in Britain (in AD 77 or 78) to be immediately faced by a rebellion of the Ordovici. They had wiped out a cavalry *ala* (unit of 500 or 1,000 men) and in doing so had inspired others to rebel. Agricola gathered together detachments of legionaries and auxiliaries to launch a surprise attack resulting in the almost total destruction of the Ordovici fighting forces. Having realized where the centre of resistance was, he moved quickly against Anglesey, thus destroying the centre of Celtic opposition, a task that had been left unfinished by Paullinus's precipitous withdrawal to put down the Boudiccan rebellion.

He then spent time concentrating on reforming the civil administration, a task for which he had been prepared by his governorship in Aquitania. He therefore employed the correct officials for civil business, not freedmen or slaves. Every governor was allowed to bring his own officials and friends and presumably these are the ones referred to when Tacitus said that 'he preferred to appoint to official positions and duties men whom he could trust not to transgress'. When Cicero was governor of Cilicia he had been accompanied by his son, his nephew and a relative of his friend Atticus. He wrote to his brother Quintus that a good governor should take particular care in choosing his friends, as he was responsible for everything they did. This Agricola was obviously anxious to do. He reduced the corn levy and prevented the abuse of making the Britons buy back corn that they had already supplied in order to fulfil their quota of supplying it. They had also been ordered to take the corn to bases a long distance from where it was grown and to avoid this they had to bribe tax officials.

In between other campaigns he turned his attention to carrying out a policy of Romanization. This included educating the children of leading Britons, teaching them Latin and introducing them to the civilizing ways of Rome. Tacitus said that so successful was he in this that they became fluent in Latin, the toga was frequently to be seen, attendance at Roman baths was popular and smart dinner parties, presumably following the custom of reclining, took place. Tacitus commented that the Britons believed this to be civilization when in reality it was slavery. Tacitus might sneer but different and reasonably decent housing, cleanliness, social activities in bathhouses and orderly administration might be preferable for a younger generation to living in Celtic huts, being subject to tribal warrior authority and not being certain of their status in society. The disadvantages of being subject to Roman rule would come when less scrupulous governors were in control.

In AD 79 Agricola turned his attention to the north, advancing on both the western and eastern sides of Britain, laying out a series of roads and forts aimed at suppressing any resistance. He then offered reasonable peace terms to win over hostile tribesmen. Succeeding campaigns took him as far north as the Tay estuary by AD 81 and a series of forts were laid out along the Forth–Clyde isthmus. In doing this Agricola was intent on subduing the more northerly tribes, the Votadini, Selgovae and Novantae. His tactics were again to lay out a network of roads and forts. He tried to win over the tribes but his efforts had little success and he was forced to rely on military control.

About this time Agricola contemplated an expedition to Ireland, urged on by the arrival of an exiled Irish prince. Tacitus said that Agricola remarked that Ireland could be reduced and held by a single legion or a few auxiliaries. Given the warlike nature of the Irish tribes this would have been improbable and Agricola's reputation was saved by the fact that such an invasion was never undertaken. Roman troops were never based in Ireland although a 16-hectare (40-acre) fortified promontory at Drumanagh near Dublin has been claimed to be a Roman fort. It could equally well have been a trading settlement. Other Roman finds in Ireland also indicate that there was some trade between the two areas.

Agricola had enough to do taking the army further north into Scotland. He sent the fleet ahead to raid and plunder along the coast, thus spreading uncertainty about Roman intentions and also spying out the land. He also began to establish forts to block the entrance to each glen to contain the tribes and prevent them communicating with each other. A large fort was built at Inchtuthil on the Tay, probably for Legion XX to guard a passage through the Tay gorge at Dunkeld. This would allow him to move troops swiftly through the highlands. This action alarmed the most northerly of the British tribes, the Caledonii, who made common cause with other forces and elected Calgacus as leader. He gathered together an army of 50,000 tribesmen. These halted Agricola's advance so that Agricola was deter-mined to bring them to battle. In AD 83 Calgacus awaited the

Roman forces on high ground, placing his charioteers in the front. It is not clear where the Battle of Mons Graupius took place. A claim can be made for the hill of Bennachie as Agricola put his infantry in front of him with a camp in the rear and the fort of Durno (Aberdeenshire) is four miles away.

Agricola had about 8,000 infantry and 5,000 cavalry, including 'the bravest of the Britons and those whose loyalty had been proved during a long period of peace'. As was usual in Roman battle tactics he sent in the auxiliary cohorts of the Batavians and the Tungrians first. They took the brunt of the attack. Later Agricola deployed the cavalry to attack the flanks of the enemy while the legions remained stationary. The result was inevitable. Tacitus said that 10,000 Britons were killed for the loss of 360 Romans, presumably from the auxiliaries.

Agricola quickly moved to subdue the Boresti, whose territory was probably in the Moray area, and sent the fleet to sail around the northern coast of Britain. It performed the remarkable feat of sailing round the north of Scotland, receiving the formal submission of tribes in the Orkneys and sailing a short way down the west coast before returning to a base on the River Tay. The oarsmen reported the water to be sluggish and heavy, indicating that they had difficulty with the strong currents in those seas.

As far as Agricola was concerned the whole of Britain was now conquered and all that was needed was to consolidate his position in the following year. This was not to be. Agricola had been governor since AD 78, a longer term than any previous governor and this length of service in one province could be dangerous as it allowed a military general to secure the loyalty of his troops, replacing that of loyalty to the emperor. Domitian had become emperor in AD 81 and he was unwilling to commit more forces to the conquest of Britain. He, too, may have thought Britain was subdued. Agricola was recalled to Rome in AD 83 to 84. Tacitus implies that Domitian passed over Agricola for the position of proconsul for both Africa and Asia and hints that his death was hastened by poison.

The comment about the position of proconsul may be a little unfair. Agricola's career had been almost entirely in Britain and, though he had thought the province was conquered, this was not the case. However, his achievements in Britain were remarkable. On the military side he had doubled the area under Roman control, established a network of forts and roads into Scotland designed to subdue the northern tribes, used sea power to circumnavigate the north of Britain, recruited Britons into the auxiliary and revised Roman battle tactics, making the auxiliaries expendable troops by placing them in front of the legions. On the civil side, he had advanced the policy of Romanization. Agricola had encouraged the building of forums, temples and other public buildings and amenities of urban life. As Tacitus writes, he had reformed the administration and encouraged the sons of Britons to 'embrace the liberal arts. The result was that in place of distaste for the Latin language came a passion to command it. In the same way our national dress came into favour and the toga was everywhere to be seen.'

Two inscriptions relate to Agricola's governorship. One, dated AD 79, is on a lead pipe supplying water to the fort of Chester. The other is more significant. This is part of an inscription from the forum at Verulamium, also dating to AD 79, commemorating the erection of a basilica and indicating that Verulamium was a *municipium*. The erection of a forum and a basilica were definite signs of the progress towards the adoption of a Roman form of civil government. Allowing for the enthusiasm of a son-in law it would seem that Agricola had advanced the policy of Romanizing the Britons, relying on the younger element to overcome the prejudices of the older generation clinging to a Celtic lifestyle.

After Agricola there was a retreat from Scotland, which was probably due to the fact that the Romans were concentrating on the Danube where they had to put down a rebellion in AD 86. Legion II Adiutrix was withdrawn from Britain where it had been stationed at Chester. Its place was filled by Legion XX, which was pulled back from Inchtuthil. That fort was completely dismantled. Wroxeter was also abandoned as a fort and became the capital of the Cornovii. In spite of Tacitus's comments in his *History* that Britain was immediately conquered and let go (*perdomita Britannia et statim omissa*), the permanent occupation of Scotland would have required a large number of auxiliary and legionary troops. Some of these were needed elsewhere and the Roman high command possibly felt that the tribes in northern Britain had been temporarily subdued. It may also have felt that there was nothing to be gained from advancing further into Scotland. The land was poor, there were no minerals to be mined and occupation would be more of a burden than an advantage.

Little is known historically for the remainder of the century. One governor of Britain, Sallustius Lucullus (AD ?84–96), roused Domitian's wrath and was put to death as he called a new kind of spear 'Lucullan' after himself. He may, however, have been suspected of trying to gain the loyalty of the military forces in Britain for himself. Nevertheless two forts, Ardoch and Newstead, remained as outposts in the Scottish lowlands to keep the Selgovae in order and other forts were strengthened to keep lowland Scotland under control until about AD 101–105, when Newstead was demolished and other forts were burnt or abandoned. This retreat from lowland Scotland was possibly because Emperor Trajan recalled troops from Britain to fight in the Dacian wars. The Tyne–Solway line along the road called the Stanegate, created by Agricola, seems to have then become a line of demarcation and a policing boundary.

The Romans concentrated on rebuilding and extending the main forts and fortresses – Caerleon (AD 99–100), Chester (AD 102) and York (AD 107–108). Forts were also renovated in Wales and a new fort was built at Hardknott in the Lake District to keep watch on the Brigantes. At some time Legion IX was withdrawn from Britain, accompanied by three auxiliary units, probably to serve on the Rhine frontier. Lincoln became a *colonia* about AD 90 and Gloucester also became a *colonia* in Nerva's reign (AD 96–8). These were not only to provide retired veterans with urban property and agricultural land but also to act as models for the benefits of a civilized way of life. They also kept a watchful eye on neighbouring tribes – Lincoln on the Brigantes and the Parisii and Gloucester on the Silures.

At this time, however, the main Roman interest was centred on the Danube frontier where in AD 89 Domitian led a punitive expedition against Decebalus, who had attacked Roman territory and broken a treaty. Decebalus was confirmed as king of Dacia but the growing threat of his army resulted in Trajan invading his territory in AD 101. Decebalus committed suicide, his decapitated head was displayed on the steps of the Capitol and Dacia was made a province. Later, Trajan made Arabia into a province on the death of the Arabian king who had ruled a friendly client state. The empire expanded further in AD 114 when Trajan led an expedition against the Parthians using Armenia as a base. He then moved southwards into Mesopotamia but was checked by trouble in Cyrenaica, Egypt and Palestine. He moved legions to crush these revolts while he proceeded to annex Mesopotamia and Armenia into the empire. But in AD 117, while on campaign, Trajan fell ill and died. He had not named a successor but Hadrian, then governor of Syria, was acclaimed emperor by his legions on a rumour that on his deathbed Trajan had named him as his successor. Once his authority was assured Hadrian turned his attention to strengthening the empire and his decisions included the province of Britain.

5

CONTROLLING THE NORTH

By the end of the first century legionaries and auxiliaries had become more of a garrison army than an advancing one. Fortresses and forts had been established and many now had civilians living within a *vicus* (a settlement attached to a fort), often these being the unofficial wives and children of the soldiers. Britain appeared to be fairly quiescent, although in AD 118 the governor Quintus Pompeius Falco faced problems, possibly a revolt by northern tribes.

With the accession of Hadrian the Roman Empire ceased to expand. Hadrian intended to make a tour of the empire in order to consolidate the provinces and to weld their disparate peoples into a populace that would owe total obedience to Rome. From now on the emphasis was on achieving sound government and internal peace. Not that this seemed likely at the beginning of his reign. Hadrian faced a conspiracy by four of his senior commanders acting on the assumption that Trajan had not named Hadrian as his successor. Their revolt was stopped when the Senate condemned them to execution. This disloyalty reinforced Hadrian's desire to promote a central loyalty to Rome rather than give more power to individual generals.

The swift scotching of the conspiracy meant Hadrian was able to begin his tour of the provinces in AD 117. Britain was on his itinerary but Falco's suppression of a northern rebellion enabled him to postpone his visit until AD 122. He appointed as governor of Britain his loyal friend and capable general Aulus Platorius Nepos, who had been governor of Thrace and then of Germania Inferior, both provinces providing suitable preparation for Nepos's new role. Nepos arrived first in Britain, closely followed by the emperor, who brought with him Legion VI Victrix, either with the firm intention of using it to secure the frontier or to replace Legion IX. There has been speculation as to the fate of this legion, that it suffered a defeat and was disbanded or that it was transferred to the Rhineland. Later it disappeared from the army lists while campaigning in the east.

Hadrian's visit lasted only a summer but had significant results. His two aims were to improve civil administration and to create some form of permanent defence in the north from where the greatest danger came. The *Scriptores Historiae Augustae* commented that in almost every city he gave public games and 'he built public buildings in all places and without number'. This seems to have been the case in Britain. The *civitas Cornoviorum* built a new forum at Wroxeter and London completed the building of a new forum and basilica. A giant statue of the emperor was erected there of which the head survives. Small centres, such as Caistor-by-Norwich, were encouraged to build civic buildings, especially forums.

In his second aim Hadrian made great use of the army. It was not to be used as an attacking force but to provide a defensive structure. It is not clear if Hadrian had envisaged a wall before he visited Britain or if he grasped the strategic importance of one when he arrived. The cryptic reference in the *Scriptores Historiae Augustae*, written in the fourth century AD, summed up the emperor's visit in two sentences: 'the Britons could not be kept under Roman control' and Hadrian therefore 'set out for Britain. There he corrected many abuses and was the first to build a wall, 80 [Roman] miles long, to separate the Romans and the barbarians.'

The Wall as built was 120.6 km (76 miles) long from the Tyne to the Solway and was to be a permanent undertaking. This made sense as the distance was the shortest line from sea to sea across the country and the wall could make use of the huge crags, forming natural defences. The fact that this wall might divide the British tribes did not enter into the Roman calculations. As it was it became a barrier dividing the warring tribes of the north from those in the south and in doing so split the Brigantes. It is difficult to know why Hadrian envisaged such a formidable undertaking. A precedent might be seen in the 30-kilometre (19-mile) stretch of turf wall erected by Julius Caesar to block the advance of the Helvetii to the Jura Mountains. Roman frontiers were mainly roads and rivers. Agricola's frontier had taken the form of a road, the Stanegate, which developed into a boundary relying for its control on information gathered from the natives by troops living in forts at Carlisle, Corbridge and Chesterholm. These also acted as supply bases. The German frontier consisted of a ditch and a palisade, later replaced by a bank. In Raetia and Africa stretches of stonewall were supported by a number of blockhouses. Hadrian's Wall was a formidable undertaking that took six years to build, AD 122–8, and was subsequently altered.

The literary evidence may be slight but there is no doubt as to the physical evidence. An inscription, later embedded in the wall of the church in Jarrow, indicates that Hadrian was personally involved in the planning of the construction. It stated that once the barbarians had been scattered and the province of Britain recovered (which may refer to the AD 118 rebellion), the Emperor Hadrian added a frontier between the shores of Oceanus for 80 (Roman) miles. The army of the province built the Wall under the direction of Aulus Platorius Nepos. Other inscriptions found along the Wall make it clear that those builders included Legion II Augusta, Legion VI Victrix and Legion XX Valeria Victrix together with auxiliary cohorts, each allotted certain sections. Local people must also have been commandeered into working parties. Nepos was in charge of the work, remaining as governor until AD 127, therefore being responsible for much of the construction of the Wall, together with subsequent alterations to the plan.

There were four elements to the Wall: a stone wall, a ditch, a road (the Military Way) and an earthwork (the Vallum). This was not just to be a frontier but an indication of the power of Rome and its control of its territories. The work took a long time. A great deal of stone had to be quarried and dressed to enclose a rubble core. Lime needed for mortar was produced from abundant limestone burned with charcoal, but the process might take two to three weeks before the lime was ready to be mixed with sand and water. Work probably took place in the summer months, as mortar would not set in severe winters and the frozen ground prevented digging ditches.

The Wall took advantage of a ridge giving a view northwards and rising at its centre to run along a series of basalt cliffs known as the Whin Sill. It began in the east at Newcastle where a bridge was constructed across the Tyne. For the first 45 Roman miles (161 km, 41 miles) the Wall was stoutly built, being 3.1 m (10 ft) wide and 2.7–4.6 m (12–15 ft) high. On the top there was probably a palisade or a parapet. Beyond that, at the western end, suitable stone was less available so 31 Roman miles (46 km, 29 miles) were constructed of turf blocks 6.2 m (20 ft) wide and 3.7 m (12 ft) high, again with a parapet. Some time later, probably after the Antonine Wall was abandoned, the Turf Wall was replaced by a stone wall 2.6m (9 ft) wide. Another modification over the extension of the Wall from Newcastle to a fort at Wallsend (4 Roman miles).

Aerial photograph of Housesteads Roman fort from the south-east. Hadrian's Wall forms the north wall of the fort. The latrines are at the lower right of the fort. Since this photograph was taken, more buildings have been excavated

The Wall was also planned to have fortlets (milecastles) at intervals of one Roman mile, with two turrets between them. The milecastles were approximately 18 sq. m (194 sq. ft) and were constructed regardless of any irregularity in the ground. Each of these seems to have had two barrack blocks inside capable of holding eight to sixteen men, possibly more. Access to the Wall was gained by a staircase. That they were intended to act as independent units and be self-sufficient is indicated by the presence of a bread oven, usually placed in a north-west corner. A gateway through the Wall allowed troops to go north-wards to check any rebellion; one in the fort's south wall gave access to a road leading to the Military Way. Both gates acted as checkpoints for people passing through and, as on the German frontier, allowed them to proceed under guard and possibly paying a toll. For people accustomed to wandering freely and transferring animals from lowland to highland pastures this could have caused resentment at having to be beholden to Roman troops and moving through an unnecessary barrier.

The turrets, which were 6 sq. m (65 sq. ft) and built of stone even on the Turf Wall, acted as watchtowers and signalling platforms. Access to the rampart walk on the Wall was by a wooden ladder. There was a gateway in the south wall but none through the Wall itself. The turrets would also provide shelter with cooking places and small rooms. A reconstruction at Chesterholm consists of two storeys with a platform at the top surrounded by rampart walls. Each turret was in sight of the next so that continuous observation could be made along the Wall and to the north.

The construction of the Wall was not, however, straightforward. The soldiers began to lay the construction of what is now called the Broad Wall but about AD 124 a decision was taken that such a width was unnecessary. The foundation of this wall had been laid up to the River Irthing when the order was given to reduce the width to 2.5 m (8 ft), probably to increase the speed of the work and also to save on stone and the core material of the wall. Some turrets had been built with their wings ready for the Broad Wall to be bonded to them. An order was also given to move some forts up to the Wall to provide a stronger defence and allow troops to move swiftly into action.

The legionaries and auxiliaries had originally been intended to remain at forts already established along the Stanegate. These included Corbridge and Vindolanda, but the new forts were intended to cut through the Wall as at Chesters and Birdoswald. Housesteads was built on the Whin Sill where the drop from the fort was at its steepest and therefore the fort lay alongside the Wall with its north wall being part of the Wall itself. At four

Hadrian's Wall: the narrow wall on the broad foundation, Willowford

forts, Birdoswald, Chesters, Great Chesters and Housesteads, milecastles had already been built; these were obliterated. If the forts at Carvoran and Newcastle are included the number of forts equalled 17, 12 of which had been originally planned. These forts housed auxiliary cohorts 500 or 800 strong. At Carvoran there was a garrison of Hamian archers while at Benwell in the second century there was a vexillation (a detachment of soldiers) of Britons obviously raised within the province. An *Ala Petriana* (an auxiliary unit) of 1,000 men was stationed at Stanwix on the western part of the Wall. The forts along the Stanegate continued to be garrisoned to provide defence to the south. To the north forts were situated at Bewcastle, Netherby and Birrens, probably part of the original scheme. Later Risingham and High Rochester were established to the east of these. This meant that the area of lowland Scotland could be patrolled to check any trouble amongst the northern tribes.

This was not the only defence for the Wall. To its north was a ditch running 6 m (20 ft) from the face, except where there were precipitous slopes. In front of the Turf Wall it narrowed to 1.83 m (6 ft). The dimensions of the ditch varied from 9 to 12 m (29.5 to 40.5 ft) and the depth varied from 2.5 to 3 m (8 to 10 ft). The ditch had already been constructed when the forts were moved up so had to be filled in at the relevant points. At the eastern end, near Newcastle, excavation has revealed several areas where pits had been dug with a stake placed in them (*lilia*) to give additional defence.

To the south were two more elements of the Wall. One was a linear road (the Military Way). This does not seem to have been part of the Hadrianic system but a road was necessary to allow men and supplies to reach the forts. Side roads branched off from the Military Way to the forts. This road may have been constructed twenty years later. The other was the so-called Vallum, which also does not seem to have been part of the original plan but was added while the Wall was being constructed. This ran parallel to the Wall on the southern side at an average distance of 60 m (197 ft). There has been a great deal of discussion about its purpose. It might not be considered defensive as it consists of a ditch averaging 5.5 m (18 ft) wide at the top, 3.1m (10 ft) deep and 2.1 m (7 ft) wide at the bottom. The earth thrown up on either side was covered with turf blocks to prevent these banks from eroding. The whole distance across would be approximately 37 m (120 ft). A recent suggestion has been that it allowed men who patrolled the area to walk in the ditch without being seen. It is more likely that the Vallum prevented access to the Wall except at certain points, thus providing a controlled zone on the south up to the Wall. In that case it could be considered defensive.

When access across the Vallum was needed, cobbled causeways were provided. An excavated one can be seen at Benwell fort. Here, on top of the causeway, are the remains of two pillars, the bases of an impressive gateway. There was no doubt where a controlled zone began. Waggons and supplies could safely shelter in it at night. Such an undertaking, however, might indicate that there was hostility amongst the tribes to the south against this formidable barrier that curtailed their contact with their northern kin. This particularly applied to the Brigantes, some of whom were displaced to ensure the building of the Wall.

The whole system was further modified in the mid AD 120s with the establishment of a fort at South Shields where supplies could be landed. This was replaced by the present stone fort in the mid 140s. On the western side the system was extended to run along the Cumbrian coast for about 42 km (35 miles), probably to monitor movement across the Solway Firth. There was no wall but a series of fortlets and turrets would have provided a frontier, especially if they were joined by a palisade of some kind. The fort on the headland at Maryport allowed a wide view across the Solway Firth. Other forts at Burrow Walls, Beckfort,

Moresby and Ravenglass could check for pirates along the coast. These were linked by roads to inland forts at Papcastle and Old Carlisle. The latter was a cavalry fort that would have allowed a swift response to be made to any threat along this coast.

This frontier was a massive undertaking involving legionaries, auxiliaries and local labour. It was part of Hadrian's strategy to protect the frontiers of his empire but it was not merely a protective and defensive structure, although the wall certainly provided a fighting platform. The frontier supervised and controlled movement at certain points, at the milecastles and Vallum crossings, and, linked to the outpost forts, provided surveillance over lowland Scotland. The Wall must certainly have been a provocation to the northern tribes, but it served its purpose until the third century, allowing punitive campaigns in the north even though there were some reversals, as in AD 180 when Chesters, Rudchester and Corbridge were destroyed in raids. There were also some positive effects. The prevalence of so many troops in the area stimulated the economy for they needed supplies from the local tribes, especially leather for clothing, weapon coverings and tents.

The extension to the west protected the tribe of the Carvetii from hostile raids and their fertile land produced grain for the army. The *vici* attached to the forts also gave protection to civilians as well as opportunities for trading. Soldiers below the rank of centurions were forbidden to marry, but the men made liaisons with local women who lived in the *vici*. Marriage or cohabitation was finally legalized in AD 197 by Septimius Severus, who, according to Herodian, 'gave soldiers permission to wear gold rings and to live in wedlock with their wives'. Liaisons were unofficially encouraged because male children, emulating their fathers, might provide recruits for the army.

Formidable though the frontier might have been it was not the final defensive structure of Britain. Nepos's command in Britain was terminated for unknown reasons, possibly because alterations to the Wall were costly. He was replaced by Sextus Julius Severus but only for a short while because he was withdrawn from Britain in AD 133 to put down a revolt at Bar Kochba in Judea, a result of the destruction of a temple to Jupiter Capitolinus on the site of the Temple of Jerusalem. The outbreak was put down with much bloodshed the following year. The next governor in Britain, P. Mummius Sisenna, was responsible for more changes to Hadrian's Wall, replacing the Turf Wall by a stone wall, part of which was built in front of the Turf Wall.

Hadrian died in July AD 138. The succession should have passed to Lucius Aelius, whom Hadrian had adopted in AD 136 and granted the title of Caesar, but Aelius had died which meant a reorganization of the succession. Hadrian chose Antoninus probably because of his loyalty, but it was by no means clear that this would be accepted in the empire. Antoninus (AD 138–61), given the epithet 'Pius', probably because of his devotion to the empire, although he preferred to live in his villa rather than traverse his domain, was determined to make his authority obvious from the beginning of his reign.

The *Scriptores Historiae Augustae* commented that he waged a number of wars but all of them through his legates. Quintus Lollius Urbicus, his legate, 'overcame the Britons, and built a second wall of turf after driving back the barbarians'. Urbicus had fought in Judaea and been governor of Germania Inferior, a posting that always provided a good training for governing Britain. He arrived in Britain in AD 138, determined to restore order and bringing with him military reinforcements from the two German provinces.

The victory over the Britons was commemorated on coins showing a seated Britannia. Another source, Pausanias, writing in the mid second century, said that Antoninus 'never willingly involved the Romans in war, but he deprived the Brigantes of much of their territory because . . . they had invaded the territory of Genounia, which was under the control of the Romans'. The name Genounia is not mentioned elsewhere and there has been speculation as to where this might be. It has been suggested that this territory is not in Britain but in the Alpine region of Raetia where there was a tribe called the Brigantii whose neighbours were the Genauni. The attacks in Britain may have centred further south than the Wall on the less warlike and therefore unsuspecting tribes of the Cornovii or the Coritani. At this time, however, the *civitas* of the Carvetii was created in the Cumbrian area, which became part of the territory of the Brigantes.

Urbicus's first task was to strengthen the northern defences. Building took place at Corbridge, increasing the size of fort for use as a supply base. Dere Street would enable supplies to be conveyed to the north. The forts of Risingham and High Rochester were strengthened and Roman troops advanced into Scotland, probably in order to quell any sign of unrest linked to the trouble south of the Wall or by attacks by the Selgovae and the Novantae in the Scottish lowlands. The Roman high command then rethought its position and Antoninus Pius may have decided to emulate his predecessor and thus make his bid for glory. In order to contain the lowland tribes Lollius Urbicus was ordered to build another wall, the Antonine Wall, stretching 60 km (37 miles) between the Forth and the Clyde. This Wall was begun in AD 142 but was not finished until AD 158; Urbicus was recalled before the earthwork was completed, leaving succeeding governors to work on the Wall.

As stone was scarce in the region the Wall was built of turf on a stone foundation. It was 4.3 m (14 ft) wide and probably about 3.1–3.6 m (10–12 ft) high, with a rampart walk of 1.83 m (6 ft). Culverts were provided through it to drain off any water ponding up behind it. In front was a ditch averaging 12.3 m (40 ft) wide and 3.1 m (10 ft) deep. Six forts were built along the Wall as part of the original design, with regularly spaced small fortlets between them, but before the Antonine Wall was finished more forts were added, with all of them, except Bar Hill, using the Wall itself as their northern rampart. These were held by cohorts 500 strong, although Castlecary housed a garrison of 1,000 men.

The spacing between the forts was 2.4–4.8 km (1.5–3 miles), far more closely spaced than on Hadrian's Wall. This may have been to forestall attacks by hostile tribesmen either of one tribe against another tribe or against the Romans. Some forts were very small; Duntocher was only 0.2 hectares (0.5 acres). Outside the walls of Rough Castle pits filled with stakes (*lilia*) were dug, a defensive tactic used outside the fort of Newcastle. Inscriptions recall that the Antonine Wall was built by troops of Legion II Augusta, Legion VI Victrix and Legion XX Valeria Victrix, who were already skilled in this form of building. Help was given by auxiliary cohorts, in particular the Sixth Cohort of Nervians and the first Cohort of Baetasians.

Signal platforms were provided and a supply road ran along the Wall and often passed through the forts as the *via principalis*. The flanks of the Wall were protected with a large fort at Whitemoss on the south side of the Clyde and an outpost at Lurg Moor beyond it. On the eastern side forts at Carriden, Cramond and Inveresk prevented any invasion from the Forth. North of the Wall Agricola's forts of Ardoch and Bertha were reoccupied and others were placed at Strageath, Cardean and Dalginross in order to keep watch for any sign of rebellion.

Recent aerial photography has recorded fourteen marching camps near the Wall. The construction parties may have used these while the Antonine Wall was being built. No Vallum was constructed, as there was no need for a military zone. Instead the forts had defended annexes where supply waggons, traders and travellers could take shelter. While the Antonine Wall was in use, there was no need for Hadrian's Wall. The Vallum ditch was filled in certain parts and the mounds broken through.

Troops were moved north to provide garrisons for the forts on the Antonine Wall.

The whole of the Scottish lowlands could now be patrolled and any threat from the Selgovae, the Novantae and the Votadini immediately put down. Advances could also be made to the Dumnonii and the Venicones further north if need be. That Urbicus did intend to restore order was shown by his treatment of the northern tribes. *Numeri* (a unit of auxiliaries of ethnic origin) of Britons appeared on the German frontier after 145, probably consisting of young men out to cause trouble but with their warrior ardour deflected away from their native tribes. Those who remained appear to have been subdued by the control exerted by Roman forces between the two walls. Yet there may have been an ulterior motive on the part of the emperor. Did Antoninus Pius feel that he had to flex his military muscles, using the building of the Antonine Wall both to control the northern frontier and as a propaganda coup? The emperor could claim that he was transferring young headstrong men out of the province and recruiting their fighting spirit into the army. He issued commemorative coins between AD 143–4 on which were displayed Britannia and Victory.

Yet the Antonine Wall was not destined to be held for long. In the 150s another governor, Julius Verus, was reoccupying forts in the Pennines and beginning to refurbish Hadrian's Wall. The Antonine Wall was no longer regarded as the frontier but it is not clear when it was abandoned. A series of coins stamped with a defeated Britannia, issued AD 154–5, must indicate the successful suppression of a revolt. It is probable that soon after, about AD 158, the order was given to move back to Hadrian's Wall. The decision to retire was probably part of strategic planning with the object of not stretching the Roman forces. They would now rely on the outpost forts to control the lowland tribes. This may have been done with reluctance and while Antoninus was alive there may have been a reoccupation in the early 160s. At one time it was suggested that there was a later reoccupation of the Antonine Wall in the 180s but this theory has been dismissed.

From the 150s there appears to have been unrest elsewhere. Many towns began to erect walls, especially in central and eastern Britain. These fortifications have been suggested as belonging to the period when Clodius Albinus made his bid for the empire but new evidence suggests that they were begun long before this. Some of the walls may have been erected because of civic pride but the expense entailed indicates that there was a feeling of threats against urban life.

A curious feature is the number of fires that occurred in Britain in the middle of the century. For example, there was a major fire in London about AD 150–55, in Verulamium about 155–60, Alcester 150–88 and Towcester in the 160s. In addition a large number of villas were burnt down in the territory of the Catuvellauni and the Trinovantes. These problems may have been the result of an outbreak of tribal warfare, possibly by the Brigantes, frustrated by being corralled into their territory and moving south to take advantage of attacks on their more peaceful neighbours. The Brigantes extended as far south as the Peak District so unrest could easily have spread into the midlands and further south. This activity may indicate that the Romans had still not subdued the Celtic warrior propensity for raiding neighbouring tribes.

Antoninus Pius died in AD 161 and was succeeded by Marcus Aurelius. His reign coincided with attacks on the Rhine and the Danube, which meant that attention shifted from Britain. In an attempt to enlist the cooperation of the barbarian tribes Marcus tried a new policy. He transferred them south of the Danube and resettled them in the area provided that they would guard that frontier. In Britain there seems to have been further trouble, which necessitated consolidation of forces. In AD 163 Calpurnius Agricola was appointed governor and inscriptions reveal that he pursued reconstruction of the forts on Hadrian's Wall and in the Pennines. These included Ribchester, Ilkley, Lancaster, Old Penrith and Brough-on-Noe.

Marcus Aurelius needed troops elsewhere in the empire and withdrew troops from Britain, so the Antonine Wall was finally abandoned, although the lowland forts continued to be held. From now on, however, Hadrian's Wall was to be the northern frontier. Imperial attention had switched to the Danube area and the east. To replace some of the troops Marcus sent 3,500 Sarmathian cavalry, who had been recruited into the Roman army during Marcus's engagements in the east, to Britain. It is not clear where they were stationed but some of them later settled as veterans near Ribchester, so they may have been deployed on the northern frontier or in the Pennine forts. It is possible that they were drafted into this region to keep some control over the Brigantes, who had never been reconciled to Rome.

After this time the immediate history of Britain is unclear. That the Brigantes were still not subdued was indicated in the 180s when there was serious unrest during the reign of Commodus. Dio Cassius said that the greatest war was in Britain. Tribes crossed a wall that separated them from the Roman army and created great damage, even killing a general and his troops. Commodus sent Ulpius Marcellus against them. Dio Cassius goes into great detail about his character, stating that although he was totally incorruptible he would act without mercy when needed. He permanently fasted, could go without sleep more than any other officer and would send orders to his commanders on wax tablets during the night to confirm that they were still awake. Nevertheless, he was a capable soldier, as Dio said that he inflicted major defeats on the barbarians in Britain.

The wall which was overrun would probably have been Hadrian's Wall and indications of destruction have been found at some sites. The strategy of the northern tribes seemed to have been to make sorties and retire – pinpricks rather than an invasion. This meant that no side could gain a decisive advantage. The lowland tribes still obviously resented being corralled between both walls and later beyond Hadrian's Wall, especially the Brigantes, who had been divided by its building. These attacks meant that the Wall garrisons had to be constantly alert. Calpurnius Agricola set in motion restoration to repair any destruction and then led a punitive expedition into the lowland area. An altar at Kirksteads, erected by Legion VI, records a successful engagement beyond the Wall. Another, once in Hexham Abbey, now lost but originally from Corbridge, recorded that a prefect of cavalry killed a band of Corionototae, a tribe unknown but presumably from beyond the Wall. That this was successful is indicated by the commemorative coins which were issued, yet the destruction caused by the barbarians must have been substantial for the outpost forts of Birrens, Newstead, Risingham, High Rochester and Cappuck had to be abandoned.

Ulpius Marcellus's character and overbearing nature affected the army. He was recalled after his successes and Dio said that as he was on the point of being executed Commodus spared him because of his singular abilities. The army in Britain had one of its usual revolts and elected Priscus, a legionary commander, as emperor. Priscus knew better than to accept this and refused the honour. This both reflected on what had been done before and what was to come. From now on any emperor had to be wary of the attitude of the army and had to take steps to ensure its loyalty. A strong emperor would have ensured this; a weak emperor would be at risk.

A curious incident concerning the army in Britain indicated this. In 182 Commodus had appointed Perennis as Praetorian Prefect. Perennis gradually took on most of the government of the empire while Commodus indulged himself in acting out a role as a gladiator and pursuing other activities. Perennis began to replace senators, who had always been commanders of legions, by equestrians, probably hoping thereby to secure their loyalty. This obviously affected the careers of young men in senatorial families who had expected to follow the *cursus honorum* (the career progression). A furious reaction occurred and rather surprisingly a deputation of 1,500 men from Britain went to Rome in AD 185 to protest about this. Dio said that Commodus met them and asked what they had meant by this. The deputation stated, perhaps rather cunningly, that they had heard that Perennis was plotting to make his son emperor. This was enough for Commodus, who promptly handed over Perennis to his Praetorian Guards, who tortured him and put him to death.

Commodus, however, had taken note of this action. He sent Helvius Pertinax to Britain as governor with orders to restore discipline in the army. At first all was well: he put down rebellions amongst the lowland tribes; coins were issued in AD 186 commemorating this victory. He quelled the mutinous troops but then seemed to have exerted such disciplinary methods that one legion revolted and attacked him and his bodyguard. He had to punish this mutiny severely, which caused further army unrest, so much so that he had to withdraw from Britain. Decimus Clodius Albinus replaced him but in AD 192 Commodus was assassinated, troops in Rome elevated Pertinax to the purple and the train of events in the struggle for the imperial throne would have their impact on Britain.

6

CONTRAST:
REVOLTS AND PROSPERITY

Pertinax had been made emperor by the action of the Praetorian Guard. In December AD 192 Aemilius Laetus, Prefect of the Guard, had conspired with Marcia, Commodus's concubine, to kill the emperor. The Guard then made Pertinax emperor, as he assured them he would give each man 12,000 sesterces. Pertinax, however, later not only refused to pay this but he also tried to stop the Guard seizing plunder for themselves. They therefore elected Sosius Falco, one of the consuls, to be emperor, when Pertinax was in Ostia dealing with the food supply. Pertinax returned, exiled Falco, but neglected to take precautions for his own safety and was killed. The Guard then auctioned off the city and empire. Didius Julius won the empire by offering each soldier 250,000 sesterces. This was to no avail. He did not get the support of the Guard, who murdered him. News eventually reached Septimius Severus, a member of a wealthy North African family who had been governor of Pannonia in AD 191 and who controlled the Danube legions. He was pronounced emperor by his soldiers at Carnuntum in Pannonia. He moved swiftly to Rome and subdued the Praetorian Guard by tricking them into parading without their weapons so that his soldiers could surround them, 'netting them', as was said, 'like fishes in a circle of weapons'. The Senate proclaimed him as emperor and a new dynasty was established.

Severus now had to deal with events that had taken place in the empire. The weakness of Didius's claim had seemed obvious to other legions in the provinces, and both Pescennius Niger in Syria and Clodius Albinus in Britain had stated their own claims to be emperor. Probably these men had already planned their future moves beforehand. Severus first concentrated on subduing Pescennius Niger, who seemed the more dangerous threat. He had proclaimed himself as emperor at Antioch and controlled ten legions. To Clodius, who had only three legions, he gave the rank of Caesar, assuring him, according to Herodian, that he needed such a man of nobility and even allowing him to strike coins and erect statues to himself. Severus had no intention of letting him keep this title for long, but it gave him the respite he needed to move against Niger and defeat him near Issus in Cilicia. Niger fled but was captured somewhere between the Euphrates and Antioch and beheaded. Clodius, meanwhile, accepted Severus's blandishments, but he also had greater ambitions, proclaiming himself as Augustus in AD 194. He also suspected that Severus might try to assassinate him and therefore refused to accept any embassies from Severus.

Herodian stated that Clodius, on hearing that Severus would be moving against him, tried to take the initiative. Taking troops from Britain, in AD 196 he crossed to Gaul and based himself at Lyons, but few troops joined him there. At first, he gained the initiative in several skirmishes but in a huge battle, which Dio Cassius described in detail, stating that there were 150,000 troops on each side, Clodius's forces were defeated and he committed suicide 'in a house situated besides the Rhone'. The

Scriptores Historiae Augustae preferred to say a slave stabbed him and that he was taken half alive to Severus, who ordered him to be beheaded and his head sent to Rome.

Whatever the outcome, Severus was now undisputed emperor and free to pursue his own agenda. He immediately sent an equestrian, Sextus Valerius Marcellus, as procurator to Britain to hunt down Clodius's supporters and ensure that the province would be loyal to the new emperor. Measures included confiscation of the estates of those who had supported Clodius, one of whom seems to have been the owner of the Lullingstone villa. In this Sextus was aided by the new governor, Virius Lupus.

Clodius's attempt to gain the empire had led to a vacuum in Britain. Tribal revolts had broken out in Wales and Scotland; forts on Hadrian's Wall and in the Pennines were attacked; the Wall itself was destroyed in parts. Severus sent Virius Lupus, yet another governor from Germania Inferior, which seems to have been a training experience for governors in Britain, to restore order. He paid off the tribe of the Maeatae, the most hostile in the northern area, which had allied with the Caledonii, and began repair work on the northern forts. This included buildings at Chesters and Housesteads and granaries at Birdoswald and Corbridge. To subdue hostile tribes beyond the Wall the fort at Risingham was refurbished. Not all of his work may have been due to destructive attack. Restoration of fort buildings was constantly needed because of natural deterioration and Lupus's work may have been part of this. Between AD 198 and 209 the fortresses of Chester and York also underwent restoration.

Lupus remained as governor until AD 201. After him several short-serving governors succeeded until in AD 206 Lucius Alfenus Seneco arrived. He began restoring the forts on the Wall but Herodian said that he then sent word to Severus that the Britons were in revolt, overrunning the country, looting it and causing widespread havoc; he required additional forces and a visit by the emperor. Severus decided to come to Britain even though he was ill and suffering from gout. Herodian said that the emperor regarded such a visit as an opportunity to add to his military glory. Both he and Dio Cassius also emphasized that Severus was concerned about the conduct of his sons, Caracalla and Geta, and this would be an opportunity to get them away from their pursuit of a dissolute life in Rome and subject them to military discipline.

Severus arrived in Britain in AD 208 accompanied by his wife, Julia Domna, his sons Caracalla and Geta, and many high-ranking senators. For most of the journey he had needed to be carried in a litter and Dio Cassius commented ominously that he made the expedition to Britain even 'though he knew he would not return'. He brought reinforcements with him, including levies raised in Gaul, and established his headquarters at York. He made extensive preparations for the campaign, creating a huge storage depot at South Shields where twenty granaries were built. From here grain could be transported in ships along the coast to Cramond and further north to provide supplies for his army. He dismissed envoys sent by the Britons and, taking his elder son Caracalla with him, moved into Scotland.

Severus established a large base at Carpow on the estuary of the River Tay. This could easily be reinforced with supplies. At Carpow, the main buildings had stone foundations indicating that it was to be a permanent base from which to keep a watchful eye on the northern tribes. Camps established during his campaign are to be found in the eastern lowlands, skirting the Grampians.

The emperor found it no easy task as he passed through forests and over swampy areas, with the enemy melting away in front of him and any of his army who straggled behind being cut down by the Britons. Dio Cassius put the Roman losses at 50,000 which, even allowing for the usual exaggeration, would seem to be a considerable number for it might be equal to ten legions.

Rather vaguely, Dio then reported that Severus 'neared the furthest point of the island' and 'having being carried through the whole of the enemy territory' in a covered litter he returned, having forced the Britons to cede a large piece of their land.

The next year the Caledonii joined the Maeatae in revolt. Exasperated, Severus ordered Caracalla to lead his troops to attack and 'kill everyone even the child carried in its mother's womb'. Caracalla had his own agenda, preferring to win the loyalty of the troops to support him and, as Herodian said, 'regarding his father, who had been a long time dying, as a troublesome nuisance', even trying to persuade the doctors to hasten his death. Severus still prepared himself to go on the campaign but died at York; Dio Cassius recorded this as being on 4 February AD 211. His last, cynical words were 'live in harmony with each other. Give money to the soldiers and despise everyone else.'

One curious anomaly concerning Severus's visit to Britain is a statement in the *Scriptores Historiae Augustae* that 'he built a wall across the island of Britain from sea to sea, and thus made the province secure – the crowning glory of his reign; in recognition thereof he was given the name Britannicus'. *Britannicus Maximus* appeared on inscriptions in AD 210. The information about building a wall appeared also in an account by Eutropius in his fourth century *Breviarium Ab Urbe Condita*, stating that Severus built a wall for 132 miles from sea to sea. The same information was stated by other writers until Bede writing in the eighth century AD referred to it as a rampart made of turf, 'raised high above the ground like a wall. In front of it is a ditch from which the turf has been taken and on top of it are fixed stakes made from the hardest wood.' The literary evidence contradicts the archaeological evidence and subsequent writers have tried to reconcile the contradiction by supposing Hadrian had built an earth rampart to which Severus added a stone wall. This is now no longer tenable and Hadrian must be credited with building Hadrian's Wall, although Severus may have rebuilt parts of it.

On Severus's death Caracalla and Geta were declared joint emperors but Caracalla attempted to get the army to recognize him as sole emperor. This failed, so he cut his losses and, according to Dio Cassius, 'made peace with the enemy', presumably the northern tribes. He withdrew from their territory, moving back swiftly to York and thence to London. Carpow was abandoned but he seemed to have created some form of lasting peace for there is little reference to trouble in the north for the next seventy years. Coins stamped with the words *Victoriae Britannicae* were struck, indicating victory in Britain.

The refurbishment and rebuilding of sites allowed peace to be achieved. To ensure greater control, although some of the Wall turrets were abandoned, the milecastle gateways were narrowed and sections of the Wall were reconstructed. Many forts also needed restoration of their buildings not necessarily because of enemy action but because they simply needed repair, like the gateway at Chesterholm and the granary at Great Chesters, where an inscription specified that it had collapsed through age. Refurbishment took place at Bewcastle and Netherby, and High Rochester and Risingham were extensively rebuilt, thus ensuring almost complete control of the area beyond the Wall.

Each of these forts housed a *cohors equitata milliaria* (a thousand strong), which meant they could put sixteen *turmae* (cavalry squadrons), each of thirty men, into action at one time, thus providing a formidable group. In addition, Risingham had a *numerus Raetorum Gaesatorum* (Raetian Spearmen) and a *numerus Exploratorum Habitancenses* (company of scouts from Habitancum), and High Rochester a *numerus Exploratorum Bremeniensium* (company of scouts from Bremenium). The Raeti Gaesati would be able to reinforce the garrison and the scouts would provide vital information on suspicious movements or events taking place in the region, as well as recruiting civilian agents to help them. The Raeti Gaesati was an interesting group. Its members are described as spearmen but the name seemed to be akin to a weapon used by the Celts and called in Irish texts, the *gae bulga*. This consisted of a spearhead above a large number of barbs. When the weapon entered the body it could not be pulled out without mangling the flesh. Diodorus Siculus also mentioned spears, some having straight heads and some twisting round, 'its purpose being to thrust and mangle'.

Before he left for Rome, with his mother and his brother Geta, Caracalla divided Britain into two provinces. Herodian had credited Severus with doing this as early as AD 197. The emperor may have decreed it but Caracalla probably decided the details about AD 212. He had arranged his brother's murder in February of that year: Britain seemed to have taken the news of Geta's murder badly and the troops were restless. Dividing the province, however, would have made it difficult for a governor previously in overall control to lead a revolt against the emperor. An inscription set up in Rome dating to this time was by the Provinces of Britain confirming their loyalty and devotion. The term 'provinces' is definitely in the plural, indicating that a division had taken place. Accordingly, Britannia Superior, that is the part of the province nearest to Rome, had two legions, one at Chester (Legion XX Valeria Victrix) and one at Caerleon (Legion II Augusta). A consular governor stationed in London administered this. Britannia Inferior was the northern province and had a governor of praetorian rank, who would proceed to a consulship after he had given up office in Britain. It had one legion stationed at York (Legion VI Victrix) but as it covered the Pennines and the Wall it also contained a large number of auxiliary troops. York seems to have also been the administrative centre for it was not only the site of a legionary fortress but also the extramural settlement had been granted the title of *colonia*, no doubt a result of Severus's visit.

This administrative arrangement would certainly make control of the province easier, especially as it would prevent a governor from having total control over the army and the civilian administration of the province. It contributed to the next fifty years of relative peace, allowing Britain to enjoy a period of prosperity. Severus had made a similar division in Syria in AD 194 and Caracalla was to make one in Pannonia in AD 212. These divisions were also intended to prevent a governor taking out of Britain a large army and being a menace to the central authority of Rome.

In AD 212, Caracalla issued an edict that had considerable consequences for the provinces. On a papyrus found in Egypt in 1991 is written a copy of the so-called *Constitutio Antoniniana*. In it Caracalla stated:

> I am now granting to all those non-citizens who dwell within the borders of the empire the rights of Roman citizenship including all those who live in cities of whatever kind . . . It is most proper that the general populace should also henceforth share in the joy of my victory. This edict accords with the greater glory of the Roman people.

This may have meant little to Romans in Rome but it meant a great deal to provincials. It was intended to create a pride in those provincials who had felt themselves inferior to Roman citizens and excluded from the rights granted to those they may have still considered their oppressors. On the downside the decree brought them into the taxation system and this may have been intentional. In fact, Dio Cassius indicated that it was a cynical move aimed solely at raising taxes, especially as it made more people liable to inheritance taxes. How far it affected Britain is uncertain but from then on all free born inhabitants in Britain were assumed to be Roman citizens and all people part of one vast empire.

In Britain, troops were gradually withdrawn from the northern regions. Whatever arrangements Caracalla had made they seem to have worked; Carpow was abandoned, probably about AD 215, and defence concentrated on Hadrian's Wall. The Vallum was gradually slighted but cavalry units were attached to the Wall garrisons. They could more easily move into the lowlands if there was trouble. Troops may have brought their families with them from their homelands or intermarried with local women. They would have lived in the *vici*. Increasing emphasis seems to have been placed on *exploratores* or scouts, who patrolled beyond the frontier to collect information and give warning of attack.

Even so, the main forts were not allowed to fall into disrepair. Evidence of improvements and restorations is indicated in inscriptions. Between AD 213 and 225 there are numerous examples, including an enormous hall at Netherby in AD 222 and more granaries at Great Chesters in AD 225. An aqueduct was built at South Shields in AD 222–3. A gateway at Chesterholm was recorded as being rebuilt from the ground in AD 223. Beyond the Wall restoration took place at High Rochester and Risingham, including rebuilding of a *ballista* artillery platform.

There is also evidence of reconstruction of forts in Wales, at Caerleon in particular. This was probably part of a general restoration scheme, for attention had been concentrated on the northern frontier for many years. Other forts receiving major repair work were Caernarfon, Caersws and Castell Collen.

The area that appeared to cause most concern was in eastern Britain. A new fort was established at Brancaster (Norfolk) and a new headquarters building was provided for the fort of Reculver. Forts were provided at Caister-by-Yarmouth (Norfolk) and in Suffolk at Dunwich and Walton Castle. The last two have now disappeared beneath the sea. There is no literary evidence to indicate why these forts were built but they may have been in response to pirate raids on the coast. They also indicate that more trouble might have been expected in that area in the future.

The third century as far as Britain was concerned appeared to have been a relatively prosperous era. Many towns and small settlements added walls to their defences. Verulamium built its walls about AD 230. Alchester and Dorchester-on-Thames (Oxfordshire), Great Casterton (Lincolnshire) and Mancetter (Northamptonshire) added them about the same time. Canterbury waited until AD 270. This does not mean that these towns were in danger of attack. Adding walls to a town was a source of civic pride, perhaps as a result of the general granting of Roman citizenship, and permission had to be granted for their construction. What it also indicated is that money was available both for their building and their upkeep – an indication of the prosperity of the century. Rather curiously, a large number of hoards – over 600 were buried in Britain between AD 250 and 300 – have been described as hoards to avoid robbery. If the province was relatively peaceful, it is difficult to understand why so many hoards were buried, with the intention of being retrieved. A hoard found at Frome (Somerset) was so large (52,503 coins) that if it was the intention to retrieve it the most sensible thing would have been to divide it into portions. The possibility is that this was a generous offering to a deity and other deposits were ritual offerings.

Much of the wealth probably came from an increase in trade, especially between Gaul and Britain. Indications of this trade can be found in inscriptions, the most famous probably being that of a dedication in AD 237 by Marcus Aurelius Lunaris to Boudiga, a deity of Boulogne. He describes himself as a member of the *seviri Augustales* (the custodians of imperial worship, who were usually wealthy freedmen) of Lincoln and York in the province of Britannia Inferior and thus had trading connections, if not shipping agencies, in both these towns and in Boulogne. Another merchant was Marcus Verecundius Diogenes, also a *sevir* in York, who seemed to have provided shipping space for other merchants. Yet another merchant at York, Lucius Viducius Placidus, a trader from Velocasium (Rouen) who dedicated an altar to the goddess Nehalennia at Colijnsplaat on the island of Domburg, shipped goods to Britain. So did other devotees of Nehalennia: Gaius Aurelius Verus, Publius Arisenius Marius and Marcus Secundinus Silvanus, a merchant from Germania Inferior who was a trader in chalk. There was obviously continual trading across the Channel.

The emphasis on York indicated the importance of rivers for trading. Merchants could take advantage of the navigable River Trent to send goods into the midland areas of Britain. A canal, the Fossdyke, enabled barges to move from the River Trent to Lincoln. York was the headquarters of Legion VI but the civil settlement, which had developed from a *colonia*, was obviously an important adjunct. Goods would have included wine, salt, pottery, olive oil, the all-important fish condiment liquamen, timber and metal goods.

Not only York was important. London had become the largest town in the province by the late first century and it continued to expand and develop. Imports not only included basic necessities of life but also more exotic goods – ivory from North Africa, amber from the Baltic, and gold and other precious metals and stone, either in the form of finished goods or the material with which to make or assemble them. A gold-refiner's workshop was excavated in the Cannon Street area and a gem-cutter's shop in Eastcheap. Glassmakers' and pottery workshops were common. Building stone brought from other parts of Britain – Kentish ragstone, Lincolnshire and Northamptonshire limestone – was used to construct the large forum, the amphitheatre and the numerous temples. Decorative stone included marble from Purbeck and farther afield – from Carrara in Italy, Asia and the eastern provinces. With these came also craftsmen, especially mosaic makers. To this quantity of goods must be added imports of wine, food, textiles and house commodities such as lamps and metalwork.

That Britain was prosperous is indicated by evidence from villa excavations. Many of these country estates were rebuilt or extended in the third century. Villas such as Latimer and High Wycombe (Buckinghamshire) were enlarged and enhanced with mosaics; the villa at Great Witcombe (Gloucestershire) was expanded in AD 250–70; Rudston and Langton in Yorkshire were extended; and inhabitants of villas in the Cotswolds region employed mosaic workers from Corinium (Cirencester) to provide richly decorated floors and walls. Some of these, such as the villa at Chedworth, had thriving businesses attached to them. It has been suggested that some villas built in Britain resembled those built in north-east Gaul and the Rhineland which included a central hall, as seen in villas built in Gloucester and Somerset. This might be due to an influx of refugees escaping problems in Gaul in AD 260–80, so the style may represent transference of an archaeological style from Gaul to Britain.

It is clear that both urban and country life seem to have been prosperous in the third century. Trade and agriculture flourished. Britain seemed to have been remote from the chaos that shook the empire after the murder of Caracalla and the attempts to gain imperial power. Emperor Alexander Severus's murder in AD 235 led to struggles for power from which Gordian III emerged, only to be murdered in AD 244. Further crises in the empire led to a series of short reigns. None of these appeared to have affected Britain until AD 260, when the death of the Emperor Valerian led to a revolt in the Danube provinces. A usurper, Postumus, declared a Gallic Empire as an independent unit; this included Germany, Gaul, Spain and Britain. Britain seems to have accepted this and to have been free from any disruption. Postumus was murdered in AD 269 to be succeeded by Victorinus and Tetricus. Inscriptions on milestones, especially along Ermine Street and the road leading from

Clausentum, a port near Southampton, record some of their work in Britain.

In AD 270 Aurelian became emperor, the Gallic Empire collapsed and Britain was once more subsumed into the Roman Empire. Aurelian, however, lasted only five years before his assassination and a period of turmoil led to the murder of his successors Tacitus and Florianus. Probus assumed power in AD 276 and over the next six years succeeded in giving the empire some stability, though not in Britain, where there was rebellion. Probus sent Victorinus, a Moorish officer, to sort out this problem. Zosimus said that Victorinus put down the rebellion by a clever trick but unfortunately does not elaborate on this. Probus also used Britain as a place to send captives including Burgundian and Vandal prisoners, intending that they should settle in the province; whether the intention was to get rid of them or, as Zosimus said, to use them to assist in putting down the rebellion is not clear. Probus lost the empire to Carus, his Praetorian Prefect, in AD 282 and Carus's son Carinus took charge of the western part of the empire, assuming the titles of Britannicus Maximus and Germanicus Maximus.

Stability was not restored to the empire until Diocletian secured the imperial throne in AD 284. The next year he appointed Maximian as Caesar, his deputy with control over the western part of the empire. A year later, because of his successful rule in Gaul, Maximian was elevated to the position of joint emperor. A signet ring found in Britain portrayed their relationship. Diocletian was represented as Jupiter making decisions while Maximian was Hercules roaming the world to protect the empire against the forces of destruction. As Maximian had married Diocletian's daughter this also indicated the link with Hercules as a son of Jupiter.

Maximian's main task was to prevent pirate raids, which were increasingly occurring along the coasts of Britain and Gaul. This brought him into conflict with M. Aurelius Mausaeus

Carausius, a Menapian from a region within modern Belgium. With his command covering the coasts of Belgica and Armorica and probably Britain, he was in charge of a fleet to drive off the pirates, mainly Franks and Saxons.

From his base at Boulogne, Carausius was successful in putting down piracy, so much so that he made himself a wealthy man. He was accused of letting pirates raid the coast, then capturing them when they left, and seizing their booty. This did not fit in with Maximian's scheme of government for the west. He put a price on Carausius's head whereupon Carausius, in either AD 286 or 287, sailed for Britain and declared himself emperor. Britain was now a province worth governing, as it was one of the most secure, prosperous and relatively peaceful in the empire. Why, therefore, it supported Carausius is not clear. He may have secured enough wealth to pay subsidies to troops to bring them over to his side or the troops in Britain may have become alienated towards, or indifferent to, the present imperial government. Carausius might have been an officer in a Roman legion for part of his career and was therefore known to the troops. Civilians, such as wealthy villa owners or merchants, may have resented paying taxes to Rome and taken an opportunity to rid themselves of this burden.

Maximian could not move against Carausius immediately as he was concerned with suppressing rebellions on the Rhine frontier. By 289, however, he had gathered a fleet but Carausius's sea tactics ensured that he drove off the Roman fleet and Maximian appears to have been unable to secure a decisive victory. Instead, he put the best face he could on the matter and gave Carausius the title of Augustus. How far Carausius's empire extended is uncertain. He had control of Britain and possibly the coastal areas of Gaul – coinage found in northern Gaul has his name stamped on it. The coins had been struck at several mints, one being in London and another at Rouen. He needed this coinage to pay his troops but the coins also show his imperial expectations. Early ones depict him clasping hands with a figure of Britannia and the legend '*Expectate veni*' (Come, we have expected you). Others legitimate his authority with the words '*Pax AUGGG*' (Peace of the three emperors).

Carausius's empire was not destined to last. He was assassinated by Allectus, his financial officer, whose plot against him succeeded in AD 293, probably because Carausius had been weakened when Constantius, elevated by Maximian to the post of Caesar, seized Boulogne. This had loosened Carausius's grip on the coast of Gaul. Constantius was now determined to seize back control in Britain, but he did not organize an attack until AD 296, possibly finding it difficult to raise sufficient ships until then. He divided his fleet into two separate parts. One, led by Constantius himself, sailed from Boulogne towards the Thames estuary; the other, under the command of the Praetorian prefect, Asclepiodotus, sailed from the Seine estuary. He was extremely lucky for a thick sea mist enabled him to avoid been seen by Allectus's fleet, which was stationed off the Isle of Wight. He landed somewhere in the region of the Solent and, once he had embarked, ordered his men to burn the boats. He may have wished to prevent the enemy getting hold of them or perhaps he did not have enough men to leave some to guard the ships. Burning the boats also ensured that his men knew there was no way back.

Constantius's fleet had been delayed by bad weather and only a few ships got through to land troops near Richborough. The greater danger, however, came from the troops of Asclepiodotus, who was advancing towards London. Allectus may not have been with his fleet but was somewhere in the south-east, for he was able to raise an army to meet the oncoming forces. The two armies met either in Hampshire or West Sussex. The battle resulted in the total defeat of Allectus and his subsequent death. The remnants of his forces retreated towards London, only to be trapped by those soldiers who had managed to land from Constantius's ships. Allectus's forces included Frankish soldiers who sacked the city before probably intending to return to their homes across the North Sea. They were slaughtered without mercy.

Constantius quickly sailed for Britain and was able to enter London in triumph. A bronze medallion, struck at Trier, records his entry. On one side is the head of Constantius with his titles. The other shows him riding into a walled city identified by the letters 'LON' for Londinium underneath. Before the wall kneels a figure with arms raised in supplication at his entry. His fleet, represented by a boat, has obviously sailed up the Thames. The inscription *Redditor Lucis Aeternae* (Restorer of the light that burns for ever) indicates the gratitude of the citizens.

Constantius immediately focused his attention on ensuring control over the army as well as securing the defences of the province, for Irish pirates were now menacing the west coast, the Picts were restless in the north and there were also pirate attacks on the eastern seaboard. A number of forts had already been constructed on the south-east and south coasts of Britain and these were reconditioned. These have been called the Saxon Shore forts but they were not built at the same time to form one coordinated defensive structure. Brancaster (Norfolk) and Reculver were built about AD 230. To these were added Burgh Castle (Norfolk), Walton Castle (Suffolk), Bradwell (Essex) and Lympne (Kent) in the 270s. At that time the small fort of Richborough was given more defensive walls and Dover was refortified. Carausius may have added Portchester but the fort of Pevensey (East Sussex) was not built until AD 370.

These were not forts in the strict military sense of housing units of troops trained to attack. Their stout walls and formidable turrets seem to have been designed for defence. *Ballistae* and catapults could be placed on these turrets. Soldiers and their families, who normally lived outside the forts, could take shelter in them. Their defences were against raiders coming across the

North Sea, drawn by the wealth of the province. Yet raiders could easily slip between the forts and land anywhere along the undefended parts of the coast so it would have been necessary to construct a unified system of command that would ensure the defence of the whole eastern coast and its hinterland. It is also possible that a line of watchtowers was constructed along the Thames estuary, as one has been excavated at Shadwell. London would have been a great prize for seaborne raiders and early warning of their coming was essential. The western coastline was not left unprotected. Forts were built to guard the estuaries from Cardiff to Lancaster from raiders coming from Ireland and Scotland.

All these forts would have had to be used by the fleet. The *Classis Britannica* (the British fleet) already had bases at Dover and Richborough and after Carausius's rule the latter became its chief base. Gaius Aufidius Pantera, prefect of the fleet, dedicated an altar to Neptune at Lympne, which suggests it was another base. Other forts would have provided facilities to moor and repair ships. It would have been easy to link the forts by sea and arrange patrols along the coast. There is no evidence of a road system linking one with another. In the south roads lead from Richborough, Dover, Reculver and Lympne to Canterbury, which has been suggested as being an off-duty station for the troops.

The northern frontier required extensive restoration, not because of destruction, but from decay. There had been no programme of repairs since Severus's reign. It was time for intensive refurbishment and this was continued beyond Constantius's visit. Some forts had their garrisons reduced; at Wallsend and Chesters buildings were demolished in one area of the fort and not rebuilt. In other forts, buildings were abandoned. It has been suggested that these open spaces were to house the tents of mobile forces that could move out quickly to put down uprisings. Constantius appeared to have ordered forts to reduce in size their principal buildings, as happened at Great Chesters and Housesteads. At Birdoswald the *principia* (headquarters), the *praetorium* (commander's residence) and the baths needed extensive repair.

There were also differences in how the troops were housed. At some forts, such as Housesteads, rather than restore the barrack blocks, 'chalets' were built, laid out in rows, as if indicating that soldiers and their families could live there. Alternatively these may have housed the *exploratores* (scouts) whose duties took them into the Scottish lowlands. Restoration was also made to the south of Hadrian's Wall at Lanchester, Binchester, Malton and Ilkley. In addition the walls of the fortress of York were rebuilt and the riverfront enhanced with a series of multangular towers, both for protection and to demonstrate the power of military might. This restoration took place over a long period and extended into the fourth century.

Constantius returned to Gaul in AD 297 to concentrate on the problems there. He took skilled men from Britain to rebuild part of the city of Autun in France, which may indicate that the towns in Britain had not suffered during Carausius's rule. A panegyric on Constantius Caesar, compiled in AD 297, recorded that the Britons had greeted him, 'with great joy after so many years of most wretched captivity . . . At last they were free, at last Romans, at last restored afresh by the true life of the empire.' Allowing for the hyperbole it would seem that a new era had begun in Britain but to ensure that it would continue to be a prosperous province its defences had to be secured. That all was not yet secure is indicated by the return of Constantius in AD 305 to sort out further problems in the north.

7

TRANSITION:
THE END OF ROMAN BRITAIN

Constantius had to leave Britain in AD 297 to deal with events in Gaul. Soon after Diocletian and Maximian abdicated and Constantius was proclaimed as Augustus with control over the west while Galerius ruled as Augustus in the east. One of their purposes was to separate the civil and the military administrations. The provincial governor was no longer a legate at the head of his troops but a civilian officer with total control of administration and the empire was split into dioceses under the control of *vicarii* (governors).

Renewed fighting in the north of Britain forced Constantius to return in AD 305 to lead a campaign against the Picts who had moved towards Hadrian's Wall from their area of eastern Scotland. His son Constantine joined him but the details of their campaign are unclear. A panegyric to Constantius suggested that he penetrated into the furthest parts of Scotland, probably moving up the east coast. Other literary sources suggested that he moved north against the Picts and the Caledonii, and pottery evidence from this period found at Cramond on the Forth and Carpow on the Tay suggests that if he did move north he was making use of the fleet to bring supplies.

Either Constantius did not intend to complete the conquest of the north or he realized that he could not do this. He returned to York where, in AD 306, he died. According to Eutropius, his son Constantine, the offspring of a somewhat undistinguished marriage, was made emperor. Zosimus added a little more. He implied that Constantine had joined his father in Britain with the intention of seeking the empire. When Constantius died the next choice to succeed him as the western Augustus was Flavius Valerius Severus, Constantius's Caesar. In Rome, the Praetorian Guard had already moved to declare Maximian's son, Maxentius, as Augustus and this was supported by the Senate. The army in Britain, deciding that the son of Constantius was capable of ruling, had declared him to be emperor but for a while he was forced to accept the lesser rank of Caesar. Severus eventually was accepted as Augustus and Constantine became his official Caesar, which gave him some legitimacy. In AD 307 Maxentius moved against Severus and deposed him. Constantine gathered troops from Germany, Gaul and Britain, marched from Gaul across the Alps into Italy and decisively defeated Maxentius and his troops at the Battle of the Milvian Bridge in AD 312.

Constantine was, however, forced to share authority with Licinius as co-emperor. They divided the empire between them with Constantine basing himself in Milan not Rome. In AD 324 Constantine finally seized complete control and forced Licinius to commit suicide. Licinius had based himself at Byzantium on the Bosporus and in AD 330 Constantine moved his court there, proclaiming it to be the New Rome, and with great ceremony decreed that it should be called Constantinople.

Eusebius said that Constantine did return to Britain at least once in his reign but once 'he had subjugated it' he returned to Rome and concentrated his attention on other parts of the world. Coins produced at the London mint were struck with the legends *Constantinus Aug*(ustus) and *Adventus Aug* (the arrival of Augustus). The implication is that there were problems in the province but what they were is unclear. There may have been other visits. Coin evidence suggests that these were in AD 307, 312 and 314. He also declared himself *Britannicus Maximus*, suggesting that he had won a victory.

It may have been on one of these visits that he made changes to the government in Britain. About AD 312–14 Britain was split into four provinces, which are recorded in the Verona List. Two might have been named after the two Caesars – Maxima Caesariensis and Flavia Caesariensis; the other two were Britannia Prima and Britannia Secunda. Maxima was to the south-east with its capital as London. Prima was in south Wales and the south-western part of Britain. An inscription found at Cirencester, which formed the base of a Jupiter column, was dedicated by 'Lucius Septimius . . . Governor of Britannia Prima', which seems proof that Corinium was the capital. Flavia Caesariensis, possibly created from land in both the provinces of Britannia Inferior and Britannia Superior, covered the centre of Britain from north Wales to the Lincolnshire coast with its most important town of Lincoln as the capital. It may have included some of East Anglia in its territory but Maxima Caesariensis may have included the whole of that area. Britannia Secunda covered the northern area of Britain including the Wall with York, headquarters of Legio VI, as its capital.

Confirmation of these provinces is given by the report on the bishops attending the Council of Arles in AD 314. Eborius was Bishop of York in *provincia Britannia*. Restitutus was Bishop *de civitate Londiniensi* (London) in *provincia suprascripta*. Adelphius was bishop of *civitate colonia Londiniensium*, probably a mistake for *Lindinensium* as Lincoln was a *colonia* while London was not. He was accompanied by a priest and a deacon, which might indicate his superior status.

Collectively these provinces formed one of the twelve dioceses of the empire so that Britain was ruled by a *vicarius*. The British diocese was under the overall command of the Praetorian Prefect of Gaul who also controlled Transalpine Gaul and Spain. This effectively eliminated the direct access that governors of Britain had once had to the emperor. Equally, it increased the possibility of more taxation being imposed on the diocese, money that was needed to support the military forces.

Constantine also seems to have instigated other reforms such as improving the road system, judging by the number of milestones attributed to his reign and the following one. These would have helped communications between the forts. The army was reformed following the work which Diocletian had begun in two areas. Firstly, the officer class became more professional so that now they served their entire career in the army without alternating it with civilian office. Secondly, greater mobility was ensured with increased mobile field units (*limitanei*) being placed on the frontiers and their hinterlands. Evidence for this comes from the *Notitia Dignatatum*, which listed chains of commands and detailed civil and military officials of the empire and the units controlled by them. This is assumed to have been completed by AD 395 with corrections and alterations over the next thirty years. How far it was kept up to date is uncertain.

The forces in Britain were listed under three commands. The south and east were under the command of the Count of the Saxon Shore (*Comes Litoris Saxonici*) who obviously controlled the Saxon Shore forts and the areas between them. The northern area, which included Hadrian's Wall, was under the control of the Duke of Britain (*Dux Britanniarum*) with his headquarters at York. Both of these commands had extensive forces on which they could call against attacks from the sea or from the north. Much later, probably on the command of Stilicho in AD 395, a new command was instituted, the Count of the Provinces of Britain (*Comes Britannarium*). These commands came into being over several years. Constantine had given the first two commands roving commissions by creating more cavalry and infantry regiments. The army had moved from being a garrison army to mobile units trained to move swiftly to counter any attack. These commands were not linked to the civil administration but covered wide areas across frontiers.

Constantine died in AD 337 and the empire again fragmented when his three sons divided it between them. Britain, Spain and Gaul were under the control of Constantine II, who invaded Italy in AD 340 to attack his brother Constans, who ruled Italy, Africa and the Illyrian provinces. Constantine II was defeated and killed at Aquileia. In spite of this warfare Britain seems to have remained relatively peaceful until about AD 342 when Libanius reported that Constans crossed to Britain in mid winter 'with everything, cloudy, cold, and swell roused to total fury by the weather'. Julius Firmicus Maternus confirmed his 'crossing the swelling, raging waves of Oceanus, in winter time, a deed unprecedented in the past, and not to be matched in the future'. As the Romans disliked crossing the sea during the winter storms the implication is that the revolt in Britain was serious; in fact, Libanius said that Constans did not announce his coming or give any warning. Possibly Constantine II had withdrawn troops from Britain in his bid for complete command of the empire and the northern tribes had taken the opportunity to revolt.

One result of this visit was that Constans undertook a reorganization of the army. He created a native force called the *areani*, believed to be scouts, who, knowing the region, could range over large areas of land collecting information from the fellow natives. Ammianus Marcellinus said that it was their duty to 'hasten hither and thither over wide spaces to give information to the generals of rebellion amongst neighbouring people'. In order to make peace more secure Constans may also have made a treaty with the Picts in Scotland and strengthened the forts of Richborough and Portchester.

Constans was assassinated in AD 350 by Magnentius, commander of part of a field army. Two other candidates appeared as Augusti – Vetranio in Illyricum and a nephew of Constantine in Rome. Both of these were quickly disabused of their pretensions and Britain was under the rule of Magnentius. He removed troops from Britain, which may have resulted in an uprising in the north when the outpost forts of Risingham, High Rochester and Bewcastle were burnt in the AD 350s. Magnentius was defeated by Constantius II in AD 353 and extensive reprisals were taken against those Britons who had supported him.

Paulus, Constantius's Secretary (*notarius*) and a Spaniard whose ruthlessness had earned him the nickname of *catena* (the Chain), was sent to Britain to investigate this support, and to root out heretical opinions and anyone who opposed the unity of the Christian church. This he proceeded to do with intense zeal. He exceeded his duty, throwing freeborn men into prison, putting others in chains, fabricating evidence against them and, as Ammianus Marcellinus said, creating manifest slaughter and distraction. He returned to Rome with many prisoners, who were tortured; other men were proscribed, driven into exile or executed. Ammianus said that no one recalled anyone being pardoned if they were once accused. Not even Martinus, the *vicarius* who governed Britain, could protect anyone as Paulus threatened to take him in chains in front of the emperor. He attacked Paulus but was unable to do any damage because 'of a weakness in his right hand'. He therefore 'plunged the drawn sword into his own side' and the last chance of protecting Britain had gone.

Even with all this turmoil Britain still seemed to remain relatively prosperous. Constantius had appointed his cousin Julian as Caesar in AD 359 with the task of governing Gaul and Britain, as well as campaigning beyond the Rhine. Britain was able to supply Julian with grain for this campaign. He gathered together a fleet of 800 ships, some of which were built specially for this purpose, to transport the grain and so much was supplied that he constructed granaries in which to house it. Julian realized the value of this. In AD 360, according to Ammianus Marcellinus, the Picts and the Scots united and attacked in the northern area near and on Hadrian's Wall. This was in winter, but Julius, who had his own problems in Gaul and could not leave because of the revolt of the Alamanni, dispatched Lupicinus, his commander-in-chief (*magister militum*), to settle the problem by force or negotiation. He took with him auxiliary troops of Heruli and Batavians and two units of *numeri* from Moesia, crossed from Boulogne to Richborough in the depth of winter and went to London in order to assess the situation. Unfortunately Ammianus did not give any further details about this mission but the problem seemed to have been solved and Lupicinus returned to Gaul within a few months, only to be arrested as Julian, who had been declared Augustus by his troops, felt that Lupicinus was preparing to join Constantius. Constantius died in AD 361, plunging the empire into civil war from which Julian emerged victorious.

This may have set off another revolt in Britain. Ammianus recorded attacks on the northern frontier and there seems to have been little help from the central command. Julian died in AD 363 and the reign of his successor Jovian lasted only a year. The empire was now divided between Valens in the east and his brother Valentinian in the west. The enemy on the fringes of the empire may have sensed a certain weakness. There were constant attacks across the frontiers of Gaul and on Britain. In AD 367 the situation became highly dangerous. There was a concerted and violent attack on Britain by the Picts from the central lowlands and highlands, the Scotti from the lowlands, the Attacotti (possibly a tribe in Ireland or the Western Isles) and the Saxons from Germany, which was highly dangerous as the barbarians acted seemingly as one unit. Ammianus called it a *barbarica conspiratio* (barbarian conspiracy). This may have implied that a single leader, who welded these disparate groups together, was organizing these attacks, and even more importantly had kept Rome in ignorance of his plans. This personality is not known but the events foreshadowed the age of barbarian leaders such as Alaric, who would one day lead their disciplined hordes against Rome.

If the main attack in 367 had been a concerted effort, individual raiding parties soon split into small groups intent on plunder rather than conquest. The Picts and the Scots raided the north coastal areas and the Attacotti, creating destruction over a wide area; the Franks and Saxons pillaged the coasts of Gaul and probably the coast of Britain. The result was a disaster on a huge scale. Hadrian's Wall was overrun, not surprisingly as the fort defences seem to have been neglected. Nectaridus, Count of the Saxon Shore (*Comes Maritimi Tractus*, or *Comes Litorus Saxonici*), who may also have commanded the western coastal forts, was killed and Fullofaudes, Duke of Britain (*Dux Britanniarum*), was ambushed and captured. The crisis was the more alarming because the *areani* had treacherously deceived their paymasters by passing information to the barbarians on condition they got some of the spoils. In addition large numbers of deserting troops raged over the country but their intention was to plunder, not to seize political control.

Attempts by the central command seemed at first to have been half-hearted. Valentinian I, who was then in Trier, sent Severus, his Count of the Household Troops (*Comes Domesticorum*), to sort out the situation, but he was recalled when Valentinian fell seriously ill at Amiens. Another official, Jovinus, his Master of the Cavalry (*Magister Equitum*), replaced him but was also recalled. Finally Count Theodosius was chosen, whom Ammianus described as a man 'with an excellent military reputation'. Theodosius was the father of the Emperor Theodosius in whose reign Ammianus was writing, hence possibly the eulogy for the count. Nevertheless his command seemed to have been what was required. He collected together what Ammianus described as 'courageous young men' from legions and cohorts and sailed from Boulogne to Richborough. Auxiliary cohorts of Batavians, Heruli, Jovii and Victores (about 2,000 men) quickly followed him and once the army had landed it set out for London. Theodosius divided his army into several detachments to act as field armies, ordering them to stop the looting and prevent the raiders from reaching the coast. Any booty recaptured was restored to their owners if he could find them, except for some moneys that he kept to pay his troops. He offered pardon to deserters, many of whom accepted the offer. He next asked for Civilis, a man noted for his skill in law, to be sent as governor and also asked for Dulcitius, a general well tried in warfare.

Theodosius was able to spend the winter preparing his troops for action and generally raising their morale. He then had to contend with a revolt in AD 368 by Valentinus, a Pannonian who had been exiled to Britain, a fact he resented, who tried to bribe soldiers to support him. Theodosius heard of this plot, quickly put it down, and delivered Valentinus and his compatriots to the Emperor Valentinian for punishment as well as suppressing all enquiries into the conspiracy in case it provoked others to rebel.

Restoration may have taken a considerable time but by about AD 369 Theodosius was able to concentrate on 'restoring cities and forts of the garrisons'. Several towns already had defensive walls, probably because of the unsettled nature of the country. Ditches had been deepened and walls erected, and presumably Theodosius encouraged these precautions. Sometime between AD 341 and 375 London added bastions to its walls. Towns such as Caerwent in south-west Wales, which had provided thick stone walls, also built semi-octagonal projecting towers. Towers and bastions would support *ballistae* capable of firing arrows, darts and boulders. The emphasis was on defence rather than attack. Many towns also seem to have recruited a militia (*laeti*) to provide a protective guard. These may have come from rearming members of British tribes who still retained their Celtic spirit or from mercenaries who increasing sought employment in what was seemingly becoming a restless province.

London was renamed Augusta, presumably to give it enhanced importance, and shortly after AD 367 a fifth British province – Valentia – was created, named in honour of the reigning emperors Valentinian and Valens. Ammianus described it as being 'a province which had fallen into the hands of the enemy and been completely restored to its former state'. The *Notitia Dignatatum* recorded a consular governor but it is uncertain where the province was situated. One suggestion is that Britannia Secunda was split into two with the western part being called Valentia with a capital at Luguvalium (Carlisle). Another suggestion is that it was the eastern part of this territory with York becoming its capital. Yet a third is that it covered the area of Wales but this would mean taking part of Flavia Caesariensis and Britannia Prima, and, unless Wales had been overrun by the barbarians and become difficult to police, this seems unlikely. London also had a governor of consular rank and as it had grown in wealth and prestige – it was the largest provincial city north of the Alps – it no doubt had a status beyond that of a small province and was probably the administrative capital of the *vicarius*.

On the military side the treachery of the *areani* meant they were completely disbanded and the outpost forts of Hadrian's Wall were abandoned. Arrangements were made with the lowland tribes to make them into client states, which could form buffer areas beyond the Wall. One of these was the Votadini. A great hoard of silver found at Traprain Law hillfort, a stronghold of that tribe, may have been a payment made to ensure their loyalty and buried for safety. Later one of their tribal chieftains named Paternus appears in their genealogy as Padarn Pesret, the second word indicating that he wore a scarlet cloak, an insignia in Roman terms of a military general. Possibly similar arrangements were also made with the Dumnonii in the Strathclyde area.

Hadrian's Wall now had less importance as a barrier as the Picts were more adept at raiding by sea along the coasts. Some forts were reconstructed including Halton Chesters and Rudchester, and civilians moved into them from the *vici* to have more security. This is also clear at Benwell and Housesteads, where parts of the walls were rebuilt. Some elements of civilized life were retained: Chesterholm had its headquarters building restored with two latrines and a hypocaust. To the south restoration took place at Chester-le-Street, Papcastle, Bainbridge and Ilkley. At South Shields an assembly hall was converted into a grain store as if preparing for a siege or a campaign against raiders from the north. The scale of the reorganization and reconstruction indicates that the concerted barbarian assault had been considered a grave military attack on the Roman forces.

To give warnings of future raids Theodosius provided signal stations. Two have been found on a road in Cumbria at Wreay Hall and Barrock Fell but the larger number were on the Yorkshire coast from Huntcliff to Filey, as the greater danger was from raiders from the North Sea. The tall cliffs would have allowed the defenders to spot raiders quickly and possibly send warnings to the fort at Malton from which a message could be sent to York. Excavations at Scarborough indicate that the signal stations took the form of a tall watchtower 30 m (98 ft) high, surrounded by a walled courtyard and a ditch. An inscription at Ravenscar recorded either a building of the tower and fort (*turrem et castrum*) about AD 367–8 or a rebuilding about AD 395.

The towers may have been under the command of the *Dux Britanniarum* or the *Comes Litoris Saxonici*, who may also have organized a naval operation described by the military writer Vegetius in his *Epitoma rei militaris* (Military Affairs). He recorded that the Britons had fleets of galleys, the smallest having a single bank of oars, the largest having twenty oars on each side, which were intended to seek out the enemy ships before they reached the coast and to determine where they would land. To prevent these ships being seen by the enemy they adopted a kind of camouflage. Their boat, sails and riggings were dyed sea green and the sailors also wore sea-green clothing so that the ships would not be seen either by day or night. This last statement indicates that there was still an overriding fear that Britain was not safe from invasion by Franks and Saxons so a constant watch had to be maintained.

Once he had restored the province to order Theodosius was summoned back to Rome. According to Ammianus he 'left the province, dancing with joy, having distinguished himself in a series of great victories . . . and with good will on all sides he was escorted across the Channel'. When he arrived at the emperor's court he was greeted with praise and was immediately given command of the cavalry.

Theodosius's reconstruction appeared to have been extremely thorough, providing protection over the next twenty years. Meanwhile, after Valentinian's death in AD 375, his sons, Gratian and Valentinian II, divided the empire of the west between them. But Gratian did not know how to handle his army and problems arose concerning his commands. In AD 378 the Romans suffered a catastrophic defeat at Adrianople where two-thirds of their eastern army was destroyed. Troops had to be brought from the west, which included those in Britain. In addition provincial barbarians led by their own kings and chieftains filled the ranks. In Britain there were campaigns against the Picts and the Scots led by Magnus Maximus, a Spaniard, who had been with Theodosius in Britain in AD 367–9 and had been sent back to organize the province's defences. He was successful in these campaigns but was resentful that he had not been promoted to higher office. In AD 383, making himself popular with the troops and taking advantage of their resentment against Gratian, he got himself acclaimed emperor. He left for Gaul, taking with him a large number of troops from Britain, probably from some of the forts in Wales and the northern Pennines that were now abandoned. When he arrived in Gaul, he was joined by some of the troops in Germany. Gratian confronted him in battle but many of his troops deserted to Maximus so that he was forced to flee towards the Alps. Maximus sent his cavalry officer Andragathius after Gratian, who was caught and killed, and forced Theodosius (the son of Count Theodosius and emperor of the east since 379) to accept him as emperor in the west, where he proved his worth by holding Gaul against the barbarian invasions. This did not satisfy him and he invaded Italy in AD 387 driving Valentinian, who still had vestiges of his rule there, out of Italy to seek refuge with Theodosius in Constantinople. Theodosius was then forced to intervene and a decisive encounter took place in AD 388 at Aquileia where Magnus was defeated and executed. In AD 394 Theodosius had to intervene again in Italy in order to counter an invasion of the Goths. In this he was successful and managed to unite the empire, but he died in January 395 and the empire was divided between his two sons, Honorius and Arcadius, both already acclaimed Augustus. Honorius took the western empire, reigning from AD 395 to 423, a considerable length of time for an emperor, but over that time he had to face a series of crises, some of which affected Britain and included its loss as a province.

Gildas, writing in the sixth century AD, indicated that Magnus had removed so many troops from Britain that the Picts and the Scots were able to raid Britain in huge numbers. The Irish made raids along the west coast from Cumbria to Wales. They attacked inland as far as Wroxeter and then began to settle in Wales, possibly as a result of military weakness due to the removal of troops from this area. Legion XX had probably been withdrawn from Chester about this time, as was Legion II Augusta from Caerleon. Small garrisons of auxiliaries seem to have remained in some forts in Wales, including at Forden Gaer and Caernarfon, but it would seem that the Picts, unchallenged, raided as far as the south coast.

Gildas said that the Britons, 'promising unwavering and whole-hearted submission to Roman rule, if only the enemy could be kept at a greater distance', continually implored Flavius Stilicho, a Vandal general, to send an expedition to help them. He was married to Theodosius's niece Serena, and was the power behind the throne of the young Honorius. By now the Roman military command was relying on the support of those barbarians who had once been despised. Large companies of Franks and Alamanni had become part of the army in the west and barbarian names were now common in civilian and military commands. Many of these barbarian groups cooperated on a purely cash basis, and the Romans had to accept this partly because of their own shortage of manpower and partly because the Roman nobility declined to give either money or potential recruits from their estates. This, however, resulted in a certain tension, as the Romans were never able to have full confidence in these new mercenaries and allies.

Claudian, Stilicho's court poet, indicated that Stilicho 'had a care', which ensured 'Britain should not fear the spears of the Scots nor tremble at the Picts'; according to Gildas, Stilicho did send help (a 'legion') with the result that many of the invaders were killed, which seemed to provide some respite. Possibly some troops were still able to provide a defence. He also reported that another mission was sent to help Britain but as he also mentioned that the Britons were ordered to build a wall 'from sea to sea between cities, which happened to have been placed there through fear of the enemy', it is not clear if his accounts are accurate. The wall referred to must be Hadrian's Wall and the 'cities' are presumably the forts. The original building of the Wall had been lost in antiquity and Gildas was probably trying to explain when it was built. His statements might be explained by crude inscriptions found in the Wall, which indicate that construction units were provided by the *civitates* of the Durotriges and the Catuvellauni. These may have been fighting units transferred to the north to repair the frontier and reinforce its garrison.

Rome, however, was more concerned with other barbarian invasions. The empire was being menaced elsewhere and in AD 401 more troops, mostly from the forts in Wales and the Pennines, were withdrawn to help stop the advances of Alaric, leader of the Visigoths. From then on there were successive withdrawals so that Britain was denuded of troops, which led to more attacks on Britain. Irish attacks on the south coast by the Irish king, Niall of the Nine Hostages, may be dated to AD 405 but before that there is evidence of the destruction and burning of villas in the Somerset and Gloucestershire regions, probably by Irish raiders. Keynsham villa was burned about AD 378, Kings Weston about AD 384; and Atworth, Box, Colne, North Wraxall and others in those areas suffered the same fate.

St Jerome, writing about AD 415, stated that Britain was a 'province fertile in tyrants', and this seems to have been the case. There were a succession of usurpers of which the first was Marcus, who was elected by the army in AD 406, but within a year he had been deposed and killed. In AD 407 Gratian, described as 'a citizen of Britain', was elected and as quickly dispatched. The army then elected a soldier, who took the name Constantine III, probably believing that this name would help him to achieve the empire. The fifth-century historian Orosius said that he was 'elected from the lowest ranking soldiers, solely because of the hope attributed to his name and not because he had achieved any honour'. He proved, however, to be an effective military leader. Despite the previous withdrawal of troops he was able to take even more troops from Britain, possibly attracted by booty and adventure, and crossed with them to Gaul.

Events, however, had overtaken the empire. On a bitterly cold 31 December 406, when the Rhine was frozen, a vast number of Alans, Sueves and Vandals crossed the river and spread across northern Gaul. Constantine took advantage of this, quickly established an administration in Gaul, and then began to bring the invaders under control. He was not entirely successful but it was sufficient to ensure his authority. He then sent his son Constans and his general Gerontius south to invade Spain. By AD 408 Spain was in his grip. He had won support because he realized that the best chance of defending the west lay in strong government in Gaul, Spain and Britain. Honorius, in AD 409, also accepting the inevitable, recognized the validity of Constantine's rule, proclaiming him as Augustus and seemingly agreeing to a united Gallic–Britannic province with Constantine as a legitimate emperor.

Problems in Italy were to devastate this arrangement. In AD 410 an alliance between Alaric, leader of the Visigoths, and Honorius broke down. Alaric led his force into Italy and sacked Rome, with his Gothic troops doing the greater damage. Alaric died the next year but this did not spare Rome as his brother Athaulf led another army into Italy leading to confusion and tumult which resulted in Honorius's loss of confidence in Stilicho and his subsequent execution. Meanwhile Constantine was losing control of events in Gaul. He had recruited barbarian troops into his army but, when German barbarians crossed into Gaul, they failed to oppose them, instead concentrating on plunder. Constans's troops in Spain also got out of control. He blamed Gerontius who promptly rebelled and supported a soldier, Maximus, as a rival emperor. He allied himself with barbarian invaders who captured and murdered Constans. They then moved into Gaul at the same time as Constantine, wanting more power, was leading his forces into Italy. Hearing this Constantine returned to Gaul but was besieged in Arles by Gerontius. At the same time the Burgundians invaded Gaul with the intent of settling there.

Constantine's empire was disintegrating and his British forces were losing faith in him. Whether he knew it or not there were also serious attacks on Britain, which led to the Britons withdrawing their support from Constantine. Zosimus described them as 'throwing off Roman rule and living independently, no longer subject to Roman law and reverting to their native customs and setting up their own administration as well as they could'. This indicated that they expelled the Roman administrators, which was to have serious consequences later.

Zosimus said that Honorius sent letters to the cities of Britain, bidding them to fend for themselves, which implies that they had appealed to him for help. Any attempt to help was now out of Constantine's control. Honorius's army advanced to Arles, defeated Gerontius's forces who were besieging the city and forced Constantine to surrender. Constantine was executed and Gerontius escaped to Spain where some of his troops, hearing of his defeat, besieged his house. Realizing there was no escape and yielding to the entreaties of his wife he beheaded her and committed suicide. This Gallic Empire had now been destroyed.

Honorius seemed to have made no attempt to bring Britain back under Roman control. He had no troops available to do this and was concerned with containing events in Gaul where the real power was in the control of the Burgundians and the Visigoths. In fact, Procopius, a sixth-century historian who was prefect of Constantinople during Justinian's reign, said that the Romans were never able to recover Britain, which from then on remained on its own, subject to various usurpers (tyrants).

It would seem therefore that from AD 410 the Britons had to rely on their own precautions against any raiders. Direct Roman rule in Britain had ceased to exist, brought on by a succession of rebellions against the central authority. There was no withdrawal of Roman authority. Britain had gradually withdrawn from Rome. Britain, on the extreme north-west of the Roman Empire, may never have been fully assumed into that empire possibly because the whole population have never been fully Romanized. Celtic tribal authority was allowed to continue when towns became *civitas* capitals. Britons in remote areas continued to follow their own way of life. It was in the towns and the villas that people had become most attracted to conditions that seemed to offer a better way of life.

Towns hoped that stout walls would protect them; their citizens might raise a militia or hire mercenaries. That this was possible for some towns is shown by a visit of Germanus, Bishop of Auxerre, to Verulamium in AD 429. According to the Gallic cleric Constantius of Lyon, Germanus had been sent to Britain to counter the Pelagian heresy. This has been spread by Pelagius, a Briton, who decreed that man was responsible for his own actions and by his own free human will and God-given nature would determine his own salvation. This was in direct opposition to St Augustine's view that man was utterly dependent on the divine will and the grace of God, because the frail nature of his being makes him unable to achieve grace and salvation by himself.

The Pelagian heresy gained a strong hold on the upper classes in Britain and it may have been this belief that helped them to take matters into their own hands for their defence – to exercise, in fact, free will. After Germanus's arrival his preaching seemed to have checked further spread of these heretical opinions. He then visited the shrine of St Alban at Verulamium to hold an assembly, which suggests that the town then had some form of government to organize this. This is confirmed by the fact that he healed the daughter of a man having tribune power, that is, a man having military leadership in the Roman sense. Shortly after, Germanus won a victory over a raid by the Picts and the Scots, by leading the Britons into battle and urging them to cry 'Alleluia' at the moment of attack, an action which went back to the Celtic custom of shouting a battle cry when they attacked enemy forces. Constantius also states that Germanus made a second visit to Britain in AD 437 but, as he was involved in mediation in Amorica at that time, this visit seems unlikely.

Yet Saxon raids continued. The Yorkshire signal stations came under attack at least twice, Huntcliff and Goldborough being savagely destroyed. Hadrian's Wall ceased to function as an effective barrier. Forts remained in use but each may have organized its own defence. The soldiers had always been paid in coinage sent from Rome that then filtered through the population as goods were bought outside the forts. Coins from Roman mints began to cease after about AD 402. This cessation of money being sent from Rome or from the mints may have been because transporting coinage may have become too difficult and risky when crossing Gaul. Cash was also required elsewhere in the empire and Stilicho may just have stopped payments, believing it was a waste to send coinage to Britain. Local mints did not supply coins either because of the lack of good metal or because of difficulties in production. Whatever the reason the lack of coins particularly affected the civilian settlements round the forts. These had an artificial economy kept going by the pay of the troops. When monetary contact ceased the inhabitants drifted away, leaving only a handful of people to occupy the forts for defence or shelter, hence the lack of settled communities round the forts. After AD 407 Britain existed on coins already in existence or on barter. Military groups would probably seize supplies where they could. Army units would hold together for security and companionship but any military force under direct Roman military control was disintegrating.

The situation may have resembled that described in Noricum by Eugippius in *The Life of St Severinus* during the AD 470s. When coinage ceased to arrive, military units disbanded and left their posts. A neighbouring king then crossed the Danube and took over military control of the Romanized towns and the population, organizing them into defensive groups. If the same thing happened in Britain when coinage did not arrive, soldiers would leave their posts. Towns and villa owners in Britain may then have hired soldiers for protection as happened in other parts of the now disintegrating empire. These may not have been regular Roman troops. Instead troops in legions and auxiliary forces were being increasingly replaced by barbarians or by mercenaries, who were employed as *foederati* (warriors from barbarian tribes who fought in exchange for a subsidy). These may not have been paid but have received grants of land in return for military service.

Some form of town life probably continued in most cities. London and the former *coloniae* – York, Gloucester, Lincoln, Colchester – have remained as towns, while some forts such as Chester and Exeter were now civilian towns. Even smaller towns such as Dorchester-on-Thames and Catterick survived. Some did not. Wroxeter and Silchester were abandoned and Verulamium moved its site to centre on the shrine of St Alban. What form of town life remained is uncertain. Deposits of dark earth in towns such as Canterbury, Gloucester, Lincoln and Winchester have been suggested to be evidence of farming in the centre of what was once a thriving urban area. These patches may, however, be evidence of collapsed buildings as they are full of pottery, bone and charcoal. Refugees fleeing into the towns would have made camp in any abandoned buildings, moving on when conditions became too disgusting, a feature noted in towns that have been partially destroyed in recent centuries. In Cirencester, debris analysed in the amphitheatre suggested that people had once gathered there for shelter. In London the great basilica had been abandoned; the quays, not maintained, had crumbled. The city, once the largest north of the Alps, had gradually contracted and, although some people lived in its ruins, excavations have proved that the Saxons preferred to live to the west of the city in what is now the Aldwych and Covent Garden areas.

Gildas suggested that it was not only town life that had disintegrated. Potential conflict of interest was based on the defence of food supplies, for large-scale agriculture had been abandoned: 'So the Britons began to attack each other and in their efforts to seize some food dipped their hands into the blood of their fellow countrymen. Domestic turmoil worsened, foreign disasters resulting in no food except that which could be obtained by hunting.'

Villa owners continued to work their land as and where they could. Some owners probably moved to what they thought was the safety of the towns. Others continued to live in crumbling buildings. Rooms, which once were highly decorated to the pride of their owners, were now used for other purposes – a corn drier was put in a bath wing at Atworth (Wiltshire), fires were lit on the floors of the living rooms at Ditchley (Oxfordshire). At Lufton (Somerset) a hearth was built on a fine mosaic and an oven was carved into a floor in another room. The collapse of the Witcombe villa can be noted by roof tiles used as a floor and fires being lit on mosaic floors. There was now no satisfaction in keeping up a Roman lifestyle. Either their owners had given up the effort or squatters had taken what shelter they could. Life was now a struggle for existence.

Central administration had broken down. Local landowners were reluctant to take high office because of the cost. There was no longer a pride in being part of the governing structure. The expelling of Roman administrators during Constantine's reign in Gaul meant that the network of central authority had been rejected and men with experience of high office were lacking. Few men wished to take up office because of the cost and the responsibility. This meant that local arrangements had to be made, differing from place to place. The fact that Honorius sent letters to the cities of Britain, ordering them to take measures on their own behalf, was merely a form of words; he assumed the cities were still in existence and well-managed but he had no knowledge that was the case.

It might be argued that Britain, lacking official contact with central Roman authority, began to break into its tribal areas. Tribal disputes may explain the appearance of linear earthwork defences. The Wansdyke could be explained as a frontier between the Durotriges and the Dobunni. Bokerley Dyke would have separated the Durotriges from an advance by the Belgae or vice versa. The Fleam Dyke, with a probable date of AD 350–510, marked the boundary of the borders of the Catuvellauni and the Iceni, and Beecham Dyke and the Foss Dyke also protected the Iceni in the fen area. Grim's Dyke, north of London, would have protected the capital from attacks from the north. These might be expected to protect areas from attacks by the Saxons.

There were, however, other problems. Raids by the Picts and the Scots were becoming far more frequent. They came first as raiders and then as settlers. The Britons were forced to seek help from the Saxons against the Picts and the Irish, and the earliest Saxon settlements may have been at the invitation of the Britons to give protection. Traditionally the date of the arrival of the first Saxons, as given by Bede, basing his work on Gildas, is AD 449. Archaeological evidence has proved that settlement had occurred well before that date. A group of Saxon settlements south of London may have been linked with a group placed there to guard the city.

Possibly these raids and settlements forced the Britons to make one last attempt to get the central Roman power to supply aid. Gildas said that a message was sent to Agitius, consul for the third time, 'in the following terms, "to Agitius come the groans of the Britons . . . the barbarians drive us to the sea; the sea drives us back to the barbarians; between these two we are either slaughtered or drowned." Yet for all these pleas no help was forthcoming.' This can be dated to AD 446 and refers to Aetius, who was then the leading military man in the army of Rome. He was credited with defeating Attila and his Huns in AD 451, only to be stupidly murdered by the Emperor Valentinian in AD 454, who thus lost control over his army.

Britain also had new rulers. Gildas mentioned a proud tyrant, whom Bede identified as Vortigern, a Celtic name meaning

'High King'. Nennius, in his *History of the Britons*, also mentioned him and he may have been born about AD 360 and died in the late AD 430s. Nennius said that the Saxons, under their leader Hengist, came to Britain as exiles and that they were welcomed by Vortigern, who allowed them to settle on the Island of Thanet in return for military assistance. Unfortunately an agreement that they should be paid and fed broke down. In addition, Vortigern fell in love with Hengist's daughter, married her and gave the district of Kent to Hengist as a bride price. Whatever the truth, Vortigern seems to have been unable to prevent the Saxons from landing. Forty boatloads were mentioned and more arrivals meant that the Saxons soon spread across the land.

The *Anglo-Saxon Chronicle* confirms this story, stating that Vortigern (Wurtgern) invited Hengist and Horsa and their warrior bands to Britain to provide protection again warrior bands roaming the country. It may be argued that Hengist and Horsa are not the actual names; as nicknames they both indicate 'horse'. Whatever the case, the *Chronicle* said that they accepted this invitation but then set up their own kingdom in Kent holding the area by defeating the Britons at battles at Aylesford (AD 455), where Horsa was killed, and at Crayford (AD 456). They apparently came as *foederati*, indicating that they had obligations with subsequent rewards to guard Britain. Gildas said that they were given generous amounts of food but complained that these rations were not enough, saying that if they were not increased they would break the treaty. Soon they took up their threats with actions.

From then on Saxon penetration of the island seemed inevitable. Gildas mentioned the arrival of Aelle in AD 477, who founded the kingdom of Sussex, defeating the Britons at the Battle of Anderida (Pevensey) in AD 491. The *Anglo-Saxon Chronicle* recorded that in AD 495 Cerdic and Cynric landed in the West Country and founded the kingdom of Wessex. These accounts of the invasions are very speculative, especially as the *Chronicle* stated that landings were in two or three ships. It would have been impossible for such few men in these ships to win decisive battles. Nevertheless, they indicate some folk memory and it would be futile to deny that the country soon succumbed to Saxon invasion and settlement. Some Saxon settlements have been found as far inland as Dorchester-on-Thames. Possibly these were founded by men hired as *foederati*.

One name that emerges from the history of this time is Ambrosius Aurelianus, also called Arthus. Little is known of this man and his history has become irrecoverably entwined with medieval legend and romance so that it is difficult to untangle fact from fiction. As King Arthur, he was immortalized by Sir Thomas Malory in the fifteenth century in his work *Le Morte d'Arthur*, with an elaborate account of Arthur and the Knights of the Round Table, thus intermingling fact and fiction. The historical Ambrosius was a warrior, probably trained in Roman military tactics, who led mounted bands of Britons against the Saxons. The *Historia Brittonium* called Arthus *Dux Bellorum*, reminiscent of a Roman military title. He was associated with twelve battles and probably led mounted horsemen, well trained, who could easily rout a force of foot soldiers. Eight of these battles took place at fords where foot soldiers would be at a disadvantage. These victories culminated in a last great battle, about AD 500, at Mount Badon (*Mons Badonicus*), an unidentified site but probably somewhere in the south-west. Gildas said that 'after this there was peace' and about AD 540 spoke of 'our present security'.

This, however, was merely a respite because soon the Saxon conquest was renewed. By AD 600 most of Britain had been divided into Saxon kingdoms. The Saxons did not attempt to emulate Roman customs and institutions, and it would appear that the Britons had not so assimilated Roman institutions that they wished them to continue. The Anglo-Saxons imposed their own law, language, political systems and material values on Britain. Roman Britain, whose official contact with the Roman Empire had ended about AD 410, merged irrecoverably into Saxon England.

8

OFFICIAL AND CIVIL ADMINISTRATION

When Britain became part of the Roman Empire it was one of forty provinces in an empire stretching from the Atlantic to Asia Minor and covering almost all of the then known world. To govern such a disparate number of people the Romans devised an administrative system, which separated military and civil commands but ensured that men who wished for political advancement had been trained in both those areas. This career structure was the *cursus honorum*. Men who wished to follow this route were expected to spend time being trained in strategy in military posts and serving in civil positions, as a *quaestor*, an *aedile* and a *praetor*, giving them experience of legal training. They would be appointed as military tribunes in their twenties and in their thirties might expect to be in command of a legion (*legatus legionis*); usually by now they would have served as one of two consuls elected each year in Rome. Under the empire the consulship became nominally an honorary position but it still carried immense prestige, giving entry to the most important military and administrative posts. During the Republic the provinces were under the control of the Senate which appointed the governors. After Augustus became emperor he allowed the Senate to continue appointing the governors of settled provinces but kept under his control the provinces where, because of possible unrest, large numbers of troops had to be stationed.

Governing the provinces, however, was not entirely a matter of officials being sent directly from Rome to control barbarian or inferior peoples. By the first century AD there was a general assumption that Roman culture and the benefits of that culture could be assimilated in many provinces with the cooperation of the leaders, usually the wealthy nobility. Tacitus addressed the opposing points of view of conqueror and conquered. In the *Agricola* the speech he gave to Calgacus, the Caledonian leader who faced Agricola at the Battle of Mons Graupius, accused the Romans of being power-hungry: 'Neither east nor west has been able to satisfy them. Alone of all men they covet rich and poor nations with equal passion. They rob, slaughter, plunder and they call this empire. Where they make a wasteland, they call it peace.'

In his *History*, however, Tacitus accused the Gauls of always having war and tyranny until they yielded to Roman authority, and stated that if the Romans were driven out the Gauls would return to war. Peace was therefore a result of Roman control. In return for this peace, he said, the Romans, by right of conquest, imposed on the Gauls one demand: that they paid the cost of keeping that peace, 'for peace amongst different people cannot be maintained without troops, and troops cannot be maintained without pay, and pay cannot be found without taxation. In all other results we are equal. Therefore love and cherish peace and the city of Roma which you and I, conqueror and conquered hold with equal rights.' It was therefore the duty of Rome to govern provinces fairly and justly so that they could participate in the Roman peace.

The implication behind this, although not stated, is that the Romans ruled these provinces by right. Roman writers indicated that Rome's destiny was to be ruler of the world. Virgil made Jupiter declare, 'I set upon the Romans neither bounds of space nor of time. Your task shall be to govern all the peoples of the world in your empire. You will impose a settled pattern of peace, pardon the defeated and reduce the proud.' Livy stated bluntly: 'the city of Rome shall be the capital of the entire world . . . no men or power shall be able to resist the military might of Rome'. Behind this, however, were the cynical motives of many politicians whose political and economic fortunes could be enhanced by wars of conquest and who might themselves be appointed to govern a province.

Britain was never entirely a peaceful province. To ensure that peace was kept there were always three or four legions stationed there, together with a large number of auxiliary units, some for lengthy periods of time. Legion XIV was part of the invasion force but was withdrawn in AD 66 to take part in Nero's campaign against the Albani of the Caucasus. On the other hand Legion II Augusta took part in the invasion of AD 43 and was last recorded at Richborough in the *Notitia Dignatatum* at the end of the fourth century. Legion XX also took part in the invasion and was known to have been on Hadrian's Wall in AD 262–3. Some of the auxilia also remained in the province for long periods and were joined by other units. The presence of so many troops ensured that Britain was thus an imperial province, which came directly under the control of the emperor.

The governors of imperial provinces took their *imperium*, their command in military and civil matters, entirely from the emperor who in theory ruled provinces by the authority given to him on his accession. Not surprisingly, many had already gained extensive experience. Suetonius Paulinus had suppressed revolts in the Atlas Mountains and Platorius Nepos had been governor of Thrace and then of Germania Inferior before they came to Britain. They were drawn from the senatorial class and were expected to have property to the value of a million sesterces. Probably this was another reason why at first it was impossible for Britons to rise to high positions, although men from other provinces could do this: Trebellius Maximus was born in Toulouse and Agricola was born in Forum Julii (Fréjus). It was also often useful for a man to have a patron or excellent imperial or senatorial connections – Petillius Cerealis was a close relative of Vespasian; Lollius Urbicus had served with Julius Severus in the Jewish War. As many of these men had been ex-consuls before serving as governors it meant that in some ways their powers almost ranked with that of the emperor. This could not be tolerated and so, while in position, they ranked as pro praetors and were designated as *Legatus Augusti pro praetore*. Their previous holding of a consulship meant that many were referred to as *consularis* and this seems to have been particularly the case in Britain.

A governor was usually appointed for three years. Trebellius Maximus had six years as governor in Britain and Agricola had seven, but this was unusual. A governor was allowed to bring with him his own staff to help with the administration. One of these would be a *quaestor*, sometimes a relative, who would act as a personal secretary. He might deputize for the governor if he was absent but so might one of the legionary commanders, who were expected to provide total loyalty on any military campaigns. As well as professional officials there might also be a group of friends (*amici*) and advisers who hoped for favours from a governor both for themselves and for other friends and relatives. If this group were not reined in there could be trouble. Tacitus makes it clear that Agricola understood this in the first year of his governorship and that he was a stern disciplinarian. Rather surprisingly he did not make use of slaves and freedmen but seemed to have had a professional staff drawn from the army. Mention is made of him choosing centurions and other men whom he could trust and who would not abuse their positions. This kind of staff, which could provide a mini court, was relatively small, although later governors increased their numbers.

Agricola's career indicates that a governor was not a professional administrator. The office was accepted as part of a career structure. For some, such as Agricola, it was the apogee of a career and thereafter he could live in honourable retirement in Rome. For others it might have meant appointment to another governorship. Several moved from Britain to become governors of Upper or Lower Germany. A few might have become proconsuls of Asia and Africa. The number of men who held these positions, possibly 200–300 of a small elite group, out of a population of 50–60 million in the empire, indicates the assured mentality of the Roman administration but it was always backed by an efficient military power.

To provide help on the legal side a *Legatus Augusti Iuridius* was appointed. This was a vital office when questions of property had to be decided. The appointment was another stage in a career structure. This man had been a legionary legate, presumably with a flair for giving legal advice and, as the post gave him a good training in noting how a province should be governed, he would then expect to be appointed a provincial governor. At least five are known in Britain between AD 75 and 190. One, M. Vettius Valens in the AD 130s, was later appointed Patron of the Province of Britain, a title conferred by the Provincial Council, although it is not certain what this title or its duties actually entailed. The authority of a *Legatus Augusti Iuridius* can be recognized in the fact that another, M. Antius Crescens Calpurnius, in the 180s became acting governor of Britannia when, as Dio Cassius reported, the tribes in the island 'killed a general and his troops'.

Tacitus's comments about the situation in Gaul indicate that taxation played a decisive role in keeping the peace in a province. In those provinces under imperial control the *quaestor* did not act as a financial secretary as this might give the governor too much power. Instead the emperor appointed fiscal procurators from men of equestrian rank. These had to hold property with a value of at least 400,000 sesterces and many were men who came from the provinces. They might also be freedmen, probably in the imperial service, who would be regularly employed in the provinces to watch over the emperor's interests. The actions of the first procurator known in Britain, Decianus Catus, contributed towards the problems leading to the Boudiccan rebellion and his hasty exit from the island left the way open for his successor, Julius Classicianus; the latter's power seemed to have been such that he was able to have the governor recalled to Rome. Classicianus came from the Trier area and was therefore more likely to understand Celtic tribal feelings in Britain, an indication of the flexibility of Roman forms of government.

Evidence suggests that the procurator's office was established in London. Julius Classicianus died in office and his tombstone was found outside the walls of the city. More explicitly, tiles stamped PPBRILON meaning *P(rocuratores) P(rovinciae) BRI(tanniae) LON(dini)* have been found there, and also at Brockley Hill (Middlesex), where there was a tilery producing these products. A wooden writing tablet, found near the Walbrook river, was inscribed with the words *Pro(curators) Aug(usti) P(rovinciae) dederunt Brit(anniae)*, meaning the Procurators of the Province of Britain issued this. Such a document must have been issued directly from the procurator's office.

There were also other posts designated to procurators or their staff. At Combe Down (Somerset) an inscription mentioned the restoration of a headquarters building, possibly the main one on an imperial estate, which was often under the supervision of imperial procurators. This particular inscription by Navius identifies him as an imperial freedman and assistant to the procurator who had restored the building and dedicated it to the welfare of the emperor, probably Caracalla or even

Elagabalus. Procurators were also in charge of mining areas, which were most important in the Roman Empire.

The duties of the procurator included collecting direct taxation and administering imperial estates. When provinces were first brought into the empire there was considerable advantage for an ambitious politician, ignoring any legal or moral restraints, to advance his fortune. The Augustan reforms checked this and limited any Roman official's exploitation of the provinces for the emperor's own advantage. Taxation was now under imperial control and was based on land (*tributum soli*) and persons (*tributum capitis*), with extra taxes on the sale and emancipation of slaves and on inheritance, although the last did not apply to Britain.

Every five years a census was undertaken throughout the empire, conducted by a censor, a man usually appointed from the army and given the title of procurator. This was to ascertain both the number of the population and the property that a man held. Two censors are known in Britain. Gnaeus Munitius Aurelius Bassus took a census in Colchester, probably in the early third century AD, and this town would probably have accepted it with resignation as one of the burdens imposed by the empire. T. Haterius Nepos was in charge of a census in the early second century of the Anavionensian Britons, probably in Annandale in south-west Scotland, which, being on the fringes of the civilized area, might have caused these people bewilderment if not great resentment, as they may not have been used to this custom. Fringes of the empire it might have been, but it indicates how far the jurisdiction of Rome extended. The bulk of the money in at least the first two centuries AD went to the support of the army, which also had to be paid in kind – food, hides for leather, minerals and building material.

Later, as the Roman administration became vitally short of money, especially as the barbarians were pressing on the frontiers of the empire, taxation increased enormously. Britain was not spared. In AD 353 the imperial legate Paulus, who had been sent to Britain to ascertain support for Emperor Constantius III, tried to sequestrate the fortunes of those civilians who had supported the pretender Magnentius. This was an illegal act but later problems with inflation led to taxation being imposed in kind as food was more useful than money. This may have been why Emperor Julian was able to remove so much grain from the abundant harvests in Britain to support his army in the Rhineland in AD 359.

Provinces usually had a provincial capital. It could be argued that during the first century AD the centre of government in Britain was where the governor was stationed at a certain time. This would equate with the progress of a medieval monarch, but while the monarch moved with all his court, Roman governors had a large administrative staff that often received orders from Rome and thus needed a permanent place in which to perform their duties. The main centre of government in Britain was first based at the *colonia* of Colchester, the former Camulodunum, and the chief town of Cunobelin, which had been the Roman objective during the invasion of AD 43. It was here that the Imperial Cult was centred, closely linked with the Provincial Council to which delegates were sent once a year by tribal communities. The president of the council was the priest of the Imperial Cult. He paid the costs of the council and for festivities or games held while they met. Tacitus, when commenting on the reasons for the Boudiccan rebellion, indicated that not only was the Temple of Claudius looked upon as a stronghold of tyranny but that those chosen as priests were pouring out their fortunes to sustain it on the pretext of religion. No doubt these costs were extracted from the native Britons.

The temple was rebuilt after the rebellion so the religious capital remained at Colchester, but some time later the Provincial Council seems to have met in London. The evidence for this is based on an inscription dedicated to the deity of the emperor by the Provincial Council and a tombstone dedicated by Anencletus, a slave of the province (*provincialis*), to his wife Claudia Martina, who died at the young age of nineteen. The administrative capital may therefore have moved to London where the procurator was based late in the first century. A large building found under Cannon Street station was initially suggested to be the site of the governor's palace, but reconsideration of the evidence has shown that its foundations do not form one building but can be allotted to several different ones.

The governor's staff included clerks, scribes, accountants, administrative officers and guards, in addition to their numerous assistants. Some of these men were educated slaves sent from Rome; other might be seconded legionaries. A monument erected by a group of *speculatores* to one of their members indicates the presence in London of guards. These would be groups of ten men seconded from at first the four and later the three legions in the province, who guarded prisoners and supervised executions. Their perks included any items belonging to the condemned men. In theory these should have been sold and the money sent to the emperor. Some governors did this but often it was not worth the effort to send the money to Rome and probably in a remote province such as Britain the money either went towards the governor's expenses or was kept by the *speculatores*. Amongst the lower ranks of the governor's staff were the grooms (*stratores consulares*) and evidence from a Vindolanda tablet indicates that one was based in London, having been seconded there from the northern fort. Their tasks could also include seeking out new horses for the army.

More important were the *beneficiarii consulares* who were detached from legions in order to serve the governor in some capacity. They enjoyed considerable status and were seconded from legions, often up to sixty men per legion. The governor of Britain could therefore have about 240 or, later, 180 men to do his bidding. No inscriptions to these men have been found in

London, perhaps not surprisingly as they would have been sent throughout the province or to other provinces on the governor's business.

All these soldiers would have to be housed in a military base in London. This would have been in the Cripplegate fort where they would have been joined by the governor's guard, hand-picked men from the cavalry and the infantry. The 5-hectare (11-acre) fort was built outside the city, possibly first in timber but then in stone, probably about AD 100–130. Later it was incorporated into the city when the defensive wall was constructed. The fort could have held 500 *equites* and 1,000 *pedites singulares* (the hand-picked horsemen and foot soldiers). These remained attached to their units; one of the Vindolanda documents records a detachment of forty-six troops from *Cohors I Tungrorum* and a centurion being sent from that fort to London presumably to form part of the governor's guard.

An important discovery, dating to the third century AD, was found in the remains of a series of handsome Roman buildings when excavating the site of the medieval palace of the bishops of Winchester in Southwark. This was an inscription listing soldiers from a legionary cohort, although it is not clear what that legion was. As by that date Britain was divided into two provinces they must have been from either Legion II Augusta or Legion XX VV, both stationed in Britannia Superior. Mark Hassall suggested the men could be members of a guild of *beneficiarii consulares,* and that the buildings, which contained a large bath complex might be their *schola* (clubhouse). There could have been sixty members but only the names of seven could be distinguished. The presence of soldiers in Southwark indicates that London then certainly housed the headquarters of the governor.

Britain had remained as a single province governed by a single command until the end of the second century AD. Under Caracalla's rule Britain was divided into two provinces: Britannia Inferior, with its headquarters at York, probably under the control of the *Legatus Augusti* of Legion VI Victrix; and Britannia Superior in the south with a consular governor who controlled Legion XX Valeria Victrix at Chester and Legion II Augusta at Caerleon. As suggested, his headquarters were in London and, as he was a consular governor, London was therefore probably the capital of Britannia Superior, outranking that of York.

The Diocletian reforms (AD 284–306) created two military commands, the *Dux Britanniarum* and the *Comes Litoris Saxonici*. They also divided Britain into four provinces and later a fifth was added. Maxima Caesariensis had a governor of consular senatorial rank; the other three were governed by equestrian *praesides*. Overall there was a *vicarius* (deputy) of the British Provinces who, given the status of the city by that time, must have been based in London. He would have been responsible to the Praetorian Prefect of the Gauls and his staff is detailed in the *Notitia Dignitatum*. These included a chief of staff (*princeps*), a principal assistant or secretary (*cornicularius*), accountants (*numerarii*), a minor secretary (*commentariensis*), a registrar (*ab actis*), a correspondence secretary (*cura epistolarum*), an adjutant (*adiutor*), shorthand scribes, clerks, guards and numerous minor officials. The senior official in charge of finances and the treasury (*Praepositus Thesauri Augustensis*) must also have been stationed in London. The list not only indicates the responsibilities of the *vicarius* but also gives an indication of the status of London in the fourth century.

It is obvious that by this time the financial and administrative system had changed and increased because of new responsibilities caused by the division of Britain and the probability of external barbarian raids and internal unrest. Before the fourth century the fact that the empire could be governed by such a relatively small group of officially designated people in each province was due to a form of power sharing. In Britain the Roman occupation led to an enormous urban expansion. Tribal centres in Britain before AD 43 had begun to take on some form of urban layout – Silchester had some form of street layout by 20 BC and the Danebury hillfort had houses arranged along a road – but the Romans would not have considered these as towns. They valued towns, not only for their cultural identity, realizing their potential as contributing to a Romanized form of government, but also for their economic value, their potential for taxation and their administrative function. Many officials might be from the Celtic nobility and Tacitus indicated that the Romans knew the value of educating the next generation in preparation for accepting the mantle of authority.

People living in towns also had opportunities for social and cultural amenities that could mean acceptance of Roman values even if Celtic ones still lay below the surface. More importantly, towns provided a local autonomy as a fundamental unit utilizing the native elite to take official positions allying their interests with those of Rome. Even so, compared with other provinces the number of major towns in Britain was small. Twenty-five have been suggested and after the mid second century no new large towns were created. Towns would vary in size from London's 128 hectares (316 acres) to Water Newton's 18 hectares (45 acres), and even smaller ones of half an acre, if these could be called towns.

There were official designations for towns and these allowed a town to have a different status allied to certain privileges. It is possible that a town might have petitioned to raise its status, for example from a *civitas* capital to a *municipium*. Status depended on the circumstances of the town, the area in which the town was situated and the groups of people it served. Rome established towns on new sites but also adapted and extended tribal centres in a conquered country. Although wishing to promote an urbanization policy, the Roman authorities would have wanted to make sure of the wealth and social status of those who would take office in the town.

Sometimes, for political reasons, people were removed from hillforts to towns founded in lower areas; the inhabitants of the Maiden Castle hillfort were resituated in the new urban area of Dorchester, no doubt cursing their lot but grudgingly coming to appreciate its facilities because they provided possibilities for economic growth. This might lead to increasing wealth but it could result in more taxation and, as the Romans had shrewdly realized, taxation could be more efficiently managed and collected from urban centres. Governors progressed round the towns not only to see that justice was carried out and that peace was secured, but also to ensure that taxation was professionally managed. The development of a road system ensured easier access between the towns and encouraged their development.

A *colonia* was an extension of Rome and was modelled on that city, following Roman law codes. Three had been established in Britain by the end of the first century: Colchester (AD 49), Lincoln (AD 90–92) and Gloucester (AD 96–8). These provided retired Roman veterans with homes within the site of the abandoned legionary fortresses; some of the veterans at Colchester were living in the abandoned barracks of Legion XX. By implication, however, the government of these towns and the conduct of their inhabitants were to be the model which other towns would follow – something which had to be rectified after the Boudiccan rebellion, as the activities of the people in the *colonia* of Colchester had contributed towards the rebellion. Later the title *colonia* might be conferred by a special grant. The extramural settlement at York gained this status either as a result of the visit of Septimius Severus or when it became the capital of Britannia Inferior. It has been suggested that London may also have been granted this status though it had not got it by the time of the Boudiccan rebellion, as Tacitus refers to it as not being 'distinguished by the title of *colonia*'. London, however, may have been known as a *conventus civium Romanorum*, implying that it was a town where Roman citizens lived in order to follow trading and commercial interests.

Another granted status was that of a *municipium*. This was a self-governing community, which had a regular constitution based on Roman law but was also allowed to keep some native laws. The only known certain case in Britain is Verulamium where Tacitus referred to the same fate (as that of Colchester) overtaking the *municipium* of Verulamium. It is also described as such in an inscription set up on the basilica in the forum in AD 79 during Agricola's governorship. Important timber buildings had been erected along streets by AD 50. These were destroyed in the Boudiccan rebellion but the town was quickly rebuilt. York may have also been granted this status before it became a *colonia*, for a life of Septimius Severus describes him as dying in AD 211 in the '*municipium* called Eboracum'. Foreigners, especially traders, were attracted to these towns because once they settled in them they could become citizens of *municipia*.

The other important towns were *civitas* capitals, usually the most important town in a tribal area. In areas hostile or intractable to Roman influence founding of independent *civitas* capitals would be delayed. This would account for the late development of Caistor-by-Norwich in the Icenian territory and towns in the Brigantian area. Some sites, which had developed by the Late Iron Age into what could be considered urban communities, could easily be granted urban status. Probably this happened at Silchester where an irregular pattern of streets had been established by 50 BC. Not all these pre-Roman communities were allowed to persist. Maiden Castle has already been mentioned and Danebury, which seems to have been laid out with some form of street system, was abandoned.

At least sixteen *civitas* capitals are suggested to have been created in Roman Britain. Their formation was helped by the aid of client rulers who controlled their own society. One of the earliest was Chichester where an inscription refers to Tiberius Claudius Cogidubnus, king and imperial legate. Cogidubnus had obviously been granted full Roman citizenship and undertook the governing duties of a legatus in his area, where he may have inhabited the palace-villa at Fishbourne. Verulamium was probably a *civitas* capital before it was enhanced to a *municipium*. Canterbury is known to have been developed (c.AD 80–100) from an Iron Age settlement at the crossing of the River Stour, where there was a scattering of buildings around a temple enclosure. Later towns were established in other tribal areas, once they had been deemed to be peaceful and therefore in no need of direct military control. Practical help in erecting the necessary administrative buildings may have been provided by the military but more probably by architects from Gaul and the Rhineland. Financial help would have been expected from the wealthier native nobility, who would have had to be assured of a part in the administration of the town.

The *civitas* capital of the Iceni at Caistor-by-Norwich may have been founded after the Boudiccan rebellion in the hope that it would help to pacify that tribe. This might have been difficult as a generation of young men, including future leaders, could have been lost in the fighting. The fury of the Romans would have reduced many persons to slavery, thus destroying any ambition, and it was not until the Hadrianic period that a forum was built. Wroxeter began the process towards a *civitas* capital of the Cornovii once Legion XX had moved to Chester and this was confirmed by an inscription in the forum, dating to AD 130, referring to the *civitas Cornoviorum*. Exeter developed as the capital of the Dumnonii after Legion II Augusta left that area for its new base at Caerleon when Frontinus had subdued the Silures in AD 70. Later, the Silures were provided with their own *civitas* capital at Caerwent. These sites were laid out in a form of grid pattern that may have resulted from utilizing those of the previous forts.

Hadrian's visit to Britain and the building of Hadrian's Wall, which ensured the protection of and domination in the northern areas, stimulated the encouragement of urban settlements so that a *civitas* capital for the Brigantes could be established at Aldborough, the farthest northern *civitas* capital, and possibly another at Petuaria (Brough-on-Humber) for the Parisii. The former flourished, the latter seems to have failed, probably being placed under the nearby *colonia* of York. The native *oppidum* of the Dobunni at Bagendon was abandoned in the AD 70s and the *civitas Dobunnorum* was established in the abandoned fort at Cirencester (Corinium). This developed so well that it became more important than the *colonia* of Gloucester. One late creation was the *civitas* capital of the Carvetii in the Eden Valley sometime in the third century AD.

Civitas capitals controlled sub-divisions of territory and districts (*pagi*). A writing tablet, found in London, refers to the *pagus Dibussu* in the *civitas* of the Cantiaci (Canterbury). Roman administration was particularly concerned that no area of a province should be without an administrative system in some form even if the smallest town did not include a building following the classical style.

Below these towns in status came a variety of small settlements and urbanized centres, mostly very small and serving a local area. Some grew up by fords; others were at crossroads where a market became established with market rights regulated by the state; at religious sites such as Bath and Harlow; or developed round a *mansio* (an official hostelry, created for the postal couriers, on a roadside) as at Letocetum (Wall) on Watling Street. Small industrial sites might develop some kind of urban area, even where there was a state monopoly: Droitwich (Worcestershire) and Middlewich (Cheshire) had salt industries, Mancetter (Warwickshire) had its pottery and at Charterhouse on Mendip (Somerset) lead-mining took place. *Vici* were under the control of the fort commander who might also be responsible for the settlements in the surrounding area but when the army abandoned a site a *vicus* could develop its urban potential. Those attached to the forts on Hadrian's Wall, however, ceased to exist once the forts had been abandoned. Urban communities varied in size but even the smallest might have some pretension to an administration decreed by Rome. Many were the forerunners of towns and villages in existence today.

The *colonia* were administered in full accordance with Roman law; the *municipia* and the *civitas* capitals were allowed to practise some form of native law. They would have had a council (*ordo*) of decurions (council members) who were elected from their fellow citizens. In theory the *ordo* numbered a hundred but in Britain their number was probably less. It has been suggested that at most the members reached about thirty or forty. Again, in theory, the electors were presumed to be above thirty years old and to have sufficient wealth and property; in practice it would be those men who had most influence. The *ordo* would therefore have been drawn from tribal elites who continued to enjoy their power and wealth. They would have been expected to pay a considerable sum of money for this office (*summa honoraria*) and might still have been expected to distribute some of their wealth and show favour to loyal followers but in doing so they were only following the Roman system of patronage and the Celtic tradition of supporting their tribal warriors. By the second century AD many of those in power had probably become a self-perpetuating elite. Five decurions known in Britain are all from *coloniae*. A decurion of the *colonia* of Glevum, mentioned on a tombstone at Bath, lived to the age of eighty years. Flavius Bellator at York was more unlucky, dying at the age of twenty-nine; at least two other decurions are known at York. Another, Aur(elius) Senecio, set up a tombstone at Lincoln to his well-deserving wife Volusia Faustina, who died aged twenty-six.

The *ordo* in the *coloniae* and the *municipia* elected two officials (*duoviri iuridicundo*) who controlled the members of the *ordo* and held them to account. They acted as magistrates in judging petty crimes; major crimes in civil and criminal cases had to be referred to the governor. Later all criminal cases went to the governor or were held over until he made a visit. The officials supervised the Imperial Cult through the six *severi Augustales*. Later, when towns were being menaced by hostile raids, they recruited a local militia. Every five years two men were elected as *duoviri* (municipal officers) with the additional title *quinquinnales*. They had to ensure that all vacancies in the *ordo* were filled, check public contracts and assess levels of taxation. Some of the larger towns might have had *quaestors* who kept a stricter eye on taxation. Later the imperial government created the post of curator to take responsibility for financial matters and the erection and repair of buildings. There is no record of any curator being appointed in Britain but several are known in Gaul, especially during the increasing bureaucratic tendencies of the third and fourth centuries.

Smaller towns may have had only two *duoviri* but all towns appointed two *aediles* to arrange contracts for erecting and demolishing buildings. They ensured public order, supervised water supplies, ensured the cleanliness and upkeep of streets, aqueducts and sewers, controlled markets and checked weights and measures. All these officials paid fees on election and contributed to the amenities of a town either permanently in the form of buildings or by providing entertainment, perhaps by organizing public shows or by holding public feasts. Marcus Ulpius Januarius, an *aedile* at Petuaria, presented a new stage, probably made of timber, to the town, carefully mentioning that this was at his own expense. Public works paid for by private individuals kept down local taxation, which was mainly raised from market tolls, fines for local offences and such transactions as selling water from public supplies for private use. Major taxes were collected by Rome, and were either sent to the city or used to support the army.

Towns may also have elected or appointed a patron who was expected to look after their interests. An inscription found at

Caerwent was probably from the base of a statue. It was set up by decree of the *ordo* of the Silures to Tiberius Claudius Paulinus, who had been the legate of Legion II Augusta at the nearby fort of Caerleon. He progressed to become proconsul of the province of Narbonensis, then *Legatus Augusti* of the province of Lugdunensis before returning as governor of Britannia Inferior during the reign of Elagabalus (AD 220). Tiberius may have remembered his nearby citizen neighbours and acted as patron to Caerwent on his distinguished posting to Britain.

At first wealthy Celtic nobility might have been willing to accept official positions in towns because they wished to ensure continuing prestige. Problems began to arise when Diocletian made the decurions liable for any deficit in taxation. As taxation continually increased men became reluctant to take office, especially if they were being pressed for personal taxes. The government then made the taking of office compulsory for certain groups and even made certain offices hereditary. Even if a person went bankrupt they still had to carry out official duties. Possibly men began to avoid this service by retiring to the country and concentrating on their villas, hoping to be exempt from service in towns. What had once been considered a privilege to take part in the administration organized by Rome had now become a burden and one that men were increasingly anxious to avoid. It was left to the central administration to ensure that Britain was governed responsibly to ensure its security.

9

ARMY LIFE

During the republic the Romans had created an efficient fighting machine, which resulted in the inexorable expansion of Rome until the second century AD. The Emperor Augustus, aware of the power of this force, began a series of reforms which created a professionally paid army, loyal to the emperor, and provided an officer class drawn from the senatorial and equestrian orders, following a career structure (*cursus honorum*) that included holding successive military and civil appointments. The underlying assumption was that Rome's military might was superior to any opposing force, both in her fighting techniques and by the fact that Rome was destined to rule the known world.

The Romans were a practical people. Military superiority was achieved by adapting and changing tactics, and by utilizing the manpower of other areas. Thus men from the provinces were enrolled into the army either individually or in tribal groups, some keeping their own methods of fighting so that in the auxiliary forces provincial customs and habits were accepted. Cavalry units especially were recruited from such sources and provided an essential complement to the legions, which were almost entirely composed of infantry. Native forces were recruited as professional troops and this subtly began to alter the relationship between the military and the civilian. This could be both a strength and weakness as it was uncertain where loyalties would lie. This polyglot force had to be moulded into one serving emperor and empire. In addition, it was relatively unusual for ordinary soldiers to change units and, if a unit stayed too long in one area, the men might become embedded in the community. Legion XX was established at Chester about AD 87. Although vexillations were sent to build the Hadrian and Antonine Walls and to keep order in the north, the legion remained at Chester until probably the fourth century AD. Some of the wall garrisons remained in place for many years.

The Roman military force at its greatest in Britain has been estimated to be between 50,000 and 55,000 men. Aulus Plautius had arrived with 20,000 legionaries and auxiliary soldiers with nominal strengths of 500 or 1,000 men. But legions and auxiliary forces were brought into or removed from Britain as circumstances demanded. The largest number of troops was stationed on Hadrian's Wall, and the Wall itself and the associated military zone contained perhaps 20,000 men. The number of troops stationed in Britain indicates that the province had to keep one of the largest provincial garrisons, probably the result of the hostility of its Celtic inhabitants and the fact that the Romans never succeeded in conquering the whole island. Hostile tribes in Scotland were never entirely subdued, although finds of Roman artefacts suggest that there may have been interaction between Romans and natives. Nor did the Romans conquer Ireland, which might have prevented later Irish raids on the western shore areas.

There was also the loyalty of the Roman troops to be considered. At first, men had been recruited in Italy but by the first century AD the legions had recruited men from the provinces, especially Gaul, Germany and the Belgic areas. Few troops were stationed in Italy apart from the Praetorian Guard and the emperor's personal bodyguard until the reign of Septimius Severus. Gaul had been pacified so that most of the military units were stationed in Britain and Germany, away from Rome and from the central administration.

The Roman forces were divided into two distinct parts – legions and auxiliary – having distinct roles, although their training was similar. Latin was the language of command and men were expected to take Latin names on enrolment. Probably men spoke their own language or a kind of patois but if they wanted to progress to higher duties a command of Latin would be expected. Messages sent from the Vindolanda fort were in Latin cursive script and at least twenty-five different writers have been identified. Although men were expected to worship the Roman deities with particular emphasis on the Imperial Cult they might express their loyalty to their own particular deities, probably an essential element as far as provincial troops were concerned. For many provincials, such as the Celts and the Germans who had a martial ethos, service in the army was attractive as it allowed them to continue this warlike trait. Until AD 212 service in the auxilia had the prize of a grant of Roman citizenship after twenty-five years provided that men had received honourable discharge (*missio honesta*). This was not necessarily given if they had been invalided out through necessary discharge (*missio causaria*) or had been cashiered as a result of dishonourable discharge (*missio ignominiosa*). This career, engraved on a pair of bronze tablets, a *diploma militaria*, was a valued document which could lead to further advancement or additional rewards, such as the granting of Roman citizenship to a veteran's children.

Service in the army, expected to last about twenty-five years, provided men with a settled existence, regular pay, a career structure and the opportunity at the end of service of a gratuity and a possibility of a further career. Men took an oath of loyalty to the current reigning emperor and there was always an uneasy time before a new emperor gained control. Indeed, many emperors were elected by the army and gave donations to it as a bribe for support. Until the late second or third century men could not marry, although unofficial liaisons with women were not, and indeed could not, be prevented. This created a dilemma. Married men might prefer a settled existence that prevented them from moving quickly from base to base. On the other hand, if army men had sons, these could provide recruits for the future. The Roman army was not a monastic force. Soldiers consorted with prostitutes and slaves, and with women in the *vici* outside the forts. In AD 197 Septimius Severus allowed soldiers to live with their wives but it is not certain if this legalized what had been happening for a long time or whether it implied liaisons with concubines to make a proper marriage.

That this provided a social community around and probably in the forts is not surprising. The *vici* would house a labour force; many soldiers probably had slaves, freedmen and grooms living in the *vici* and probably relatives moved nearer. Troops who had served in Britain for long periods would, on retirement, decide to settle near their camps and forts with their families, especially auxiliaries whose terms of service were registered on a diploma. This gave them citizenship, which could also extend to their children. Four *coloniae* provided opportunities for veterans from the legions to settle in these towns and have a grant of land in the surrounding area. This is not to say that there was constant harmony between soldier and civilian in Britain. The main purpose of the army was to put down revolts, keep order (the *Pax Romana*) and ensure that taxes were regularly collected, but given the interaction of soldier and civilian this might have been done with discretion.

Legionaries were recruited, as far as possible, from Roman citizens. Originally each legion in theory numbered just under

5,000 men and consisted of 10 cohorts of 480 men, each comprising 6 centuries. Each century was divided into 10 *contubernia* (units) of 8 men who shared a tent on the march or 2 rooms in a barrack block. Although again in theory each century was composed of 100 men, in practice there were only 80. Vespasian raised the first cohort of a legion to 5 double centuries, from 4,800 to 5,120 men. In addition a legion had at least 120 cavalrymen attached to it acting as despatch riders and scouts. There would also be clerks, administrators and other men with duties attached to the legions so that the total might be between 5,500 and 6,000 men.

There were other posts, which could provide more pay and give opportunities for promotion or more interesting duties, a vital necessity if men were serving in the same fortress for several years. An *immunis* had exemption from fatigues, a *sesquiplicarius* would have one-and-a-half times the basic pay and a *duplicarius* double pay. A *tesserarius* gave orders to the guards, including the day's password. An *aquilifer* was a standard bearer of the legionary eagle; an *imaginifer* carried an image of the emperor. An altar at Bath was erected to the goddess Sulis for the welfare of Gaius Javolenus Saturnalis, *imaginifer* of Legion II Augusta, by his freedman Lucius Manius Dionisias.

A *signifer*, who had double pay, was probably proud to be entrusted with the legionary standard in battle. A tombstone at Wroxeter records Marcus Petronius of Legion XIV Gemina, a standard bearer who died at Wroxeter aged thirty-eight, having served in the army for eighteen years. Lucius Duccius Rufinus, whose tombstone at York records his death aged twenty-eight, was a standard bearer of Legion IX and is depicted holding the standard with its medallions in his right hand. A standard bearer also acted as a pay clerk and keeper of records, and Lucius holds a wax tablet indicating this in his left hand. A *librarius* was a clerk, a necessary duty in the organization of the army; Martius and

Flavus are recorded as having this duty during their service at Vindolanda. The work of these men can be seen in the numerous tablets found there. Musicians (*tubicen, cornicen, bucinator*) played music on the march. There were about 180 of these varied posts in the legion and such was the competition that centurions could be bribed to promote those whom they favoured.

An *optio* served a centurion and an *optio ad spem ordinis* was awaiting a vacancy for promotion to the rank of centurion. One unfortunate man never made this promotion. His tombstone at Chester recorded him being lost in a shipwreck. A tombstone normally records *H(ic) S(itus) E(st)* meaning 'here he is lying', but in this case the *H* is missing, implying that his body was never found.

The centurions were non-commissioned officers who gained promotion after service of sixteen or more years and had held several posts. They could be directly posted from the equestrian order or be transferred between legions. T. Flavius Virilis served in Legions II Augusta, XX Valeria and VI Victrix before moving on to serve in Legions III Augusta in Africa and III Parthica in Italy over a career of forty-five years. Conversely if a man had been a centurion he could achieve equestrian status or even become a senator. Pompeius Homullus, who had been *primus pilus* (centurion in charge of the first cohort of the first century) of Legion II Augusta, became procurator of Britain about AD 85 and then was promoted finance officer to Emperor Trajan. The long career of Petronius Fortunatus, who died in Cillium in Africa, was detailed on a monument erected to him. He had served as *librarius, tesserarius* and *optio* before becoming a centurion after the short time of four years. Numerous transfers between legions throughout the empire brought him to Legion VI Victrix in York, only to be transferred again to serve in legions in the eastern provinces of the empire. After serving fifty years in the army he retired, probably about AD 206, in his seventies and died aged over eighty. A centurion could become a *praefectus castrorum*, who took charge of the camp when the legionary commander was away, but the unfortunate career of Poenius Postumus, who hesitated about bringing Legion II Augusta to the aid of Suetonius Paulinus in the Boudiccan rebellion, showed that some men might not have had decision-making qualities. Yet others could be given command of provinces, such as Egypt, where men of senatorial rank were not eligible.

A *Legatus Legionis* of senatorial rank commanded a legion. Vespasian commanded Legion II Augusta in its march along the south coast after the AD 43 invasion. Six military tribunes were also appointed, one of senatorial rank, the others from the equestrians. A senator had a broad stripe round his toga, a superior status indicated by Tineius Longus, who described himself on an altar dedicated to the Celtic god, Anocitius, at Benwell as 'having been adorned with the broad stripe and designated *quaestor*'. The other five tribunes had a narrow stripe on the tunic and these men could become officers in auxiliary cohorts and *alae* (cavalry units).

Beneficiarii would act as aide-de-camps or be sent on special duties. Gaius Mannius Secundus of Legion XX who died at Wroxeter was on a discreet mission as he described himself on his tombstone as a *beneficiarius* of the governor. Those serving in London, as already mentioned, seemed to have formed a guild there and another guild is suggested at York. These guilds would have provided a meeting place and comradeship for men separated from their own legions for a while.

Auxiliary units were usually formed from recruits from the provinces. The units were divided into cohorts of infantry and *alae* of cavalry, usually 500 strong, although some could be 1,000 strong. There could also be mixed cohorts with 120 or 240 cavalry included in the cohort. Cavalry were elite regiments, divided into 24 *tumae* under the command of a decurion, and an *ala* raised by Augustus was stationed at Corbridge in the first century AD. After service elsewhere, the *Ala Augusta Gallorum*

Petriana milliaria civium Romanorum bis torquata, as its titles proclaim, was given a grant of Roman citizenship by Domitian and awarded first one torque and then another by Trajan. It then returned to Britain and was stationed at Stanwix.

The names of the cohorts indicate where they were raised – Vangiones and Lingones from Upper Germany, Batavians from Lower Germany, Nervians, Menapians and Tungrians from Gallia Belgica, Vardulli and Vascones from Spain, Thracians, Gauls, Pannonians, Raetians – all served in Britain at some time. It was common practice to station units far from their homeland but many of those discharged from the army would settle in Britain. Men recruited into the army from Britain usually served in other provinces. An *Ala Britannica* served in Italy with Vitellius in AD 69, a *Cohors I Ulpia Brittonum* and an *Ala I Flavia Augusta Britannica* are recorded elsewhere – but *Cohors I Cornoviorum*, obviously raised from the British tribe, possibly during Hadrian's visit, was recorded in the *Notitia Dignitatum* as being stationed at Newcastle. Later regional groups became diluted as men recruited from other areas joined their ranks, although the name of the unit remained the same.

There were other units in the army, usually specialist groups. In the second century a unit of Sarmathian cavalry came to Britain in AD 175 and later was stationed at Ribchester. Most men had ridden horses but as cavalry they needed to mount horses quickly, with or without armour; recruits not familiar with horses practised on a wooden horse. Fighting from horseback without stirrups would require particular training. This was probably the purpose of a circular area (*gyrus*) about 34 m (111.5 ft) in diameter, surrounded by a wooden palisade, excavated and reconstructed at the fort of Baginton (Warwickshire). Men on horseback could trot and canter in it or break in new horses, while other men would hit weapons and shields on the wooden sides so that the reverberated noise would accustom horses to the sound of battle. Cavalry exercises included the *hippika gymnasia* where displays of horsemanship and tactical skill in weaponry were tested. Another was the cantabrian circle, an exercise calling for an observant eye and swift arm movements from two men in the centre, who were warding off javelins thrown by galloping riders.

Smaller units, the *numeri*, carried out particular tasks. A *numerus* of Syrian archers is recorded at Kirkby Thore (Cumbria) in the third century AD. The *numerus Barcariorum Tigrisiensium* recorded at South Shields in the fourth century AD acted as bargemen and lightermen on the River Tyne; there is a similar unit attested at Lancaster in the third century AD. A *numerus Hnaudifridi* recorded at Housesteads in the third century was probably named after its commander Hnaudifridus (Notfried). They may have carried out scouting duties, as did *numeri Exploratorum* stationed at Netherby, High Rochester and Risingham and in the south at Portchester. The *Venatores Bannienses*, a unit of huntsmen, was stationed at Birdoswald in the fourth century AD, presumably to hunt down men although they could have been used to bring in supplies of wild game. The Raeti Gaesati are recorded at Risingham and Great Chesters.

Volunteers joined both legionary and auxiliary forces from the age of seventeen, usually with an introduction from a patron. A tablet found at Vindolanda recorded an auxiliary prefect, Claudius Julius Karus, writing to the fort prefect, Cerialis, asking him to recommend someone named Brigionus to Annius Equester, a legionary centurion at Luguvalium (Carlisle) – 'by doing so you will place me in your debt both to his name and to mine'. Annius is entitled *centurio regionarius* – centurion in charge of the region – which indicates that Carlisle was strategically central to an area on the west of Hadrian's Wall and that this particular centurion held a powerful command, possibly in charge of taking the census in the area. The message bridges the centuries for it is in the 'Hope you are well' tradition: 'I hope you are enjoying the best of fortune and are in good health.'

Some men joining the auxiliary from the provinces were freeborn Roman citizens; others might attain this on their retirement, having served twenty-five years. One of their privileges was that they could designate heirs in their will. Vegetius, who wrote a military manual in the fourth century AD but which incorporated material from earlier centuries, said that boys from the country were the best recruits, probably because they had been toughened by agricultural work. Boys who had followed other trades such as blacksmiths, stonemasons and wheelwrights were particularly welcomed as were sons of hunters. Sons of soldiers living in the *vici* outside the forts were regarded as potential recruits. Theoretically men were expected to be at least 1.78 m (5 ft 10 in.) high but, as more men were needed in the army, Vegetius noted that recruits were taken for their physical strength rather than their height.

Once accepted, the recruit was given three gold coins and took the oath of allegiance to the emperor, which was renewed each year by the whole army. He would be tattooed on the arm or the hand, which might have been to portray his loyalty but presumably made it easier to identify him if he deserted. He also had to hand over any money in his possession either to the standard bearer or to the centurion for self-keeping, although one might speculate how much the recruit got back.

In the early days of the empire a legionary received 75 denarii on joining up and 225 denarii pay per year, but inflation soon began to gnaw at its value until under Caracalla he was receiving 650 denarii. Pay could also be given as payment in kind. On promotion to a centurion the soldier could earn 5,000 denarii. A man took an oath of loyalty to the current emperor and there might always be an uneasy period between his death and the accession of a new emperor. To ensure loyalty men were given donations and there might be others on special occasions. Stoppages were made for food, armour, weapons and clothing. About a third of the pay was compulsorily saved so that a gratuity was available on leaving the army. Until Hadrian's reign, legionaries could receive grants of land rather than money, as presumably did those veterans who settled at the *coloniae* of Colchester and Gloucester soon after the conquest. Auxiliaries received about a third less pay than that of a legionary. Soldiers supplemented their pay by asking friends and relatives for gifts. One of the wooden tablets found at Vindolanda indicates that a soldier had received socks, four pairs of sandals and two pairs of underpants. Soldiers' pay spent in the *vici* added to the economy. The Vindolanda records indicate that quite a few soldiers borrowed money, either from each other or in advance of their payday.

Soldiers seemed to have kept their money in 'arm purses', cup-like objects with a round handle and a lid. These could have been pushed up the arm to secure the lid tight. As they would have been uncomfortable to wear and could easily catch on a protruding object, a better way might be to hang them from a belt. Two, found respectively at Birdoswald and Barcombe, contained large sums of money. The Barcombe one held three aurei and sixty denarii of the reigns of Trajan and Hadrian, so unworn that it would seem this unfortunate man, possibly a centurion, had lost his pay as soon as he received it.

A soldier usually made a contribution to a guild, which provided a burial club so that he could be buried or cremated with the correct rites and commemorated on the anniversary of his death. Inscriptions mentioning guilds have been found in or near the forts of Birdoswald, High Rochester, Caernarfon, York and Lincoln. The funeral of Julius Vitalis of Legion XX, who died at Bath, had been paid for by the guild of armourers.

Training was essential and Vegetius laid it out in precise terms. Battle drill included interlocking of shields to form a cover (*testudo*) and the instinctive use of weapons to protect the body and disable the enemy. Physical exercise and marching were essential – a distance of 32.19 km (18.4 miles; 20 Roman miles) in five hours. This did not allow for halts. The full kit of armour, weapons, turf-cutter, *dolabra* (a pickaxe), saw, cooking pot, mess tin and possibly rations for three days weighed about 30 kg (66 lb). A leather satchel found at the Bar Hill fort may have been used to carry some of the gear. The weight worn by a cavalryman was about 70 kg (154 lb) and he could carry about 3–4 kg (8–9 lb) in his saddlebags for three or four days' supply.

Practice in swimming was necessary. Tacitus said that Agricola chose auxiliaries who had been trained to swim with their arms and horses when he invaded Anglesey to complete the defeat of the Ordovici. Exercise prevented boredom. Vegetius comments that, 'even in winter men were obliged to perform their drills in the fields lest an intermission of discipline should affect both the courage and the constitution of the soldiers'. Parade grounds outside forts would provide space for training and exercise. They would also be used for ceremonial occasions, including dates on which the units were raised or the emperor's birthday. At Maryport (Cumbria), buried by the side of the parade ground, was a sequence of fourteen altars dedicated to Jupiter Optimus Maximus. Each one noted the name of the unit and the commanding officer. The fact that they were unweathered indicates that the burial was deliberate so that when a new altar was dedicated the old one was buried with due ceremony. Amphitheatres outside the legionary fortresses and small auxiliary forts could be used both for military exercises and gladiatorial and other contests to provide the troops with diverting entertainment.

The essential weapons were a sword and a dagger. The defensive weapon was a shield either of oblong, circular or semi-circular shape, which covered the main part of the body. Each unit probably had several craftsmen to make or repair these; Lucius was for a time a shield-maker (*scutarius*) at Vindolanda. Weapon training was done first with wooden staves and wickerwork shields hitting against a stake. According to Vegetius these were twice as heavy as service weight. Later, real weapons would be employed. Celts, who were used to a long slashing sword, would have had to be trained in the tactics of a short stabbing sword, although the cavalry did use a longer sword (*spatha*). They were also used to throwing spears and javelins so throwing a *pilum* (a javelin usually about 2m/6 ft long) would present no difficulty. Modern experiments throwing javelins have shown that the average range is 15–20 m (16–22 yards) and that the rate of delivery can be as fast as using sling stones, although the accuracy was not as good.

By the first century AD a standard set of equipment had evolved which seems to have been made at centres in Gaul and Italy. Once the army was established in Britain armourers would provide and repair equipment at the forts, which was issued to the troops with deductions from pay. Any loss of weapons or armour merited a fine, presumably to stop weapons being sold to civilians. Legionaries wore a bronze helmet with a large flange tilted to cover the neck, flaps to cover the cheeks and a conical knob to which a plume could be attached; by the third century the helmet was becoming more conical in shape and the plume was worn only for ceremonial parades. Officers' helmets kept a large stiff plume. A helmet found at Colchester had stylized 'eyebrows' on the front. Standard bearers wore an animal skin over their helmets.

Each soldier was given a tunic, a cloak and a blanket either yearly or every two years. The linen or woollen tunic was worn beneath the armour; a scarf round the neck prevented chafing. Legionaries did not at first wear breeches but as more provincial troops entered the army they brought their sartorial customs with them and it was soon realized that in the more northerly parts of the empire the winter cold made it essential to wear warmer clothing. Armour was strapped over the tunic. In 1984, a wooden chest, buried at Corbridge about AD 100, probably to save it from ravaging Caledonian tribes, was discovered to hold two sets of *lorica segmentata*. These were strips of metal on a base of leather straps, held together by metal hinges, thus forming a hard, movable carapace round the upper part of the body, weighing about 9 kg (20 lb). Another suit consisting of the iron bands, copper alloy studs and rivets and buckles for the leather strappings was found at Caerleon. Added metal strips on the shoulders guarded against a downward sword stroke. Olive oil was applied to keep joints from rusting. Officers wore a metal cuirass shaped like a naked torso and decorated with relief work.

Dangling metal plates attached to a belt beneath the *lorica* swung loosely, possibly more for decorative effect than for protection. Mail tunics or lamellar armour replaced the *loricae* in the late empire. Tiny pieces found at Corbridge indicate that this was made of small plates pierced by holes so that they could be lashed together to form a flexible sheet of metal. Greaves worn on the legs are indicated on the tombstone of Marcus Flavius Facilis at Colchester; these shin protectors are plain but those worn by officers were decorated with lion's heads. Armour was probably too heavy to wear except in battle, on parade and during guard duty so off-duty dress would be a tunic and loincloth. While soldiers might have started out with the same coloured tunic, constant washing would have altered these colours so that a multicoloured array might have greeted a centurion. Unfortunately nothing is known about laundry arrangements but washerwomen in the *vicus* could have done this.

Thick woollen cloaks worn over the armour kept out the winter chill. The *sagum* was a rectangular shape and a hooded *paenula* drooped to a triangular point at the front. Legionaries wore brown cloaks; officers were more distinguished. Caesar speaks of his red campaign cloak. Some men may have worn the Gallic coat like the *optio* depicted on a tombstone at Chester. During the first century AD the usual shoe was the *caliga* made of hard leather with iron nails hammered so hard into the soles that they bent round. An open lattice allowed ventilation and they were held on the feet by flexible straps. The nails may have been deliberately designed to provide a crashing noise on the march and presumably intimidate people. Juvenal's advice was not to provoke a soldier in case he kicked your shin with such a boot. They might, however, cause a problem to the wearer. Josephus recorded a soldier being killed during the attack on the temple in Jerusalem because the nails on his shoes caused him to slip, leaving him unable to defend himself.

Later a new style of shoe was adopted: a single piece of leather sewn up the front and resembling a modern climbing boot. A Vindolanda tablet referred to a *balnearia* or a bathing shoe with a wooden sole, which might have been worn to protect feet from the heat of the *caldarium* of a bathhouse. In cold weather feet would be wrapped round with cloth stuffed with wool and fur although, as already indicated, socks seemed to have been available. A bronze leg, complete to the knee, found in the River Tees at Piercebridge clearly depicts a sandal and what appears to be a woolly sock. In 2010, excavations on the A1 road between Deeping and Leeming (North Yorkshire) near the fort at Healam Bridge produced a nail of a Roman boot. On the rust appeared to be traces of fibre, possibly from a sock.

Auxilia came from far more varied backgrounds so many units wore their own dress, some wearing breeches, or using their own specialized weapons that reflected their particular fighting styles. Shields were usually oval. Most infantry cohorts wore a coat of mail (*lorica hamata*), which covered the body down to the hips. Later *lorica squamata* was introduced: rows of plates joined together by bronze wire links that were sewn on to tunics. Cavalrymen wore these split down the sides for comfort. The infantry helmets were similar to those worn by the legionaries.

Numeri used on scouting duties might be dressed little differently from the native population. Specialist groups included slingers from the Balearic Islands. Modern trials held in Turkey have confirmed the efficacy of the weapon; young men could hit a mark at 200 m (656 ft) with unerring accuracy. A soldier of the First Cohort of Hamian Archers seemingly died at Housesteads where his tombstone was erected, although his regiment was stationed at Carvoran. He was wearing a conical helmet and a coat of mail over a rough tunic. His weapons were a small bow with horn strengthening the inside of the curved wood and an axe for defence in close-quarter fighting.

Auxiliary cavalry often wore helmets with elaborately chased cheek pieces, a nose guard and a jointed neck guard. These, often gilded, took the form of an ornate facemask depicting a deity or hero. Fragments of two of these helmets have been found at Guisborough (North Yorkshire) and Worthing (Norfolk) and three complete ones at Ribchester (Lancashire), Newstead and recently at Crosby Garrett (Cumbria). The latter was in the design of a youthful handsome face, polished white, with hair of golden curls. It is the only known example of a helmet with a conical or Phrygian cap decorated with a griffin, symbol of power and protection. The pride of the men in their flamboyant appearance is summed up by Flavius Arrianus of Nicomedia who was governor in Cappadocia under Hadrian: 'The most accomplished men wore gilded helmets with plumes fluttering in the wind, especially to draw the admiring glances of the spectators and these helmets fitted all round the faces so that it appeared as if the gods themselves were on parade.' On ceremonial occasions the horses would wear protective clothing like the leather headgear stamped with studded patterns found at Newstead. Metal eye-guards found at Chesters and Corbridge, stamped with a trellis pattern, indicate that horses' eyes were protected.

The tombstone of Flavinus, standard-bearer of the *Ala Petriana*, now in Hexham Abbey, depicts him wearing tunic, breeches, a mail tunic falling to the waist and a helmet with tall plumes set in the form of a high crest. Cavalry also used spears which were longer than those used by the infantry so that riders could thrust down at the enemy as Sextus Valerius Genialis does with his spear on his tombstone at Cirencester and Rufus Sita does at Gloucester. Stirrups had not yet been invented but a Roman saddle with high pommels would grip the rider firmly, preventing him from being unseated.

Discipline had to be kept, as was the case in any army and this was usually the task of the centurions. On his tombstone Marcus Favonius Facilis loosely holds his vine stick, the symbol of his office, which could soon strike any soldier who did not quickly obey his command. One punishment might also be docking of pay and this could affect his gratuity, for part of the pay was held back to provide money for his retirement.

More serious offences could be treated severely. Frontinus said that Augustus punished a legion that did not fight bravely by decimating every tenth man and putting the rest on barley bread. Vegetius said that men who did not reach the required standard in training could be given rations of barley instead of wheat. The ultimate punishment could be that a total unit was disbanded. The number of rebellions in Britain could indicate there were often problems. Tacitus recorded that *Cohors Usiporum*, raised from the Usipi in Germany, was sent to Britain for training during Agricola's governship. They mutinied and escaped by ship, only to be defeated by the Britons when they tried to get provisions from along the coast; many were captured as slaves. Their rebellion did not succeed but a powerful leader and a promise of booty could result in soldiers following men who aspired to imperial power.

There were awards for bravery according to rank, although the *corona civica*, made of oak leaves, could be the reward of any soldier who saved the life of a fellow soldier. One was won by M. Ostorius Scapula, the son of Ostorius Scapula, an early governor in Britain. Centurions were awarded the *corona aurea* of gold and they could also win the *corona muralis* given to the first man who scaled and went over the wall of a besieged fort or town. The greatest honour was perhaps the *corona obsidionalis* or wreath of grass awarded to the deliverer of a besieged army. Presumably nothing made of precious metal could ever equal the wealth of receiving this honour. Officers of senatorial rank received a *hasta pura* or silver spear. All ranks could be awarded *torques*, *armillae* (bracelets) and *phalerae* (discs), which might be given in profusion. Single *phalera* have been found in Britain and nine plain roundels from Newstead possibly formed backing for a set of these.

Although the Romans were never happy when crossing the sea, they needed a navy to transport men and guard their trading interests; merchant ships could always be commandeered. One fleet, the *Classis Britannica*, was formed to guard the coasts of Britain and northern Gaul. Agricola used it in a scouting role to aid his land forces when he invaded Scotland. As previously mentioned, it sailed around the north of Scotland and a short way down the west coast before returning to a base on the River Tay. The oarsmen seemingly had difficulty with the strong currents in those seas. The fleet was especially useful during the campaigns of the Emperor Septimius Severus in the early third century when it acted as a support unit carrying grain from the numerous granaries at South Shields. Its main base was probably Boulogne during the first century AD, but, by the second century, it had transferred its headquarters to Dover. There it was probably concerned with the extraction of iron on the Sussex Weald. Excavations at Dover revealed four pairs of barracks each divided into eight *contubernia*, and with housing for the officers and non-commissioned officers. A villa at Folkestone where tiles stamped *Classis Britannica* have been found has been suggested as the commandant's residence.

Men serving in the fleet would probably be volunteers: tomb-stones at Boulogne reveal service by a Syrian, a Tungrian and a

Pannonian. These men had the same conditions of service as the auxiliaries, although the length could extend to thirty-five years. There was no career path in the Roman navy; the rank of *praefectus* commanding the fleet was merely a step in officer career advancement. Five men are known to have commanded the British fleet, the first three being dated to the second century. M. Maenius Agrippa began his career by commanding auxiliary regiments before becoming commander of the fleet in the 130s. He seems to have been succeeded by L. Aufidius Pantera, who set up an altar at Lympne (Kent), suitably dedicated to Neptune. Q. Baienus Blassianus, a native of Trieste on an inscription at Ostia recorded a career that included commander of the British fleet and ended with an appointment as Prefect of Egypt. A tombstone in Rome records that Sex. Flavius Quietus was promoted from the rank of *primus pilus* in XX Valeria Victrix to the post of *praefectus* of the *Classis Britannica* in the reigns of either Antoninus Pius or Caracalla. The last recorded evidence of the fleet is at Arles where Saturninus recorded that he was commander of the *Classis Britannica Philippiana* in the reign of the Emperor Philip I (AD 244–9). This was following the custom of naming units after the reigning emperor.

On the march the army was based in temporary camps, which could be organized quickly. *Agrimensores* (surveyors) determined the layout of the ground, the men dug a ditch using the excavated earth to form a defence, and tents were laid out in double rows facing each other. Bracken and straw provided floor covering. The Roman term for living under canvas was *sub pellibus* (under skin). A mass of organic material found at Birdoswald was identified as being composed of triangular and square leather pieces, used in tent-making. The leather was calfskin, chosen from the back of the beast for its consistent size and thickness. One estimate is that it would take the skins of thirty-eight calves to make one tent. The tents, 3 m (10 ft) square, each housed eight men; centurions' tents were placed at the ends of the rows. Arms and other equipment were stacked in the front and the baggage train was accommodated behind. Senior officers would have still larger tents placed in the centre of the camp and that of the commanding officer could be quite luxurious. Suetonius records that Caesar carried with him tessellated and mosaic floors on campaigns, presumably both for comfort and to impress visiting chieftains.

Fortresses were permanent bases housing the whole legion, covering on average 20 hectares (50 acres); in Britain there were ten at one time or another. Auxiliary units and vexillations of legionaries and auxiliaries were housed in forts of standard measurement and in logical layout so that soldiers, who might move from fort to fort, would realize in any emergency what route they had to follow to reach their posts. The largest fortress in Britain covered over 24 hectares (60 acres), the smallest fort less than 0.20 hectares (0.5 acre). Their size varied as to whether they housed large or small military units, infantry or cavalry, or

Reconstructed west gate at South Shields Roman fort

mixed garrisons. Colchester, 20 hectares (49 acres), housed Legion XX. Hod Hill, 4 hectares (9.6 acres), housed a mixed garrison of legionaries and auxiliaries, which was necessary during the first century to ensure the successful control of that area after the invasion.

Forts were usually oblong or square-shaped with gates on each side, opposite to each other. A main street (*via principalis*) ran between the main gates in the long side of the fort and another street (*via praetoria*) ran from the front gate (*porta praetoria*), set in the centre of the short side of the fort, to join the *via principalis* in front of the headquarters building (*principia*). To the rear of the *principia* the line of the *via praetoria* was continued by the *via decumana* which ran down to the rear gate (*porta decumana*) in the centre of the second short side. The *principia*, the administrative centre of the fort, was so important that temporary accommodation was often provided while the rest of the fort was built. A defensive space, the *via sagularis*, so-called from the *sagum* or cloak which the soldier wore when he left the fort, ran between the barracks and the wall.

Buildings were of stone and timber and were renewed when necessary; many timber forts were rebuilt in stone in the second century. If a fort had been abandoned and then reoccupied the buildings were usually rebuilt to the same pattern. Timber forts would need the felling of 6.6–12.5 hectares (16–30 acres) of wood to supply the necessary material. Stone forts used material from the nearest quarry. Banks and ditches provided defence. Soldiers from the Royal Engineers, aided by Borstal Boys, built a reconstructed rampart at the Lunt fort at Baginton. This was based on the presumed Roman measurements of 5.5 m (18 ft) wide at the base, with an earth core faced back and sides by cut turfs, and narrowing to 1.8m (6 ft) at the top. It gave a height of 3.65 m (12 ft) to which a breastwork was added.

In the second century the front of a rampart was often cut back to insert a stone wall. The *Ala Hispanorum Vettonum* did this at Brecon Gaer (Powys) about AD 140. The rampart walk would continue across the gateways, two or four in number, often with double passageways, which would secure the weak entrance points. The stone pivots on which stout wooden gates would swing can still be seen at Brecon Gaer. Over the main gateway of the fort would be placed a carved stone or wooden panel giving the name of the unit and the date of its erection, which usually included the name of the emperor. The south-east fortress gateway of York was dominated by that recording its building in the reign of Trajan by Legion IX.

The two most prominent buildings were the headquarters building (*principia*) and the commandant's house (*praetorium*). The *principia* consisted of a crosshall, possibly large enough for the whole garrison to meet, an *aedes* (shrine) and a forecourt surrounded by a veranda. The *aedes*, opening off the crosshall, was the focus of the headquarters building and therefore of the fort, where standards were kept, together with a statue of the emperor and altars dedicated to protecting deities of the unit. At

Model of the Roman fort *principia* at Chester, Grosvenor Museum, Chester

Caerleon there were benches on which standards could be placed. At High Rochester an altar set up in the third century to the Genius of the Emperor and to the standards of the *Cohors I Vardulli* and of the *numerus Exploratorum Bremeniensium* may have been intended either to promote harmony between two very different units or to indicate that they shared the fort in mutual respect. Corbridge and Vindolanda had carved stone friezes showing the standards.

Statues of deities and emperors were placed in the crosshall; bases remain at Housesteads and York and fragments of bronze statues were found in a number of forts. From the forecourt rooms might lead off for other activities. One might be an *armamentarium* or weapon store, although an inscription at Lanchester (County Durham) indicates that the weapon store was a completely separate building. A well provided water for drinking or to be used in religious ceremonies. When the Bar Hill *principia* was demolished, the well was used as a refuse pit for column shafts and capitals.

At first, the regimental pay-chest, containing the funds of the unit and the savings of the soldiers, was kept in the shrine. Later these were placed in a strong room under the shrine. There was a strong door at Chesters; at High Rochester, a stone slab, balanced on iron wheels to slide it across, assured even more security. At Brough-by-Bainbridge (North Yorkshire), the pit was lined with concrete. There were huge strong rooms at South Shields and Maryport possibly because large sums of money were held at these supply bases. At Housesteads and Vindolanda excavations revealed that the soldiers' pay could be issued from counters guarded by stone screens and grills.

The *praetorium* was usually placed by the side of the *principia*. This could be a palatial building in a fortress, especially in the third century when the legate of Legion VI at York was also governor of Britannia Inferior. Every commanding officer, however, expected to have comfortable quarters, especially if he

had a wife and children, and brought many of his own possessions with him. The presence of a wife is known at one fort by an
invitation on a wooden tablet found at Vindolanda. Sulpicia
Lepidina had accompanied her husband, Flavius Cerialis, prefect
of Cohort IX of Batavians, to Vindolanda at the end of the first
century AD. A friend or relative, Claudia Severa, whose husband,
Aelius Brocchus, commanded a fort called Briga, probably
Kirkbride, near Carlisle, invited her to her birthday party on the
third day before the Ides of September, sometime in the year AD
100. If Sulpicia had accepted, a military escort would have had
to be provided across 55 km (35 miles) of rough country. This
invitation seems to have been written by a scribe, but to make
sure that Sulpicia came Claudia pressed her, saying that this
would 'make the day more enjoyable by your presence'. She
added in her own hand, 'I will expect you sister. Farewell sister,
my dearest soul as I hope to prosper, and greetings.'

Comfort in the *praetorium* would have included rooms
heated with a hypocaust. Imposing quarters were needed to
impress fellow officers, visiting officials and native tribesmen,
and to act as a model to encourage civilian guests to realize the
comforts of Roman civilization. At Caerleon the *praetorium*
included a long colonnaded area with apsidal ends, possibly laid
out as a garden, where business was concluded or where visiting
dignitaries and fellow officers were entertained before a meal.
The *praetorium* at South Shields seems to have had summer and
winter dining rooms. Even in the smaller forts auxiliary
commanders and legionary tribunes expected to be housed in
accordance with their rank. *Praetoria* seem to have been based
on the model of the Mediterranean house with rooms arranged
round a central courtyard and including a private bathhouse
like that at Chesters. Several forts have evidence for private
latrines placed within the commandant's house. If the
commandant was not married the military tribunes could have

used this accommodation as a clubhouse, otherwise they would be accommodated in courtyard houses.

Barrack blocks for the infantry could have up to sixteen pairs of rooms. The layout of these barrack blocks can be seen at Caerleon where the foundations consist of pairs of long narrow blocks 74 m (243 ft) long, facing each other and reflecting the division of the legions into double centuries. At one end were the centurions' quarters, which take up a space equal to five of the rooms allotted to the legionaries. There is a washroom, a latrine and one room heated by a hypocaust; braziers probably heated the others.

Many barracks were at first built of timber, later to be replaced by stone as happened at Corbridge. One of the Vindolanda tablets refers to a decision to be taken on the number of waggons needed to carry stone to the fort. At Caerleon timber buildings were placed on stone foundations. Shirley has suggested that a single barracks block would require wood from 300 trees. For all the timber barracks a small forest of 70,000 would need to be cut down. The number of roof tiles needed – *tegulae* (flat tiles), *imbrices* (semi-cylindrical tiles) and shingles – would be prodigious. In addition there would be constant repair and rebuilding work by skilled military men. Shirley estimated the number of man hours needed to build a fortress as 16.5 million, probably comprising two 30-week seasons of 2,000 men.

If there were only 80 men to each century extra rooms might be given to the standard bearers or *optiones*. Larger rooms, sometimes suites of rooms, were provided at the end of the blocks for centurions. Each *contubernium* of eight men occupied two rooms, one holding equipment, and the larger one serving as living quarters. Many of the front rooms have a stone hearth for cooking or heating purposes. The internal areas varied from 15 sq. m (49 sq. ft) to 30 sq. m (98 sq. ft). A veranda at the front would have provided an extension of living space. Flooring of clay or gravel, possibly covered with timber planking, would be warmer than the stone-flagged floors found at Birrens and Ebchester (County Durham) and these would have been made comfortable with skins, rugs or even bracken.

Post-holes identified at the fort of Heidenheim in Germany may be linked to the provision of bunk beds placed against the wall. Mattresses or palliasses, however, stacked during the day, could be brought out to cover the floor at night. Sleeping arrangements might depend upon the tastes of the men and the time of watch. Barracks might not have been as crowded as they seem. Soldiers posted away from the forts, would allow their comrades some extra space. Beds might be shared between men on and off duty.

Auxiliary infantry cohorts were housed in the same types of barracks but the cavalry, organized into *turmae* (squadrons), would have needed to have more space allotted. Chesters, garrisoned by an *ala* of the Second Asturians, 500 strong, seems to have quartered the men in blocks with ten pairs of rooms, possibly to store equipment more easily. At Wallsend troopers and horses were installed in adjoining rooms with grooms accommodated in lofts above these.

Given the discipline of the army in the first two centuries the rooms would have to be kept tidy, ready for periodic inspection. There must have been some sensible method of storing military equipment and personal possessions in cupboards, pits, on shelves or hanging from hooks. Eight men living together for a long time would either come to some harmonious agreement or a dominating leader would arise to assert his own discipline and force 'room duties' on to others. Off-duty games could fill hours of boredom. Counters and a board have been found at Corbridge and a bag containing nineteen gaming counters was found at Ravenglass (Cumbria); a bronze inkwell at Longthorpe may indicate that some soldiers practised writing skills. Checking armour, oiling hinges and joints and repairing leatherwork would fill up time, as would other tasks. A Vindolanda tablet mentioned builders for a bathhouse, plasterers, workers with kilns and shoemakers.

Some entertainment might have been of a more sinister nature. Excavators recently found the body of a female child, with her hands tied behind her back, buried in a corner of one of the barrack blocks at Vindolanda. The find was dated to the mid third century when the fourth cohort of Gauls formed the garrison. She might have been a slave who was killed for not doing her tasks or been sexually abused and killed by the soldiers. Whatever the situation, her body was buried hastily to avoid discovery.

Bathhouses were a vital part of any fort for they allowed soldiers to bathe, clean themselves and provide relaxation when off-duty, soothing aching limbs and chatting to friends. Usually bathhouses were placed outside forts because of the danger of fire and the fact that men could relax more easily away from authority. The bathhouse at Chesters was situated close to the river, where there was easy access to water. Vitalis, a *balneator* (bath attendant), was in charge of the bathhouse at Vindolanda situated outside the south gate of the fort. Large fortresses provided more elaborate accommodation. Caerleon seems to have had two sets of baths, an official one inside the fortress and another outside the walls, possibly to allow soldiers to have greater relaxation. The discovery of hairpins and milk teeth inside the main baths may indicate that ladies married to senior officers and their children could use them at specified times. A lead plaque found on the site might be an admission ticket. Shellfish and other food remains suggest that a snack bar was provided. Baths continued to be built throughout the Roman occupation, the last ones being recorded at Binchester in the mid fourth century.

Another essential building was a latrine. At Caerleon during the reconstruction of the fort in the second century, the opportunity was taken to construct latrines in each corner of the ramparts. They were provided in the bathhouses of Bar Hill and Corbridge. Separate arrangements were made for one at

Piercebridge, which could accommodate thirty soldiers. Some of the most elaborate remains are to be found at Housesteads, where the drains, the channel for flushing the sponges and the water tanks for washing hands still remain.

Latrines had to be kept clean but it would have been an unpleasant task. Slaves might have been available but soldiers detailed to do the work would need to be carefully supervised, especially at forts where the latrines were a series of seats built over wooden buckets. A papyrus from Egypt, giving a duty roster, included C. Julius Valens and Marcus Longinus A— as being detailed for *ad cunus* (drain duties) and *ad stercus* (latrine duties) respectively on 3 October and 6 October AD 90. The disposal of waste may not have always been carefully supervised; at Bearsden the waste debouched into the fort ditch. At several forts there was evidence that the latrine was in the veranda or in the barrack room itself.

All forts would have had an adequate water supply. Vitruvius recommends digging wells but where possible an aqueduct or leat was constructed. At Benwell, where the water brought for over three miles had become stale and flat, it was sent through five settling tanks to help it regain its sparkle. Sometimes fatigues would include carrying water. At Hod Hill water from the River Stour was the only supply, brought laboriously up the hill and poured into huge collection tanks, one of which had a capacity of 5,455 litres (1,200 gallons). At Housesteads, with a garrison of 800 men, it has been suggested that it would have been possible to collect water from the roof structures within the fort, giving a capacity of 8,000 tonnes of water collected into storage tanks. Excess water would have been used to flush the latrine in the south-east corner of the fort.

The cavalry needed stables and, where possible, these were placed inside forts or in securely guarded annexes to prevent horses from being stolen. Mules and baggage horses might have been kept in annexes and grazed outside the fort. Immediate access to the horses was necessary in an emergency and troopers might have felt happier placed near to their mounts. Celtic ponies would stand rough weather better than high-spirited ones; skeletons of horses found buried at Newstead give a range of twelve to fourteen hands high (1.21–1.42 m/48–56 in.).

Legionary forts would have had to find space for 120 horses, with remounts and those belonging to the officers bringing the total to at least 150. Auxiliary cavalry forts would have needed room for over 500 horses. Separate stable boxes were provided at the auxiliary forts of Benwell and Halton but unless the horses were sick or temperamental it would have been sufficient to tether them in rows. Drains were noted at Ilkley and Brough-on-Noe and mucking out was done daily, as Xenophon emphasized; perhaps local farmers were glad to take the resulting dung. At the legionary fortress of Usk a barrack block was reconstructed as stables by the removal of the panels between the inner and the outer rooms, and by the cutting of cesspits. The horses were accommodated in the outer part, while hay and equipment were stored in the inner rooms. In another area stables and barracks were placed back to back, a most unusual arrangement, which suggests a temporary measure. Separate tack rooms would be essential as the ammonia vapour of urine can attack leather. Troopers could keep their own gear, including parade armour, in their quarters.

Other necessary buildings were workshops (*fabricae*), which Hygenius recommends should be far away from the hospital so that the noise would not disturb patients. Identification of these can only be tentative but buildings containing smelting hearths, ovens or metalworking debris indicate repair work on armour and weapons. Sweepings from a blacksmith's forge were found at Benwell, where the cavalry regiment of Asturians was stationed. Traces of urine and excreta found in a building at Vindolanda and the bundles of leather panels found at Birdoswald and Bar Hill provide evidence for leather-working and tent-making at these forts. Hides are soaked in urine as part of the preliminary treatment. Wagons and carts would have been kept in open-fronted sheds like those deduced at Fendoch.

Granaries (*horrea*) grouped in pairs are easily identified by the remains of rows of stone or timber pillars, which allowed air to circulate underneath, and buttresses on the outer walls to restrain the pressure of the grain. At Corbridge small doors allowed access to the space beneath the floors, possibly for inspection or to let dogs or cats enter to control vermin, not an unexpected problem. Burnt grain at South Shields contained skeletons of rats, mice, voles and other vermin. Vermin might be smoked out and burnt material discovered by the sides of the granaries at Cadder and Slack was suggested to be the remains of fires for this control. The weight of the grain required heavy stone floors and buttresses placed at frequent intervals to control the side pressure on the walls. Wooden louvres were set between the buttresses for internal ventilation. Normally the floor was placed on parallel sleeper walls or pillars. Hardknott, Rudchester and Corbridge had loading platforms covered with a portico to make easier the unloading sacks of grain directly from carts.

Grain was probably kept stored in sacks or bins leading off a central passage. Tacitus in the *Agricola* said that forts in the conquered area of Scotland held sufficient supplies to feed the garrison for a year. Calculations made of grain in granaries in Britain indicate that supplies were far and above what was needed to feed a particular garrison. This may have been to ensure that sufficient food was available in case of a siege or that the garrison should never go short of food in case of a mutiny. Other provisions could be stored in these buildings – meat, dried and salted in barrels, cheese, lard, pulses, salt, amphorae containing wine, olive oil and garum. Pliny mentioned a *carnarium*, a wooden rack from which dried or fresh meat could be suspended. The *librarii horreorum*, in charge of issuing supplies, would ensure constant replacement rather than let food become bad or stale. One fort held vast supplies. In the third century South Shields was remodelled to become a supply base for the campaigns of the Emperor Septimius Severus in Scotland. At least 22 granaries were available, which, if all full, would have had capacity of 8,000 tonnes.

There was no large mess hall in a fort. Each *contubernium* had to prepare its own meal. The basic diet of a soldier consisted of corn (which could be made into soup, pottage or pasta), bacon, cheese, vegetables, oil and wine, and the cost of their provisions was deducted from their pay. An extra deduction was made to cover the greater variety of food during festival days such as Saturnalia. Boudicca sneered at the Romans when she made her speech before her final battle, saying they had to have kneaded bread, wine and oil and that if they ran short of these they perished, which seems to indicate that the military's essential ingredients were known to the Britons early after the conquest.

Pork in the form of meat, bacon and sausages, the latter being cheap and long lasting, would be standard. Bones on military sites indicate that increasing quantities of beef were provided. The Vindolanda accounts indicate large numbers of chickens being bought, possibly more to feed the officers than the men. One account dated to AD 101–104, when Flavius Cerialis was prefect of the Ninth Cohort of Batavians, refers to geese and chickens being supplied, which might have been to serve visiting officers or a visit of the provincial governor. Officers got better food, which probably included game hunted as part of their sporting activities.

Other foods were available. One of the Vindolanda accounts asked for 100 apples if good ones were available and 100 or 200 eggs 'if they could be bought at a reasonable price'. A slave was ordered to procure radishes seemingly as a treat for Saturnalia. If soldiers required snacks or a treat they could supplement their diet by buying from itinerant tradesmen or from shops in the *vici*.

Normally soldiers had two meals a day. Josephus said that the men ate when they were commanded and were expected to eat during the day sitting down but could recline during evening meals. Each *contubernium* would be given a grain ration, which had to be collected from granaries and then ground. At South Shields, bread wheat and spelt were stored in one granary burnt down in the late third or early fourth century. Near the entrance were discarded weed seeds containing corncockle, which can be poisonous if baked in bread. It has been suggested that soldiers had collected their rations from the granary and cleaned the grain where the light was better, obviously being ordered to make sure that the wheat was safe before it was ground.

A stone hand-mill was carried on the pack of the unit's mule. Grinding would be done by the *contubernium*, a strenuous job, probably taking over one-and-a-half hours to produce a decent quality of grain as it might have had to be repeatedly ground and sieved up to three times. Possibly enough flour would be ground for two to three days to save time. Water and salt would be added to knead the flour and the resulting dough would be baked in ovens situated alongside the walls of the camp or fort for baking. Meat and other foods could also be baked there. There were two kinds of bread. *Panis militaris castrensis* was black bread or hard tack and *panis militaris mundis* was baked from finer flour and served to officers. The daily ration of a Roman soldier would probably have consisted of about 850 gm (30 oz) of bread which would provide 1,950 calories.

The recommended diet for men in the British army in barracks has been estimated to produce 2,900 calories. A man on active service in the field requires between 3,400 and 3,600 calories. According to Roth, the daily military ration of a soldier in the Roman army might consist of grain (pulses or bread), meat (probably 226 gm/8oz), vegetables, cheese, olive oil, possibly 70 gm (2.5 oz), a quantity of wine between 0.54 and 0.27 litres a day, salt and other condiments. This diet would give a total of 3,390 calories and 142 gm (5 oz) of protein, quite adequate for a man living in a fort and doing heavy work.

The wine was a sour wine and if mixed with water would have doubled the quantity for drinking. The auxilia, especially those from the northern provinces, drank beer. Both beer and Celtic beer were ordered at Vindolanda, suggesting that these were different kinds of beer. One letter from Masclus, a decurion, to the prefect Flavius Cerialis indicates that supplies had run out under his command, with the implication that some should be sent very quickly.

The army diet would not be entirely a Roman one as more than half the legions and certainly most of the auxiliars came from the provinces. The legions which came over at the conquest had been based in the Rhineland and the Danube regions where their taste might have been more akin to the ethnic groups. Bones excavated at many of the forts indicate that the preference was for beef, which is more a northern than a southern taste. This was particularly apparent at Colchester in the first century AD and in the camps established by the army during their campaigns in the north. A specific change of diet has been noted on the Antonine Wall where Vivian Swan has identified pottery akin to that made in North Africa. It has been suggested that reinforcements from Britain were sent to the Emperor Antoninus Pius's troops in his Mauritanian War (AD 146-9). The survivors returned to Britain together with North African and Moorish soldiers who brought with them their own pottery for their distinctive cooking methods. A plentiful supply of herbs and spices would be available.

The army had to have fit men and this was ensured by a vigorous training routine, care in the choice of the campsite, a good water supply and a healthy diet, but men might have had to be treated in a hospital (*valetudinarium*). They would have had special food there; Plutarch and Vegetius recommended chicken. A tablet at Vindolanda reported that some of the men

were sick or wounded and at least ten suffered from conjuncti-
vitis, not surprisingly if men used a communal towel. Not every
fort had a hospital, although forts would have medical orderlies
attached to them. That at Housesteads was placed next to the
principia; at Benwell, it took the form of a central courtyard
surrounded by a double range of small rooms and had a small
latrine and a bath. Healing herbs could be grown in the sheltered courtyard. Facilities would be available to treat sick
soldiers in most forts but anyone who fell seriously ill or was
badly wounded could be transferred to the legionary fortresses
for treatment, where they were served a special diet. The large
fortress hospital at Caerleon seems to have had sufficient rooms
for each of the sixty-four centuries of the legion; later, parts of it
were heated to give greater comfort to the sick. Soldiers could
also be sent to convalesce at spas such as Buxton and Bath.

Medical staff were recorded and they probably provided a
distinct professional corps. The *optio valetudinarii*, in charge of
the hospital, supervised a staff of *immunes*, who performed
medical tasks, and *capsarii*, who dressed wounds. Roy Davies,
in his study of the Roman medical staff, suggests that there
might have been several *medici*, each having the same title but
performing different duties. A tombstone at Housesteads
describes Anicius Ingenuus of the First Cohort of Tungrians as
medicus ordinarius. It has been suggested that this man and four
others known in Britain were qualified doctors with the same
status and rank of a centurion but serving under a camp doctor.
Many doctors were Greek, like Hermogenes who dedicated an
altar in Greek to 'the mighty Saviour Gods' at Chester.
Complete sets of surgical implements have been found on continental sites and isolated implements are known at Newstead
and Housesteads.

One of the Vindolanda tablets gives a list of ingredients
brought into the fort between AD 101 and 104, which seem to
have been used as medical supplies. These include black bryony

berries used in the treatment of wounds, pitch, which was mixed with garlic for treating arrow wounds, resin, which could be mixed with garlic and sulphur for drawing out pus, and anise as a treatment for stings and insomnia. One item seems to have referred to linen soaked in honey. Honey was used for treating wounds, drawing out splinters and other intrusive objects, and for treating inflammation. Another item was *siliginus* or soft wheat. This could have been used as flour for bread but Pliny the Elder said that if the grain was roasted and ground into flour it could be used as a poultice, which seems sensible, and also to stop eye discharges.

There were also vets to ensure the welfare of the horses and mules, together with the numerous cattle, sheep, pigs and poultry on which the troops would rely for food; Abio and Virilis are recorded as vets at Vindolanda sometime between AD 101 and 105. For a favour and a cash payment, they might have attended pets kept by soldiers and the civilians in the *vici*. Candidus and Lucco are recorded as tending the pigs.

Much of the description given above could be said to provide only a typical account of life in camps and forts. Obviously not all soldiers would be in a fort at the same time. Men needed to be trained in the use of a catapult or an onager. Some would be out on patrol noting if there were threats of violence and thereby put down an incipient revolt. They could be sent out to collect taxes, fetch in supplies, supervise harvesting and organize the rounding up of cattle to provide meat and leather. About AD 90 soldiers from Vindolanda had been sent to London to provide part of the bodyguard for the imperial governor. Over 300 had been dispatched to Coria (Corbridge). Forty-six men were reported to have been sent as a guard to Ferox, probably the Legatus Legionis of Legion IX at York.

According to the Vindolanda tablets some leave was granted. There seems to have been a strict formula for applying. One tablet, requesting leave from either Flavius Cerealis, prefect of the Ninth Cohort of Batavians, or his successor, Priscinus, Prefect of the First Cohort of Thracians, gives this formula: 'I Messicus . . . ask my lord that you consider me a worthy person to grant leave at Corio (Corbridge).' This fort was only 29 km (18 miles) away so this would be a short leave. Soldiers were given rest periods, especially on days devoted to religious observances, and many may have gone to spas such as Buxton and Bath. Desertions and absence without leave, however, were not infrequent. Possibly, unless there was a state of emergency, a particular fort might have been half-empty of its garrison.

Relations with civilians might not always have been amicable. Soldiers could assault and oppress them and the law or brute force could be on their side. Their cases could be treated more leniently in law courts and soldiers were exempt from service in mines and were spared torture. Requisitioning of fodder, food and transport would have caused problems. Even so, soldiers may have visited the *vici* to be with families and friends, consort with prostitutes, drink and gamble in inns, negotiate with traders and engage in numerous other social ploys. Military and civilian life were not entirely divorced from each other and there is reason to believe that by the second century, in some of the forts, civilians were sharing in soldiers' lives not only outside the forts, but also within them.

10

TOWN LIFE

In 1936, R. G. Collingwood described his notion of what town life might have been in Roman Britain. This was based on the concept of citizenship, meaning 'the bodily presence in the city, personal attendance at assembly and law court, participation in a kind of life, which could not be lived except in towns'. Aristotle argued that what raised a man from the level of barbarism and enabled him to develop his higher faculties, 'to live well, instead of merely living', was his membership of the actual physical city. The town was therefore 'the symbol of all that was highest in human life; it raised man above the beasts of the field'. This implies not only what a person can take from a city but also what are their duties towards it. Private donors were therefore expected and encouraged to provide amenities supplementing those provided by the state and town councils. Following this principle Collingwood continued that, 'to convert Britain into a province of the Roman Empire was to civilise it in the most literal sense of the word: to furnish it with towns'. Life in a town provided opportunities for education, trade, amusement and an opportunity to partake in civil administration. It was an essential part of Roman life and one that everyone in the provinces should have emulated.

How far these views prevailed in Britain is open to question. The Britons, as had been the case in Gaul, had developed some form of urban life before the conquest. Many of the *oppida* (hillforts) were nucleated settlements. Danebury had laid out streets and distribution points for grain, Silchester had some form of street pattern, Camulodunum some form of urban structure and many settlements had become important trading posts. The Romans, however, would not accept these as communities providing civilized amenities suitable for a sophisticated life. A settlement on a hillfort, such as that at Maiden Castle, was no substitute for urban existence, as envisaged by Rome, and so the inhabitants of Maiden Castle were eventually moved to create the new town of Dorchester (*Durnovaria*). Legion XX moved from Wroxeter about AD 90 and the native population, which had once lived in the *oppidum* on the Wrekin and had then gradually inhabited the adjoining *vicus*, took its place.

For the Romans, living in a town was the only form of civilized life and Rome provided the example of mutual citizen cooperation that all towns should follow. Urban centres also were the agents for local and regional government. Towns were therefore established throughout the empire and the province of Britain was expected to have a similar development and provide administration where citizens could follow commercial, industrial and social activities. This was probably a startling experience for what had been until then a rural community. Roman administrators accepted this as a natural development but the native population must have realized that a new way of life had begun and that they could either reject it or take advantage of the opportunities offered. Nevertheless in parts of Britain, especially in the far north, the south-west and in Wales, urban communities were not established and life probably continued its rural pattern.

The development of towns was closely linked to the construction of a road network. This was one of the first priorities of the Roman administration to enable troops to move easily round a province and for imperial couriers to convey messages and orders to administrators swiftly. The *Antonine Itinerary*, which depicted roads throughout the empire in the third century AD, lists fifteen routes in Britain. The *Itinerary* sites London as the hub of seven routes and another passed through the city. These roads linked forts, posting stations (*mansiones*) and towns, enabling not only the military but also travellers and merchants to move swiftly through a province to bring their custom and goods to towns. The result was that soon after the conquest civic life began to be established in Britain.

This took several forms according to a Roman pattern: *coloniae*, *municipia*, *civitas* capitals and the expansion of the *vici*. Other towns began by providing products demanded by the military and civilians such as those in the Nene Valley, producing fine pottery, and in the Thames Valley, supplying grey wares to the Roman army. Some became market centres or were established at fords and crossroads: Caistor-by-Norwich and Mancetter produced glassware and Middlewich and Northwich (Cheshire) became important centres for salt production. Yet others developed as small towns because of their religious importance. Springhead (Kent) by the side of Watling Street had a temple precinct containing several Romano-Celtic temples, an object of pilgrimage for many Britons. Ancaster (Lincolnshire) on Ermine Street developed not only because it was on a road junction but also because it was the shrine of Viridios, a Celtic deity.

Many of these towns probably continued from Iron Age settlements; native communities carried on while having to accept Roman authority, regulation and civic forms. The development of town life was aided by the cooperation of the Celtic aristocracy, which shrewdly saw that their best chance of keeping their authority was to ally with the Roman authorities and become leaders of their local community, imitating Roman practice. The development of Silchester, Winchester and Chichester probably owed much to tribal leaders, in particular Cogidubnus, whose acceptance of Roman authority is indicated by his adoption of Roman nomenclature. Verulamium, by the side of a native *oppidum*, seems to have developed as a client town under the rule of a native British chieftain. Canterbury may have been the continuum of an Iron Age settlement associated with a religious site as a temple enclosure lay near to the centre of the first Roman settlement. The archaeological evidence indicates that from AD 90 to 120 many towns, small or large, began to develop and this development was given a boost by Hadrian's visit.

Much of the evidence for the status of towns is deduced from brief references on inscriptions but there can be little doubt that, given the evidence from other provinces, the inhabitants of Britain would have been expected to follow the conventional administrative structure of Roman urban life. The form and style of local government established in *coloniae*, populated by discharged legionary veterans, was intended to provide a model for civic life, which was to be replicated in the *civitas* capitals. These men had Roman citizenship but there would be also others attracted to the *coloniae* who would not have this status and, being second-class citizens, would be resentful, especially if they had to contribute financially to the town. This was a factor, as far as Colchester was concerned, in the discontent leading to the Boudiccan rebellion.

Britons from tribal elites became members of councils, being instructed into Roman administration. Many of the *civitas* capitals had smaller units (*pagi*) as part of their territory; annexes to forts had the title of *vici*. The *civitas* proceeded to elect their own council and two members to govern them. These members were expected to provide the social amenities of a town, as the state was reluctant to provide funding. This would account for the haphazard development of some projects as the town waited for an individual or leading families to make available funds for a building.

The main civic buildings in a town were built on a large scale and were intended to impress the inhabitants. In the first century they would certainly have made an impression on the Celtic inhabitants of Britain, especially as their construction was of stone and marble, much of the latter being imported. Even the smaller towns would have had some large buildings such as a temple. Although the smaller towns could have had their buildings strung out along a road, the major towns would have followed the Roman pattern of streets laid out in a grid system.

The most important building in a town was the forum that acted as a market place and an administrative centre. One had been built at Verulamium soon after the conquest. That was burned down in the Boudiccan rebellion and a second was dedicated in AD 79 or 81. This, 161 m (530 ft) long and 117 m (385 m) wide, might have been the work of Gaulish architects. Silchester replaced its first timber structure with a stone one, 43 m (142 ft) by 40 m (130 ft), in the mid second century AD. Caerwent, the *civitas* capital of the Silures, who had fought fiercely against the Romans until Julius Frontinus finally defeated them in the late 70s, had a much smaller, almost square, forum, 33 m (107 ft) by 31 m (101 ft). The only precise dating of a forum is at Wroxeter. A handsome, well-cut inscription recorded the dedication of the forum in the name of the *civitas Cornoviorum* to AD 129–30. This honoured Hadrian with the implication that he might have encouraged its building during his visit.

No matter what the size of the town the main buildings on the whole were laid out on the same lines. Possibly civilian architects and surveyors were aided by the military, especially as they could provide civil engineers, tradesmen and craftsmen. It would have been one way of keeping military men occupied and prevented from being bored, but craftsmen would certainly have come from elsewhere in the empire, especially Gaul. The decoration of capitals in the fora of Silchester, Caerwent and Canterbury are similar to those produced in north-eastern Gaul. Huge public structures would have taken many years to build and occupied a workforce of several hundred men. The construction of London's forum, begun after AD 100, seems to have taken at least twenty-five years.

The forum was a large square space surrounded on three sides by offices or shops behind porticos. That at Caerwent had six on the east side with wide doorways and probably others on the west. On the most important side was an aisled hall, the basilica, which was the administrative centre. Verulamium's was 36.5m (120ft) wide and 117 m (385 ft) long, the length of the forum. This would have been used for public meetings and deciding civic and criminal cases. At one or both ends was a raised platform from which announcements could be made and from which a magistrate would administer justice. Along the sides were series of offices. One centrally placed room, often called the *curia*, may have held the most important records or have been a shrine dedicated to a local deity or the tutelary goddess of the town. That at Caerwent had foundations for a stepped dais and slots in the floor to hold wooden seating or platforms. A bronze eagle found at Silchester has been suggested to be either an attribute of Jupiter or to be part of a statue representing a local *tutela* (protector of the town). Dignified though the basilica may have been at Silchester, excavations have indicated that metalworkers carried out their activities within the building, alongside the administration of justice and religious rituals.

Another important building was the market place (*macellum*). The one at Verulamium had two rows of shops facing each other across a courtyard and was situated next to a large Romano-Celtic temple, which may have been dedicated to Mercury, the patron god of traders. Leicester seems to have built a large market hall, probably in the early third century, with an overall size of 55 m (180 ft) by 29 m (96 ft). This had a wing containing rows of shops, some with plastered and painted ceilings, projecting from each end of a basilican hall. It lasted until it was burned down in a large fire in the fourth century. Wroxeter is suggested to have had a small, specialized market, consisting of small square rooms around three sides of a courtyard, built about the time of Hadrian's visit; and Cirencester built a market hall, again probably with imperial encouragement during this visit. One of its buildings had a number of pits filled with sawn and cut-up bones, suggesting this was the site of a butcher's shop. These markets would not only serve townspeople but also people drawn in from surrounding areas who would buy goods as well as bringing in market produce and other items for sale. Cirencester is ideally placed for the surrounding villa owners to convey their goods to and from the town. Leicester, however, has no villas surrounding the town so the market may have been mainly to serve the townspeople.

If there were economic considerations so also were there spiritual ones. Classical-style temples were erected, which were also part of the process of Romanization. This was particularly apparent at Colchester where a large temple on a massive podium was erected to the Divine Claudius after his death in AD 54 as part of the Imperial Cult. It stood within a *temenos* (a sacred area), 177m (581 ft) by 107 m (351 ft). The Imperial Cult was supervised by *severi augustales* and these men are known to have been at Lincoln, York and probably London. Other classical-style temples were possibly built in the main towns. One, at Verulamium, seems to have been built in the forum complex and the Cogidubnus inscription at Chichester suggests that another was there. At Wroxeter a temple in classical style had a large podium and a portico of six columns. The Verulamium forum also included two temples, one decorated with floral designs and a tessellated floor. Bath's large temple complex was linked to its healing waters and to a theatre, which could provide a setting for religious purposes and for entertainment.

The Romans were, however, tolerant where religious belief was concerned, so many towns erected temples in the Romano-Celtic style. One at Caerwent near the forum seems, on the evidence of an inscribed statue base, to have been dedicated in AD 152 to a Rhineland god, Mars Lenus, also called Ocelus Vellaunus, presumably a deity of the Silures. A small apse, a classical architectural feature, was incorporated in its design. Another temple outside the walls was of octagonal shape, which resembles one found at Chelmsford and others found in country areas. In addition to the architectural remains a large number of altars and inscriptions dedicated to deities have been found, indicating that temples and shrines were part of the fabric of a town.

Large Roman towns were provided with public bathhouses, erected at public or private expense, which incorporated places for exercises, bathing and latrines. These were particularly useful in towns closely packed with people who usually would not have had a private water supply. No doubt the Britons soon came to appreciate the facilities. One at Silchester was situated to the south-east of the forum. A huge and costly suite of baths at Wroxeter may have been built on the instructions of Hadrian during his visit to Britain, although it was not finished until the 150s. Even small towns such as Dorchester and *mansiones* like that at Wall might have the usual suite of rooms and an exercise hall. Owners of private houses and villas often included a bathhouse. One householder at Verulamium seemed to have opened a private bathhouse and latrine on a profit-making basis. Evidence from Housesteads and Caerleon suggests that the civilian population was allowed to share military bathhouse facilities. Judging by food remains at Caerleon the bathers

Second-century bath complex at Wroxeter showing the hypocausts of the warm and hot baths, divided from the exercise hall by a wall with a huge doorway

enjoyed a shellfish, chicken and mutton chop bar. Both men and women used the baths, probably not at the same time, although prohibitions by Hadrian indicated that this was taking place. A small entrance fee was charged but Juvenal indicates that children, slaves and soldiers were admitted freely.

People might have exercised in the *palaestra* (public training area) beforehand. That at Leicester, which was at least 24 m (80 ft) long, was east of the main baths and was possibly covered to protect it from the weather. At Caistor-by-Norwich a latrine was found leading off the *palaestra*. After exercising and rubbing with oils any sweat was scraped off with the strigil. Many people had their private slave to do this. It was reported that Hadrian, on one visit to the baths in Rome, noticed an old man scraping himself on a wall because he was too poor to have a slave and gave him several slaves and money for their keep. On a subsequent visit he saw several men scraping themselves on a wall. Exasperated, he commanded them to line up and scrape each other.

Bathers undressed in the *apodyterium* (changing room), placing their clothes in niches or leaving them with attendants. Not everything was secure. A curse tablet found at Bath made dire threats: 'I have given to Sulis, the goddess, the thief who stole my hooded cloak, be he slave or free, man or woman. Let him not redeem this gift except with his blood.' There seems to have been a problem with thieving at Bath judging by the number of curses on those who stole cloaks and other clothes.

Bathing started with a visit to the *tepidarium*, a warm room that could have a bath of warm water in it. Bathers next moved into the *caldarium*, where there was usually a bath with waist-high hot water. The walls of this were very thick to retain the heat so that bathers sweated to open the pores. More scraping by a strigil cleansed the body for there was no soap. Wearing of thick sandals was also necessary because of the hot floors. The bathers then moved back to the *tepidarium* before finishing in the *frigidarium* where they bathed in the cold pool. They might have a sauna in the dry heat *laconicum* or swim in the *natatio*, a large outdoor pool. Furnaces heated the baths and estimates suggest that even a small bath suite could take 114 tonnes of firewood, a denuding of 23 hectares (57 acres) of coppice a year.

The army may have been responsible for developing Bath into a spa town. Inscriptions indicate that many of the military visited it presumably to take advantage of its healing waters. The Great Bath, 22m (72 ft) by 8.8 m (29 ft) and 1.5 m (5 ft) deep, placed in the centre of a large aisled hall, 33.2 m (109 ft) long and 20.4 m (67 ft) wide, encouraged bathers to relax in its warm waters. The hall was rebuilt with a vaultĕd masonry roof in the third century AD; its appearance would be very different from the modern colonnaded ambulatory that surrounds it today. In the nineteenth century forty-five sheets of lead were discovered to have lined the base of the bath, indicating that no expense had been spared. The arrangement of the Bath complex is particularly interesting as it linked spirituality associated with the goddess Sulis-Minerva with healing and cleanliness. The pediment above the temple contained a shield within which was a striking image of a male Gorgon's head conflated with Celtic features of a wedge-shaped nose, lentoid eyes, a flowing moustache and locks of hairs, which incorporated wings and serpents. Below this are two helmets, one in the form of a dolphin, the other being a perch for an owl; both are attributes closely associated with Minerva.

As well as bathing and cleanliness, other activities took place in the baths. Tweezers, ear-picks and manicure sets indicate that there were possibilities of a massage, having hair, beard and nails trimmed and consulting a doctor. Some procedures might be very painful. Seneca, who lived above a bathhouse, complained bitterly about the noise of grunts, slaps and screams of people who were having their armpits plucked and presumably exuberant shouts and screams echoed constantly through the high rooms. John Wacher estimated that at Leicester

possibly 500 people a day might use the baths, even if the population of 3,000 to 4,000 only used it once a week. Many people
took advantage of opportunities for meeting friends to find out
the latest news, have a gossip, generally relax or carry out
business deals. Gaming boards, dice and statues of the goddess
Fortuna indicate that gambling was a frequent pastime. Much as
the emphasis was on cleanliness of the person, possibly the
baths would not be too clean unless nail clippings, hair and
other debris was cleared frequently. The warm water would
also be a breeding ground for bacteria, especially as some
doctors encouraged the use of bathing to help skin diseases.

Bathhouses were also supplied with public latrines. Wooden
seats may have been built over the drains and John Mann identified more clearly the use of the keyhole opening known to
have been placed in the side of the seating. When people sat
down they would spread out their robes or their tunics, which
would allow for a certain amount of privacy. A sponge placed
on a stick and inserted through the opening allowed them to
cleanse themselves. Afterwards the sponge was washed in the
water running along a channel in front of them. The whole
operation could take place without leaving the seat and without
disarranging any garment.

The poet Martial satirized Vacerra because he stayed in a
latrine bathhouse for hours, not relieving himself but because
he wanted to cadge an invitation to a good dinner. Commodus
is reputed to have taken eight baths a day, which might be
considered excessive, but the man who had had *balnea, vina,
Venus corrumpunt, corpora nostra sed vitam faciunt* (baths,
wines and women corrupt our bodies but these things make life
itself) carved on his tombstone in Rome had obviously enjoyed
his earthly life.

To supply these baths copious amounts of water were
needed. Most towns in Britain seem to have had some supply of
water; some tapped a spring or relied on wells as the water table

was higher than today. A large number of wells have been recorded in London and Silchester, some lined with wickerwork. At London, reused barrels, which had held wine from the Rhineland, lined the wells. A discovery in the city of four massive first- and second-century plank-lined wells led to an experiment which concluded that water could have been brought to the surface by bucket chains utilizing box-buckets. The water was drawn up by an overhead shaft and gearing worked by a treadmill.

Other towns got their supplies either by pipes or open leats. If water was delivered by the constant flow principle much of it must have been wasted but this may account for the large capacity of the leats. The aqueduct at Wroxeter provided 9 million litres (2 million gallons) a day; that at Dorchester (Dorset), covering 7 km (11 miles), brought in 59 million litres (13 million gallons) daily. At Lincoln an elaborate arrangement of earthenware pipes sheathed in concrete supplied water over 32 km (20 miles), for the last part uphill, in a manner not quite elucidated, so that it flowed by gravity into the *colonia*. One pipeline supplied the baths; another seemed to have provided water for public or private use, an arrangement suggested by the engineer Vitruvius. Wooden pipes were used at Chelmsford, Carlisle and Worcester. Lead pipes were found at Cirencester and London and, although dissolving of the lead could cause lead poisoning, a furring of calcium carbonate in the pipes could mitigate this.

Vitruvius recommended that public buildings should have a free water supply while private customers should have one at their own expense. Some households in Catterick and Wroxeter seemed to have done this but the expense would have been beyond most households. They would rely on water fetched by women and slaves from public fountains, water tanks or a local river. Water pumps were available; a reciprocating force pump, found at Silchester, which could move 22 litres (5 gallons) of water a minute, may have been used to lift water into the domestic system of a house. Most households obtained their water from wells of which there were an enormous number in towns as the water table was relatively high. At Lincoln, a huge well on one side of the forum supplemented water brought in by the aqueduct.

Water was needed to scour drainage systems such as those provided by the military authorities at York, Lincoln and Caerleon. William Stukeley, who visited Chester in the eighteenth century, said that the drains were so high that a man could walk through them and this is confirmed by the fact that those discovered at York were 1 m (3.3 ft) high and 0.4 m (1 ft) wide, large enough to be cleaned by slaves who entered through large manholes. Yet these drains debouched into the River Foss, and if the river was low the revolting debris might be left on the riverbank or collect in the river, one of the reasons why aqueducts tapped streams and not rivers. At Chichester a lining of pink mortar would have smelt foul as faeces clung to it. The purpose of removing sewage was to prevent, if possible, a smell rather than avoid a potential risk of disease. The drains at York provided evidence of moss and sponges that had been used as toilet paper in latrines. If Romano-British custom followed that in other cities, the lower half of amphorae would have been placed strategically at street corners as urinals, which would be collected by slaves and their contents sent to tanneries.

Entertainment was not confined to the bathhouses. Romans loved theatrical entertainments and expected that theatres would be provided either at public expense or by private individuals. *Aediles* were expected to do this and Marcus Ulpius Januarius, an *aedile* at Petuaria, did his duty by providing a stage (*proscaenium*), probably a wooden one, for the little town. Stone theatres are known from Canterbury and Colchester and are suspected at Chichester and Cirencester. Cirencester also had an amphitheatre, carved out of a stone quarry, just outside the town. The theatre at Canterbury was begun about AD 80–90 and may have been the result of Agricola's Romanization policy. It was rebuilt in the early third century on a larger scale and as its alignment did not approximate to the surrounding streets it may have had another building – perhaps a temple – associated with it.

Another theatre may have been at Great Chesterford (Essex) where the discovery of counters bearing numbers and letters are suggested to have been tickets because theatres usually had numbered seats. A lead disc found at Colchester with 'XIII' stamped on it might have been another ticket. Tragic and comic actors wore masks; an ivory one found at Caerleon and pottery ones at Baldock and Catterick may have been worn by travelling actors who erected makeshift stages. At Leicester one house had tragic masks painted on the walls but whether this indicated an interest in the theatre by the householder or a representation of his visit to a theatre is unknown.

The best extant theatre is at Verulamium, where the theatre was not built of stone but provided with wooden seating on earthen banks. It followed the traditional lines of being semicircular in shape with a flat surface, an orchestra, on which there would be a stage where the actors performed. The theatre underwent several developments, enlarging the stage and giving better access to the seating. By the fourth century, however, the theatre had been closed and become a rubbish tip. This may indicate a lack of interest in civic entertainment, an attack by Christians on frivolous and horrendous activities or a movement away from this area to a more sophisticated part of the town.

Additional entertainment was provided in the amphitheatres; nine have been found attached to towns. Several are situated near forts and would be used for military exercises as well as for theatrical shows. The best preserved are at Caerleon and Chester, and at the isolated fort of Tomen y Mur (Gwynedd). At Chester a stone amphitheatre, seating about 5,000 people, replaced a timber one. Amphitheatres at the towns of Silchester, Caerwent and Dorchester have been estimated to contain the total population of the towns. Silchester's first-century timber amphitheatre was rebuilt again in timber in the second century before being replaced by a masonry one in the next century.

The popularity of shows is indicated by the amphitheatre built by the small mining community of Charterhouse-on-Mendip (Somerset). Another was built near the Frilford temple, presumably to provide entertainment and religious observances for those people who came to worship at the shrine. London, as is only to be expected, was provided with an amphitheatre having earthen banks and timber seating soon after AD 70. This was soon replaced in the early second century with a stone-built one having an arena 100 m (328 ft) wide. Evidence of activity was found in human and animal bones found in a well-preserved timber drain. Spectators might have indulged themselves with fast food as a large number of Samian ware vessels found on the site could have been used as containers. The amphitheatre continued in use until the fourth century when, it has been suggested, it became a market place. London may have had unusual entertainments. A possible grave of a female gladiator has been found in Southwark. One of the eight lamps buried in the grave depicts a gladiator; another has the Egyptian god Anubis who conveyed the dead to the Otherworld. Juvenal is contemptuous of these would-be Amazons: 'who has not seen one of them smiting a stump, piercing it through and through with a foil, lunging at it with a shield and going through the proper motions? Unless indeed she is nursing some further ambition in her bosom and is practising for the real arena.'

Minor entertainments could be cockfights, boxing bouts, wrestling matches and acrobatic turns but those most appreciated were gladiatorial fights, fights between men and animals and setting animals on each other. Amphitheatres could also be used for sending condemned criminals and prisoners to their death. There is ample evidence in Rome for this though little direct evidence in Britain, but the martyrdom of the Christians, Julius and Aaron, is recorded by Gildas as being in the amphitheatre at the 'city of the legions', probably Caerleon.

There is more evidence for gladiatorial fights. An ivory knife handle from Caerwent depicts a rare example of two fighting gladiators, a winning *secutor* (armed with a sword) and a defeated *retiarius* (armed with a trident and net), a favourite theme in third century AD art. Evidence from Colchester, as might be expected, indicates gladiatorial shows. A first-century gladiatorial helmet found at Hawkedon (Suffolk) may be part of the loot seized when Colchester was sacked. A beaker depicting Salvenus Valentinus, a *retiarius*, shows him about to be crushed by the oblong shield of his more heavily armed opponent, the *murmillo* (with a sword and a fish-shaped helmet), Secundus Memnon. The names of eight gladiators on a glass cup, also found at Colchester, are a reminder that these men had individual characters as well as having their performance scrutinized for betting purposes. Another beaker shows Secundus fighting a bear and, on a pottery fragment, two lions are fighting. Animal fights were much appreciated and the Caledonian bear mentioned by Martial may have had companions who would not all have been sent to Rome. Bulls and boars could have joined bears in British amphitheatres; monster fish, like that depicted on a terracotta plaque at Colchester, probably indicated a farcical contest.

Gladiators lived apart in their own barracks and undertook individual roles wearing special parts of armour and using particular weapons. A mosaic at the Bignor villa (West Sussex) shows a trainer holding a whip and directing cupids acting out the roles of gladiators. A plaster cast in the museum at Chester, taken from a tombstone (now lost) shows a *retiarius* advancing on an opponent, his attitude recalling Juvenal's sneer in one of his *Satires*: 'See how he wields the trident and when, with trailing right hand he has cast the net in vain, he lifts up his bare face to the benches and flies . . . from one end of the arena to the other.'

In 2010 excavations at York seem to have produced evidence of a gladiatorial cemetery, mostly dating to the fourth century AD where 80 skeletons were discovered, buried 1 m (3 ft) deep. Most of the skeletons appeared to have had much bigger muscles on their sword arm, indicating a lifetime of weapon training. Some had several weapon injuries, were decapitated or killed by a hammer blow to the head, a known method of dispatching a defeated opponent. One man had a carnivore bite-mark on his arm – by a tiger, a lion, or even the Caledonian bear. One grave was that of a tall man, aged between eighteen and twenty-three, buried in an oval grave in the third century AD, killed apparently by a sword blade to the neck. The grave contained the bones of substantial joints of meat from a cow and pigs and also the remains of several horses. The beef and pork would have been the remains of a funerary feast but the horses were probably his personal possessions.

Managers did not wish to lose their men but public opinion could force a man to kill his opponent. Small wonder that a shrine to Nemesis, a goddess often implored to defeat opponents, was included in the amphitheatres of Chester and Caerleon. The writer of a curse tablet found at Caerleon borrowed or stole some clothing of his opponent in order to resort to magical practices: 'Lady Nemesis, I give thee a cloak and a pair of boots. Let him who wears them not redeem them except with his life's blood.' Yet these men did not always lead brutal lives. Evidence from inscriptions at Rome show that they married and had children.

There is little evidence of another form of entertainment – chariot racing – which was highly organized and provided spectacular entertainment. Chariots were either two-wheeled (*biga*) or four-wheeled (*quadriga*). The races started from stalls at the flattened end, with the wooden gates all opening at the same time by a mechanism formed of twisted rope. The track was probably a sandy surface on a firm base. Each race took about

Part of a mosaic pavement from Horkstow, Lincolnshire, depicting chariots racing round a *spina* with *metae* (turning posts)

10–15 minutes over seven laps and the chariots could reach a speed of 64 km (40 miles) an hour. They stayed in their own individual lane until the end of the central barrier (*spina*). Then they could move into any position, the closer to the *spina* the better chance of winning but the more dangerous position. Cutting in fouled opponents, so did crowding out and whipping an opponent's horses. A bad accident, called a shipwreck, could result in the death of a driver or a horse. It could be expensive. Juvenal comments: 'Now the spring races are on; the praetor drops his napkin and sits there in state but those horses just about cost him the shirt off his back one way or another.' As only the first chariot past the post counted and the winner had to build up a sequence of conquests, the will to win was dominant.

The only remains of a circus (*stadium*) in Britain appear to have been found south of Colchester. Dated to the late first or early second century AD, there was possibly a *cavea* (spectator area) in the form of an earthed bank revetted on each side by a stone wall and supporting ramped seating. The *stadium* appears to have been 447 m (489 yd) long and approximately 70 m (76 yd) wide and was surrounded by a cemetery with at least 500 burials. The circus was abandoned in the AD 270s probably because the wealthier citizens of Colchester found it too much of a burden to provide mass entertainment. There are hints that chariot racing took place elsewhere. On a mosaic pavement found at Horkstow (Lincolnshire) one *biga* is about to have an accident as it turns the corner of the *spina*. A wheel flies from a chariot and an attendant runs fruitlessly to catch the falling driver. Another chariot tips up as the driver fights to control it. Another mosaic pavement at the Rudston villa shows the driver of a *quadriga* galloping headlong towards a spectator carrying a palm and wreath of victory.

A less important but necessary building was a *mansio*. This was a hostelry which was intended to provide accommodation for the imperial post. A state postal service founded during the republic was reorganized by Augustus. Frequent changes of horses enabled the couriers to make swift progress, usually 7.4 km (5 miles) an hour and a courier could cover 75 km (50 miles) a day. Ordinary travellers who made use of these roads probably travelled about 30 km (20 miles) a day or less. *Mansiones*, usually placed 32–48 km (20–30 miles) apart, provided resting places for couriers and also other guests. *Mansiones*, suggested at Silchester, Caerwent and the small towns of Wall (Staffordshire) and Aldborough (Yorkshire), would have consisted of rooms and stables placed around a courtyard, with the usual amenities of a bathhouse and latrine.

Many Celts in pre-Roman Britain had lived in round houses. This was not the custom in urbanized Roman life, although some round houses seemed still to have existed in smaller towns – Alcester, Godmanchester and Baldock (Hertfordshire), for example. Many people would be drawn to the towns in search of a new lifestyle or for work. Traders, craftsmen, adventurers and even conmen, who sought opportunities in the newly acquired province, would supplement these. All these would require accommodation. As ample space was at first available in towns there was no need for apartment blocks, such as was the case in Rome and Ostia.

Yet even though streets might be laid out in rows, living conditions could be cramped and hygienic conditions were poor. Animals wandered about the streets or were penned up next to buildings. Little attempt might be made at cleaning streets – excrement from dogs and animals was everywhere and people had no compunction, as Juvenal noted, to emptying their cesspots on to the street. Recent excavations at Silchester have revealed a huge number of timber buildings packed along streets between the previously known stone houses. In the first century early houses at Gloucester and Caerwent were closely crowded together with foundation sleeper walls of stone and clay, supporting timber-framed buildings with wattle-and-daub walls, consisting of puddled clay and dung bound together with straw and horsehair. Dried clay bricks and cob were also used. Internal partitions of wood were set on wooden sills although occasionally there was a shallow stone foundation. Thatched roofs probably covered them, although after the first century tiles and stone-slabs replaced many roofs. Brick earth or lime was painted on the external surfaces of buildings to protect against the weather. Floors were of beaten earth, possibly covered with rushes or skins. Later these floors could be replaced by mosaic ones if the inhabitants sought, and could afford, a more comfortable lifestyle.

Town houses were not necessarily purely living areas. The distinction between home and workplace was not clear-cut in the Roman period. Several houses at Silchester had evidence of ironworking on their premises. Many strip houses as at Verulamium and London, and in smaller establishments such as the Housesteads's *vici*, had a workshop or retail shop attached. This would have been at the narrow end, open to the street, with the goods placed on tables or the floor and secured by shutters at night. Living quarters in these shops would have been simple. Mats were used as beds, which could be rolled up during the day. Tile-built hearths set against an internal wall or in the centre of the room provided cooking and heating facilities. There would have been a diversity of activities with commercial and industrial premises existing together. At Chelmsford some premises have been identified as pottery workshops. Verulamium had some timber-framed shops in existence by AD 49. Many were owned by metalworkers – one has been identified as a goldsmith's shop – and they were quickly rebuilt and renewed several times after the Boudiccan fire.

In London, doorways in the sidewalls opened into narrow alleys between the buildings, suggesting that these buildings were not occupied by a single family but were let to several tenants, probably of a new artisan class, who had moved into London seeking work and producing artefacts necessary to townspeople. Analogies from elsewhere suggest there would have been a huge number of bakeries and fast-food shops. The busy commercial life and importance of London are indicated by the excavation of successive river frontages situated along the north bank of the Thames, which from the first century AD were lined with warehouses and granaries.

There could have been space for walled gardens and orchards that allowed the inhabitants to provide their own produce, as happened at Silchester, where some had corn-dryers included in their buildings. Cattle byres in Silchester and elsewhere indicate that cows were kept in the town to supply milk as was common in later eras, at least until the late nineteenth century. They may also have housed oxen needed to transport heavy loads. Jashemski's excavations in Pompeii suggest that many gardens were exploited for profit, growing vegetables, having orchards or even vineyards. Owners could not afford gardens to be completely ornamental. Some parts might have provided a recreational area but gardens had to pay their way. This situation may have been replicated in Britain, especially if the owner was not the householder but a tenant. Wealthy Celtic nobles, who were used to having a large number of client retainers and who had embraced the Roman way of living, might have acted as landlords as a form of patronage.

Some large courtyard buildings on the outer fringes of towns may have been farms. Two at Cirencester strongly resemble villas and one includes a building similar to an aisled barn. The large number of animal bones found suggests that animals were slaughtered here. Just outside the Balkerne Gate at Colchester were nine raised beds of topsoil. This was a noted method of gardening by the Romans for vegetables, vines and fruit bushes. Pliny suggested that plots were given raised borders to keep in the water and paths should surround plots so that they could be easily weeded. The best size was 30 m (10 ft) wide and 15 m (50 ft) long so that beds could be watered from a path.

In the second century householders began to replace their wattle-and-daub walls with masonry, thus allowing more sophisticated dwellings, many of the courtyard variety. At Cirencester this was done fairly quickly because of the ready availability of stone. Floors were of good quality concrete, many houses overlaying them with mosaics, and the walls were of painted plaster, many depicting figurative designs showing classical mythology. At least two firms seem to have operated, providing good workmen to lay mosaics both in the towns and in the surrounding villas. Professor Toynbee has suggested that there was a sculptor's workshop, possibly run by a man who came over from Gaul or by a trained British sculptor, which produced excellent pieces now seen in the head of Minerva and the head of a river god. Even in smaller towns like Aldborough, Caerwent and Dorchester the mosaics are of high quality. The fourth-century Orpheus pavements in the western part of Britain are of the highest quality.

Where space was available, as at Verulamium and Silchester, wings were extended from the central block and a wall was built on the fourth side to form a courtyard. Some of these included bathhouses and even if the bath was intended for the family, there could be a profit if outsiders were allowed to use it. In the small town of Caistor-by-Norwich a substantial house was built consisting of a range of rooms set between external corridors and terminating in an apse at one end. Two small wings projected from the ends of the range and one of these incorporated a bathhouse. Cupboards would hold pottery and glassware, and occasionally houses had cellars for extra storage. Latrines were placed in the houses or the garden, although there would be public ones available in the public bathhouses. If not, as indicated previously, cesspots were emptied in the garden or the street. Water was drawn from wells, collected from the roof or, for a fee, piped from the public supply. Kitchens were built at the ends of houses or apart from the main block in case of fire, and rooms would be heated by charcoal on braziers, although some houses had one room in the house heated by a hypocaust.

Most towns, especially if they replaced a fort, had streets laid out in a grid pattern. The forum was in the centre of the town with streets leading from it and the town was divided into square building areas (*insulae*) by the streets. Houses were built along the streets but when they were rebuilt many may not have adhered to a consistent pattern and the result is that a rigid grid pattern was not always the norm. At Canterbury a wide lane separated two buildings but in the second century someone had obviously bought both of them for they were incorporated into one, thus blocking the lane. Smaller towns, especially roadside settlements, like Chelmsford and Towcester, developed their own street structure from the beginning.

To keep order towns were divided into wards; at least two are known at Lincoln. Each ward in a town was supposed to have its own fire brigade, which patrolled at night with axes and fire buckets, but primitive equipment could do very little. Vitruvius said that once a fire caught hold the houses would 'catch fire like torches'. Fire was always a problem. In Rome, Nero decreed that everyone should have something in the house which would help to dowse a fire. In Britain, besides minor fires, conflagrations burned down the fora of Verulamium and Wroxeter necessitating widespread rebuilding. Only wholesale destruction of adjoining shops and houses could stop the fires from spreading. If someone pulled down a neighbour's house to create a fire barrier, he could not be liable for a damage suit if his action was out of concern for the general good.

The large amount of space available for building became more restricted at the end of the first and into the second century when towns began to build defences. Verulamium had seemingly been defended from its beginnings by an earthen bank and ditch, but this did not save it from the fury of Boudicca's followers. Silchester and Winchester were also provided with defences. At first these were mainly earth ramparts and ditches but the Boudiccan rebellion, combined with a desire to emphasize civic status, meant that the *coloniae* of Gloucester, Lincoln and Colchester received walls. London was not provided with a stone wall until about AD 200.

As towns began to feel themselves threatened by a breakdown of the social order, possibly due to the unsettled years after the usurpation of Clodius Albinus, the front of many existing ramparts were usually cut back to insert a wall. In this, Britain differed from other parts of the empire where the preference was for a freestanding wall. Verulamium's walls were 2.1 m (7ft) wide with an earthen bank 13.7m (45 ft) to 15.2m (50 ft) wide behind them. Canterbury began to build an earth bank with an external wall, 2.3 m (7.6 ft) thick, in the late third century; it enclosed an area about 48 hectares (120 acres), but excluded a large suburb on the west bank of the river Stour which was thereafter abandoned by its inhabitants who sought safety within the town walls. There was an external ditch and entrance to the town was by four gates, which seem to have been simple arched openings in the wall.

Other towns' gateways were more impressive; the two main ones at Verulamium had double roadways, flanked by footways and protected by drum towers. The surviving north gate, the Newport Arch, at Lincoln still manages to give some idea of the care that went into the construction of these gates. The walls of Caerwent, built about the same time as those at Canterbury, still remain to an imposing 5.2 m (17 ft) high and 3.1 m (10 ft) thick in places. They were built in sections with their joining areas masked by a front of facing stones. The reasons given for the addition of defences and the dating evidence have to be treated with caution, as it is not clear why certain towns added their walls, especially as even very small towns, such as Irechester, Water Newton and Great Chesterford, had walls. These might have provided protection for the imperial post and travellers along major roads. Towns near the coast would feel that protection against sea raiders was a priority and banditry in some inland areas might be common. Towns were also easier to police if their gates were closed at night. As town walls had to be paid for by the townspeople, with members of the *ordo* probably contributing most of the cost, their construction, especially the addition of handsome gates, may have been a matter of civic pride as well as providing defensive structures. For travellers approaching a town, walls would be visible long before they reached it, thus creating a visual sense of urban identity.

What is clear is that by the fourth century town walls had become substantial. London had not provided a wall alongside the river, presumably because the river would give adequate protection; a riverside wall was constructed in the late fourth century to complete the land defences and this was given such priority that it cut off important and presumably essential riverside wharves. Other buildings, however, indicate that a new riverside port was constructed downriver to enable trade to continue. After the Barbarian Conspiracy in AD 367 some towns added external towers or bastions for extra defence. These were usually built so that covering fire could be provided by defensive artillery along the intervening curtain walls. New ditches then had to be provided further out than the original ones. Even the small town of Aldborough, which covered only 22.3 hectares (55 acres), added bastions at the corners of its third-century walls, rectangular interval towers along the curtain walls and a new ditch 12.2 m (40 ft) wide and 7.6 m (25 ft) from the walls. Seemingly its large comfortable houses, many of which had mosaic floors, some with colonnaded courtyards, were worth any expense to protect them.

Yet a sense of urban identity may not have been present in all respects in Britain. London demolished its forum about AD 300 and the adjoining baths fell into decay. In the late third century fire destroyed the basilica at Wroxeter, which was not rebuilt; at Caerwent the basilica was partly demolished to house the metalworkers. It could be argued that the presence of a large basilica might not have been felt to be necessary if a town could function without this symbol of civic pretension. The *ordo* and the magistrates could have operated elsewhere and be relieved of the expense of the upkeep of a large building. Existing available space was therefore reused. Other abandoned civic buildings include the theatre at Verulamium and a decaying London amphitheatre, which was systematically robbed for its stone.

Possibly this could be due to increasing Christian opposition, or a movement away to another part of the town, but the abandonment of such important buildings would more likely indicate that townspeople were no longer interested in these essential Roman entertainments. They were also expensive to maintain, which may account for the fact that almost all public bathhouses had been abandoned by the end of the fourth century. The decay of these buildings might have been the result of a decree as issued for the city of Rome that the restoration of buildings was a task for the urban authorities; no money would be provided by the state and thus responsibility fell on individuals who were increasingly unwilling to do this.

There seems also to have been a decline in the number of wealthy houses, some seemingly being divided between several families. The lack of an active population in some towns may be indicated by the decline in the number of wells known to have been in use. Aqueducts became silted up and piping was not renewed, which probably contributed to the decline of the bath system. Cleaning of the sewers at York and elsewhere was neglected. Drains around the forum clogged up at Verulamium. Roads were not maintained and were being quarried for materials. Declining urban standards are indicated by the amount of rubbish that piled up in open spaces or on sites where a house had been destroyed. A hoard of twenty bronze, pewter and iron vessels dumped in a well in the Walbrook area of London about AD 350–400/450 has been suggested to have been a ritual deposit marking a householder's abandonment of his occupation and his city.

The impression is that civic life, so valued by Rome, was valued less so in the distant province of Britain. Probably the upkeep of public buildings was too much for the small number of people who had to contribute to their cost, and pride in presenting civic amenities began to wane as taxation became excessive. By the end of the fifth century urban life, as the Roman authorities would have known it, was ceasing to exist. The Anglo-Saxon elegy on a ruined city, presumed to be Bath, spoke for many other towns in Britain: 'Wondrous is this wall-stone, broken by fate; the castles have decayed; the work of the giants is crumbling. Roofs are ruined, despoiled are the towers with their gates; frost is their cement, broken are the roofs cut away, fallen, undermined by age.'

11

THE COUNTRYSIDE

Although the Roman authorities promoted civic life as an ideal, it is clear that most of the population of Roman Britain, probably 80–90 per cent, was predominately rural based. In the areas occupied by the Romans agricultural practices centred on settlements, varying in size, function and location, isolated farms and villas. Collingwood's assessment that 'at no time during the Roman period did agriculture occupy less than two-thirds of the inhabitants of Roman Britain' still seems to stand. Many of the population, particularly in the wilder parts of the province, were concerned mainly with growing sufficient crops to support themselves. Owners of large villas, especially those with a shrewd eye to business, would have seen the advantage of sending surplus crops to market to raise cash to pay the taxes demanded by the Roman authorities, to provide the army with its needed goods and to provide the capital needed to extend and enhance their villas. Food production would have had to increase after the conquest as the number of people who were consumers rather than producers increased.

Elsewhere, in the remoter upland areas of the north, the north-west and the south-west, the Roman conquest had a limited effect. Probably little changed from the life lived in the Iron Age, although the inhabitants would have come into contact with traders who would supply them with material goods common in the Romanized areas. People in settlements continued to follow a largely pastoral way of life, making the most they could of the poorer soil. Inhabitants living in militarized zones would have had contact with the army, which could either be an advantage, or be regarded with hostility leading to indifference to the seeming advantages of a Roman lifestyle.

To the immediate north and south of Hadrian's Wall stone-built houses, often arranged around a central courtyard, were grouped within an encircling bank or wall. Some had a central courtyard, which had become 'scooped' either because the soil had been taken to add to the bank or as a result of cattle trampling down the area. At Southernknowe (Northumberland) some houses were built into the enclosure wall. Beyond the wall would have been enclosures within which cattle or sheep were kept. Some grain, probably the hardier crop of rye, was grown and ground with saddle or rotary querns. Finds of spindle whorls and loom weights indicate that spinning and weaving were main occupations, possibly not only to supply the settlement but also to trade with other communities. South of the area of Hadrian's Wall settlements with rectangular houses may suggest some Roman influence. At Birtley (Northumberland) there were four or five huts with cobbled yards. Elsewhere, in the North Tyne valley, stone huts were built, replacing Iron Age wooden ones. These may have been deemed to be more practical to the inhabitants who had seen the benefit of living in more secure and comfortable houses. Apart from in the *vici*, however, there may have been little incentive to develop large-scale trading in this area. There was a lack of urban markets and the army may have provided the only accessible consumers.

The settlement sites may either have housed nuclear families, that is father, mother and dependent children, or extended families, which included near and distant relatives. They may also have housed people who were not related but sought a leader or similar person who would give them shelter and provide security. The Celts were also polygamous; Caesar spoke of wives being shared between groups of ten or twelve men – possibly an exaggeration, but it is not impossible that in some compounds a wealthy man would have several women acknowledging him as their consort and so living in separate huts. In addition, as the Celts included a slave society, some huts may have been dwellings of slaves. This would have been the situation throughout Britain, not only in the northern regions.

The isolation of the northern areas is also paralleled in Cornwall where small, enclosed settlements continued unaltered from the Iron Age into the Roman period, as exemplified at Chysauster where a nucleated enclosure of eight courtyard houses, outhouses and a field system continued into the fourth century AD with little change. Other sites in Cornwall, the most obvious examples being at Trevisker and Carvossa, were composed of 'rounds' where the settlement area was surrounded by a circular bank and ditch. Apart from the small fort of Nanstallon, occupied for only a short time, and a possible fort and marching camp at St Austell, which was occupied until at least AD 250, there was no overall military presence in Cornwall. The Romans, however, did not leave the area, concentrating on mining tin mainly to satisfy the demands of the pewter industry. There were no ready urban markets to encourage the production of surplus food and goods.

In the far north and north-west of Scotland brochs had been built in the Iron Age; almost 500 are known to have existed. These were huge, circular, defensive towers, large dry-stone structures with walls usually 5 m (16.5 ft) thick at the base, surrounded by an outer wall, in which was a fortified gatehouse.

The wall surrounded a courtyard in which other buildings were placed. The best preserved is on the Isle of Mousa, off the east coast of the Shetland Islands, which still stands to a height of 14.1 m (43 ft). Agricola's fleet may have observed these brochs when he sent it round the coast of Britain after his victory over the Caledonii. The journey included the Orkneys where it obtained the surrender of the inhabitants.

Before the conquest many Iron Age people lived in round or long houses, either in isolation or grouped in settlements in a variety of forms, function and location. Houses were of varying sizes. Some round houses had a central post supporting the roof; others relied on the lateral thrust of the roof timbers to the walls. There are variations in design, which have been given physical presence by reconstructions such as that at Butser Ancient Farm Site (Hampshire). These relate to comments on the structure made by Pytheas, a fourth-century BC Greek explorer from Massalia who explored the west coast of Europe; Strabo and Diodorus Siculus record his account. Living in such houses the people tended their animals and grew their crops, both to supply themselves and to utilize any surplus in trade. Some produce was exported: Strabo, in his list of exports from pre-Roman Britain, mentioned corn and cattle, and wool was also an important commodity.

Settlements in the lowland areas could develop their own agricultural systems and probably had more contact with the developing towns, regarding them as marketing centres, which could take surplus products. Round houses, like those at East Tilbury (Essex), Odell (Bedfordshire), Barcombe (East Sussex) and Selhurst Park Farm (West Sussex), continued to be self supporting; Barcombe retained its round house until the second century AD, indicating that an indigenous building tradition continued long after the Roman conquest.

Often a timber house was replaced, as at Overstone (Northamptonshire), by one with stone footings. Living in these was acceptable to many people in the Roman period, as indicated by the constant rebuilding. At Odell (Bedfordshire) two circular houses, each of which was twice rebuilt, were constructed at the beginning of the first century AD within a D-shaped enclosure. These were abandoned at the end of the century only to be built in similar form, 100 m (328 ft) to the south. Several generations of one family group lived in these houses until the fourth century. Even then, they were not abandoned when a small rectangular house was built to one side, as if one generation had finally accepted a more Romanized lifestyle or they had become part of a larger estate with a bailiff installed on the premises. During the Iron Age the inhabitants kept mainly cattle and sheep but during the Roman period there was a steady increase in the rearing of cattle. Probably this was more profitable as the value of a mature cow would have been greater than that of a sheep, especially including its hide for leather, its horns for implements and its hooves for glue.

Some settlements remained villages of peasant farmers who might have been under the control of villa owners or left to follow their own lifestyle. At Scole (Norfolk) some were well spaced out with stone foundations but clay or chalk floors. The villagers followed a basic lifestyle, growing wheat, barley, oats and a few vegetables, and eating mainly chicken, pork and what they could catch from the wild. Contact with the Romans was confined to traders bringing trinkets such as bronze bracelets, rings and brooches. This level of Romanization would be applicable to many settlements.

At certain places – Brockworth (Gloucestershire), Chalton (Hampshire) and Butcombe (Somerset) – settlements seemed to have been influenced by Roman planning, being laid out in rectilinear plots, later replaced by rectangular buildings in the second century AD. These houses, set on wooden sill beams or narrow sill walls, had timber framework walls, filled with wattle-and-daub. In some parts of the Fenland it is suspected 'that cob or mud bricks were used. Clay or stone tiles were replacing thatched roofs. By the third century rectangular buildings had become the norm, and used not only for houses but also for industrial purposes. Catsgore (Somerset) had first round timber houses, then rectangular timber huts with stone footings, which were finally replaced by stone houses in the fourth century. Each consisted of two or three rooms, one of which, usually the larger, contained a hearth.

Many settlements were surrounded by a complex of fields with Celtic square fields being replaced by larger ones as improved agricultural ploughing techniques were adopted. At Brockworth the fields were separated by ditched field boundaries. The inhabitants of Thundersbarrow Hill (West Sussex) seem to have been moved out of their Iron Age hillfort but were allowed to establish a settlement attached to the fort where the inhabitants lived without being regarded as a threat to the Roman authorities. This was surrounded by a complex of square fields, droveways and enclosures either side of a main ridgeway leading down the hill. Although this settlement was very poor, it remained occupied until the fourth century AD. Water was obtained from wells; two corn-drying ovens, constructed in pits 1 m (3 ft) deep with a stoke hole built of chalk blocks, indicated that there were cornfields in the vicinity. Roasting or parching corn prevented it from germinating and lessened the risk of rotting. Every producer of corn, however, was subject to the *annona* or corn tax, which could become a burden.

Numerous finds of sheep, cattle and pig bones also indicate that livestock was a vital part of the rural economy. These animals were left out to pasture; their manure would be useful for fertilizing the fields. In winter cattle could be brought into enclosures near the settlement. Cattle were necessary for meat and milk, and oxen were useful for traction. Finds of cattle bones indicate that during the Roman period the number of cattle increased enormously. Sheep could be left to fend for themselves until there was heavy snow. Finds of spindle whorls, loom weights and bone needles indicate that spinning and weaving were normal practice in any settlement. Pigs would provide a much needed and easy source of meat; their snouts could root into the earth and they could be kept on scrub or wasteland but if there were woodland oaks this would be excellent pannage. Food supplies would be supplemented by hunting, and, for people living on the coast, fishing, gathering shellfish and scavenging would supplement the diet.

Not all the small settlements were concerned entirely with agriculture or subsistence farming. Tile-making and pottery could be important industries. South of Verulamium there were at least five sites making tiles and pottery from local clay. These were close to Watling Street and so finished goods could be easily transported to Verulamium and beyond.

People in the *vici* would almost certainly have copied some aspects of the life lived in the forts, especially if the military had helped to build their houses and lay out the streets. The forts obtained almost all the goods they needed by importing them, commandeering them or getting them locally, but soldiers would have been able to use their pay to buy services and goods from the *vici* and the *vici* relied on this for their existence. Many of the soldiers had contact with women – wives, partners, prostitutes and camp followers. Traders visited the *vici* and settled there, as seemingly did the Syrian merchant Barates from Palmyra who lived and died at South Shields with his wife, Regina, of the Catuvellaunian tribe. One of the Vindolanda tablets refers to a purchase from Taurinus of a length of yarn at a cost of a quarter of a denarius and 1 as. This was to repair the hem of Aventinus's cloak. In addition repairs were made to a money belt for Lucanus and a shirt for Crescens. The tailoring might have been done in the fort or could have been done by a specialized tailor in the *vicus*.

Vici attached to forts on Hadrian's Wall have provided evidence of industry including iron, copper-alloy, silver and gold metalworking along with commercial activities such as the selling of pottery, jewellery and food products. More entertaining services include the provision of inns, as have been deduced at Vindolanda and Housesteads. The inn at Housesteads may not have been a salubrious establishment for the bodies of a man and a woman were found sealed under the floor. As the man had the point of a knife in one of his rib bones foul play may be deduced. Some of the *vici* became large communities; that at Old Carlisle extended for at least 0.5 km (0.3 miles) along a main road leading from the fort and the regularity of the streets at Housesteads and Vindolanda suggests some military help in planning. The *vici*, however, depended for their existence on the forts. Once the forts were abandoned, so were many of the *vici* and their surrounding agricultural plots were left to decay. Those that survived did so because they could be subsumed into a fort that later became a town – Carlisle, York and Corbridge – or, like Malton, because they had expanded as a market or industrial centre.

Larger estates could be under the control of villa owners. A definition of the term 'villa' raises problems. It is a term used in classical texts and has been applied to estates in Britain because they seem to fit the established patterns of villas elsewhere in the Roman Empire. Archaeologists use the term 'villa' as suggesting some kind of status for a building in the countryside, isolated from its neighbours, Romanized in form, not part of a settlement and usually implying some form of farming establishment. It might or might not be in the hands of a resident proprietor. The owner might also have held land not as a single whole around the estate but in widely scattered places. In 1958, A. L. Rivet described a villa as 'a farm which is integrated into the social and economic organization of the Roman world'. In 1976 Percival preferred to describe it as a unit that produces a surplus, usually agricultural, which, subject to taxes, can be used for the exchange of goods and services, including luxury items, not obtained on the villa's estate. In Italy many town-dwellers had country estates, often run by a bailiff, which they could either farm intensively or use as a country retreat. Some men had more than one. Pliny the Younger owned several villas; Cicero had eight large villas, his favourite being one at Tusculum, besides smaller ones on the coast. Villa-type buildings with extensive gardens are also known to have been built in towns.

In Britain, there were probably men who resided in a town, such as Verulamium, who were supported by their rural estates. These would be farmed by a bailiff and visited occasionally by the family. Such men included tribal aristocrats and their descendents, who may have realized that a profitable lifestyle was achieved by allying to their conquerors, administrators from Gaul and Rome and men who had done well from the profits of trade and industry. Following the occupation of a province much of the land (*ager publicus*) reverted to the emperor, who could give it as a gift, let it to tenants who would pay rent to the state or allow wealthy Roman citizens to buy it. If fighting had ravaged the land it could be sold quite cheaply.

Military veterans who already had a stake in a town and had enough money on their discharge could purchase an estate but land might have been confiscated from its Iron Age owners so that a soldier or administrator supplanted the native family. Rivenhall (Essex) was an Iron Age settlement probably belonging to a Trinovantian family. This was replaced by a large village complex, either by that family or after its confiscation when it was handed over to a Roman settler. The finding of military equipment and tile stamps of Legion VI at Dalton Parlours (North Yorkshire) was suggested by the excavators to be a case of a military veteran from York taking over an Iron Age settlement site. Immigrants from Gaul and other provinces might have seen an opportunity to invest in land. In the third century AD, Britain possibly received refugees from Gaul, driven away by incursions across the Rhine frontier. The rebellions of Albinus (AD 195–7) and Allectus (AD 287–96) also resulted in more confiscations. Much of this land would have given urban dwellers opportunities for developing country properties as well as encouraging those already established in the countryside to expand their holdings.

Some landowners may have lived on the estates permanently; others, like Pliny the younger, regarded villas as a country retreat but also expected them to be a profitable enterprise. This may have been the case around Canterbury or Verulamium, where many villa owners seemingly regarded them as a secondary, private residence, farming them as a living and expecting to make a profit. They could do this by taking surplus to a market, which could be in a town but might be attached to a temple site where there were opportunities for constant trade. The lack of villas in northern military areas may be due to the lack of market opportunities.

Not all owners of villas were absentee landowners and this was indicated by the development of estates. A small house might add outbuildings, so that the term villa might describe anything from a cottage to a grand estate. Other villas show signs of continuity. The owner of an Iron Age hut might refuse to leave the house, which his father had built, but his sons, now regarding themselves as tribal aristocrats, could become increasingly frustrated with his attitude. Within two generations more comfortable accommodation was constructed. This might have been the case at Park Street (Hertfordshire) where a Belgic farmstead was rebuilt in timber, then remodelled in the later first century as a stone-built house with five rooms, a veranda and a cellar. The veranda, an advanced architectural feature in Britain, allowed easy communication to rooms as well as ensuring privacy.

In Kent villas may have been established by merchants from Gaul preferring to live near their business interests in London or at the port of entry. One at Eccles, founded about AD 65, was based on a type of hall-villa, already established in Gaul, comprising a large central hall used for both living and working quarters, set between two rooms of equal size. The owner may have made money from a nearby pottery manufactory making flagons, mortaria and platter for the military. Several owners may have been retired veterans who shrewdly took advantage of the potentials of villa life. Some in the Darenth valley exploited commercial interests; coal from the Durham area stoked a bathhouse furnace at Northfleet. The villa at Lullingstone, built about AD 100, may have been first the country villa of an important Roman administrator who may have had connections with London.

On the whole, however, villas were agricultural units and most of their owners treated their land as a business geared to greater agricultural production. The intention of most estates, large or small, was to improve and increase food supplies. Once the Romans had established themselves in Britain there would have been a need for the more constant production of food supplies and farming to become more efficient to provide a greater yield of food to supply both an increasingly urban population and a large military force. In addition, estates were expected to contribute taxes, and these became increasingly onerous by the fourth century. In both food production and contributions towards taxation, they were encouraged by the central administration, which had to ensure that the army and the non-food productive urban communities were fed. Villa owners could take advantage of all the agricultural improvements and better breeding experiments available, as well as consulting manuals written by such people as Pliny, Cato and Columella.

Some villas went in for extensive production. Hambledon (Buckinghamshire) had several corn-drying areas. Seventy bronze pens, possibly used by officials or overseers to record production, were found. The discovery of over 100 infant burials on the site has been explained as the result of illicit or discouraged unions of a workforce of slave labour. An alternative view that this was the site of a brothel, because at least 97 children died at 40 weeks gestation or very soon after birth seems to be repudiated by Hambledon being in an isolated area – brothels were usually situated in towns. The mystery has deepened as recent examination of the bones has revealed cut marks on them that suggest some form of ritual murder.

Sometimes owners embarked on enterprises to which they were not fully committed. A farmstead, excavated at Whitton, was occupied for about 300 years but it was not until the mid second century that the first masonry building appeared. Painted wall plaster shows some pretensions to a Romanized lifestyle but the two hypocausts added to heat the rooms were never fired, as if the owners had lost the will to achieve a higher standard of living.

It was in the southern regions of Britain that the greatest enthusiasm for building to greater standards of comfort was most obvious. Most villas developed by adding wings and a corridor to a simple rectangular house; the corridor was necessary to provide privacy. During the mid third century the owners of Barcombe replaced their first masonry building by a winged corridor house of fifteen rooms with substantial masonry foundations. Ranges of buildings were added to produce courtyard homes. The owners of the Gloucestershire Spoonley Wood and Great Witcombe villas added wings on three sides to create their courtyards. In the fourth century, increasingly wealthy owners rebuilt to produce one or two courtyards including a yard or a garden, adjoining bathhouses, underfloor heating and elaborate mosaic floors.

The largest villas, such as that at North Leigh (Oxfordshire), with wings on three sides and an entrance gate on the fourth, had about forty rooms. Box (Wiltshire) and Chedworth had about thirty rooms. Chedworth had two courtyards and two bathhouses, perhaps indicating separation of the owner's family from the workforce. The inner courtyard, for the family's private use, contained a large mosaic depicting Bacchus, the god of wine, with the four corners filled with personifications of the seasons. The outer one was the farmyard in which agricultural tools and vehicles were kept and where workers and animals may have been housed. The inhabitants also built a nymphaeum where they presumably worshipped the local divinities that provided constant spring water. Woodchester (Gloucestershire) is suspected of having had three courtyards.

In some villas, the workers, labourers and slaves lived in aisled barn-like structures, which became common in Britain in the second half of the second century AD. Many of these aisled houses might have been the homes of bailiffs who ran the estate for an absentee landlord who preferred to live in his town house. Cato gave detailed instructions for the duties of the overseer including an order that he must be the first out of bed and the last in. Whether these instructions were always followed in the absence of the owner would be doubtful. Barcombe added a large aisled building, 39 m (128 ft) long, 17 m (56 ft) wide, with at least two rooms having tessellated floors, indicating more superior accommodation for a villa official. This could also have been the case at Llantwit Major (South Glamorgan) where the main house was left to fall into ruin but the aisled house was retained. Other aisled farmhouses were developed as housing for productive agricultural units. These were rectangular buildings with the interior divided by posts, which gave greater support and width, into a 'nave' and 'aisles'. Both could be partitioned off to make separate rooms, divided by doors or curtains. Even small bath suites could be added. These would shelter the owner, farm-workers and animals.

At Thruxton (Hampshire) the main building on a second-century estate was an aisled hall divided by two rows of posts. In the early fourth century a range of three rooms was organized within the south-east end. One of these, projected beyond the outer wall, had a handsome mosaic depicting Orpheus in the central roundel. This might have been a dining room but the presence of a deep shaft filled with animal bones and a nearby grave with a first-century inhumation may indicate that this could be an ancestral cult room. Other rooms had chalk floors, but the rest of the house was filled with kilns and ovens to enhance agricultural production. At North Warnborough (Hampshire) the excavators have suggested that the finds might indicate two distinct living areas on either side of the house, one for male and one for female activities. The latter included possible kitchen areas indicated by a hearth and quantities of animal bones and oyster shells. A range of four rooms at one end may have housed stalls for livestock. A variation of this at Stroud (Hampshire) seems to have had the aisled house divided into two distinct suites of rooms for two families.

Some aisled buildings may have been given over entirely to animals with the aisles divided into stalls. One at Bignor (West Sussex) might have been used for the storage of grain and fodder, although possibly there may have been lofts above for this purpose. Others, like those in the Nene Valley, seems to have been used for industrial purposes. Holcombe (Devon) had an ironworking furnace and other sites have produced hearths and ironworking tools. At Halstock (Dorset) an aisled building was given over to corn-driers.

Many owners exploited and developed their villas, probably as they achieved greater prosperity and possibly as they withdrew from activities in towns. Owners in the south-western part of Britain attracted architects and craftsmen to build and decorate their villas in the classical style. At least sixty villas include apsed dining rooms, some, like that at Keynsham (Somerset), of a sophisticated hexagonal pattern. The capitals of the colonnaded veranda were finished in Corinthian style, while moulded pilasters, decorated cornices and balustrades provide architectural sophistication. The Woodchester villa added a great mosaic pavement, 15 sq. m (162 sq. ft), in the mid fourth century AD, set in a huge square hall 225 sq. m (2,400 sq. ft). Like the pavements of many other villas in the area, it features Orpheus with his lyre taming a procession of animals that circle round him. The hall had flanking rooms and courts decorated with mosaic floors and marble statues; even the corridors had underfloor heating. This villa may have belonged to a man who had risen to high office and therefore insisted on having all the benefits of Roman civilization. The design of the pavements suggests that a talented artisan from Cirencester, who also worked on other floors in the area, constructed them.

One of the largest villas, so large that it has been called a palace, was at Fishbourne. Originally built in the AD 60s as a large house with a bath suite and a garden it was enlarged after AD 75 with four main wings laid out round a formal garden, with flower beds, shrubs and trees. In the centre of the west wing was a large reception hall approached through an entrance porch 12 m (40 ft) high. On either side of the hall were suites for the family and guests. The whole building contained mosaic floors, plastered walls and vaulted ceilings, covered in paintings. Much of the building material was imported and probably many of the artisans and builders came from the continent. The south wing seems to have contained the owner's private apartments, adjacent to a bathhouse. These rooms faced south towards the sea where there was a quay for boats and barges. Only someone who was in great favour with the Roman authorities and who was in receipt of their generosity could have built a villa of such luxury so soon after the conquest. The most likely candidate was Cogidubnus, whose willingness to aid the Romans was thus amply rewarded, but Fishbourne might have been the home of an early Roman administrator, even the first governor of the province.

The courtyard houses in Britain differed from those in Mediterranean regions in that the main entrance faced into the courtyard; in the Mediterranean regions the main door faced to the open countryside. This could be explained by the fact that British villas were not constructed as a whole but added ranges of buildings to the original corridor wing. These wings may have been added to house other members of a nuclear family, extended family groups or favoured servants and slaves.

J. T. Smith has suggested that some villas were held in joint or multiple occupancy, being divided into individual units, each the home of one 'nuclear family'. Plans of some villas do suggest that they may have been two or more parts of an economic whole, with the division indicated by the placing of a water tank, or a shrine utilizing the concept of protection, at the place of contact. The theory may have substance if the term 'extended family' is used rather than 'nuclear family'. The Gayton Thorpe villa (Norfolk) may have been two houses or occupation units, each having a portico or wing room, placed side by side, but joined by a connecting block to form a whole. Two families might have lived here, even perhaps a marriage where the man had two wives, each with a separate family. Some villas may have housed different households because of divided inheritance.

The villa at Great Witcombe, built during the mid second century and altered later, has a north range acting as a corridor, with only a single room in the middle and two larger houses situated to one side. At North Wraxall (Wiltshire), on the other hand, a large central hall dominating a series of small rooms could mean that the extended family continued the tradition of a Celtic social group living together. This theory may be extended if farm compounds are taken into consideration. At Bradley Hill (Somerset) there were seemingly two separate houses and a barn. Catsgore may have developed into six individual farm compounds; one of these was larger than the others and has been described as a villa.

In the Verulamium area villas seem to have been spaced at regular intervals along the rivers Bulbourne, Gade, Ver, Colne and Chess, suggesting some form of controlled planning. Villa economy, however, required sufficient land to sustain an estate and to allow it to function as a self-contained unit. They also needed at least thirty to forty individuals to enable it to be worked as a viable unit. This number would allow for one extended family unit or two or more distinct but separated households. It would enable a unit of forty workers to run a property of 270 hectares (667 acres). The unit does not include the workers' families who might have helped on the estate, for children were expected to work at a very early age.

The development of a villa from the Iron Age to the fourth century may be seen at Gorhambury (Hertfordshire), which was originally a first-century ditched, Iron Age settlement enclosure. Soon after the Roman conquest, a house was built of six rooms with corridors at the front and the rear and a cellar at the south end. In addition there was a stone-built granary, a corn-drier, a small bathhouse and a building that may have been used for industrial use or housed the workers. Further timber buildings were placed in an outer enclosure. In the second century, the house was rebuilt further to the west and enlarged to include an integrated bathhouse; the outer bathhouse was demolished. Improvements were made to buildings in the outer enclosure where two buildings were constructed, one perhaps being for a bailiff. Another one was a barn and a new bathhouse was obviously intended for the use of the workers on the estate as it was at the farthest end of the outer enclosure where their activities would not disturb the inhabitants of the main house.

The total extent of the Gorhambury estate at its greatest has been suggested to be 1,000–1,200 hectares (2,500–3,000 acres), of which 180–300 hectares (400–750 acres) could be arable, the rest pasture and woodland. Finds included six ploughshares and several ox goads. The aisled barn would have housed possibly at least six oxen. Oxen are used mainly as draught animals drawing carts or used in ploughing. They had to be trained to walk in pairs; when one died the other could not be paired with another one and its value was only as meat. The estate seems to have grown emmer and spelt as main crops, with the surplus possibly being sent to market. Probably sheep, cattle and pigs were kept. Woodworking tools found on the site may indicate the estate made use of the surrounding woodland, cutting timber and sending it to Verulamium where there would always have been a demand for building materials.

After AD 335, the estate was obviously run down, the only rebuilding being two barns. The villa was abandoned but one building was kept in repair, possibly to house a bailiff. The decline may have begun as early as AD 197 in connection with the defeat of Albinus and his supporters having part of their estate confiscated or being heavily taxed, for there was little improvement or change on the estate after that time. Verulamium also erected defences to guard the town and this required taxes to be obtained not only from the townspeople but also from the surrounding villa owners.

This mirrors villa economy elsewhere. During the third and fourth centuries many villas were expanded or constructed on new sites, adding such luxuries as elaborate mosaic floors and painted wall plaster. Bignor (West Sussex) was enlarged with a handsome bath suite and furnished with superb mosaics, including one showing cupids imitating fighting gladiators, which could have equalled those in Rome and which were probably made by a craftsman from Gaul. The equally superb mosaics at Littlecote Park (Wiltshire) were housed within equally elaborate architecture including a room with possibly a dome. Early in the fourth century a villa at Gadebridge (Hertfordshire), which had expanded rapidly in the second century, added a huge swimming pool 20 m (66 ft) long, together with a new wing, possibly to serve the estate workers or as a commercial enterprise. Smaller swimming pools may have been built at Great Wymondley and High Wycombe. Villas in Britain seem to have thrived during this period, especially increasing their corn production, and, as previously mentioned, in AD 359, according to Zosimus, the Emperor Julian was able to supply his armies at the estuary of the Rhine with 800 shiploads of corn from Britain.

This prosperity was not to last. Either the villa owners over-stretched themselves or their economy began to suffer because of the difficulties of the fourth century. All but one of the buildings, a small two-roomed cottage, at Gadebridge had been demolished by about AD 354. It has been suggested that the owner had been a supporter of Magnentius and that he had suffered as a result of the reprisals taken after his defeat in 353. Stock enclosures were left as if the villa was now in charge of a bailiff or a small family running it for an absentee family. Elsewhere, occupation at the Park Street villa finished about AD 367, possibly because of the chaotic circumstances of that year. In the fourth century, there was increasing inflation, debasement of currency and a lack of demand for services.

Landowners found it increasingly difficult to maintain villas, especially if they had a town house as well. Many villa owners moved into the towns. Some were forced to flee their homes and bury their wealth. The Mildenhall Treasure (Suffolk) was deposited in the earth soon after AD 360 but its owner never returned to collect it. Estates could be broken up with the villa owners prepared to give land to their workers and let them cultivate their own plots in return for money payments or the estate was left in charge of a bailiff who ran it with a skeleton staff.

Imperial estates run by procurators, like that at Combe Down, were created from land confiscated after the conquest of a country, especially if the land was very fertile, forested or had possibilities of mineral exploitation. To forestall such a takeover Prasutagus had left land to Nero under his will, to no avail, and after the Boudiccan rebellion more land may have been confis-cated from the lands of the Iceni to create an imperial estate.

There was an absence of villas on Salisbury Plain and Cranborne Chase, an area of more than 2,330 sq. km (900 sq. miles), but which contained peasant holdings. This land may have been an imperial estate given over from the late second century to stock rearing. Another region which may have had intensive stock rearing is in the Fens, where large areas between settlements were divided by dykes. A large quantity of pottery cheese-strainers was found in the area. If cattle and sheep were reared here this would indicate that milk was made into cheese on a considerable scale. The hides of the cattle would also provide the army with leather and the rearing of horses would supply their mounts. In addition extensive production of salt took place in the Fens.

Excavations at Stonea near March have revealed a settlement, which, though seemingly unique, may have been paralleled by others yet unknown in Britain. The east side of the settlement was laid out in a grid of streets between AD 130 and 150; these were lined with rectilinear wooden buildings with thatched roofs. On the west, a complex of building was created in the centre of which was a stone tower, possibly rising to three storeys. Its importance was indicated by the fact that the stone had been brought from quarries in the Peterborough area, 40 km (25 miles) away, possibly by means of a canal cut between Flaggrass and Stonea. This structure, with mosaic floors, painted plaster walls and glazed windows, has been suggested as the administrative headquarters of a Fenland salt industry. In front, linking it to the settlement, was a paved area probably intended as a market place. Close by was a small temple possibly dedicated to Minerva, patron of traders and craftsmen, as small helmeted bronze busts of this goddess were found in the vicinity.

In the flat areas of the Fens the tower would have been an impressive structure even if the workmanship was so shoddy that it had to be altered a short time after it was constructed. It lasted until about AD 220 when it was demolished, possibly because the administrative area was moved to Water Newton or Godmanchester (Cambridgeshire). There is little evidence of grain production but huge quantities of animal bones were discovered, especially of sheep and lambs. As a large quantity of spinning and weaving equipment was found it has therefore been suggested that the site produced fleeces, wool and cloth. In addition large industrial salt production took place at Norwood and smaller sites occurred along the fringes of tidal water-courses. The salt seems to have been used to preserve young lambs ready for distribution elsewhere. The whole enterprise was so extensive that it must have been under imperial control, possibly determined by Hadrian during his visit to Britain.

Regions called *regio* covered both communities and political organizations. Centurions administered these regions like an imperial estate. A *centurio regionarius* based at Carlisle (Luguvalium) is mentioned on one of the Vindolanda tablets. An inscription at Ribchester recorded that in the third century Aelius Antoninus *centurio legionarius* of Legion VI Victrix was *prae(positus) numeri et regionis* (commander of the fort garrison and the region). A second centurion, Titus Floridius Natalis, was also described in similar terms, which indicates that the area was an imperial possession at least in the third century.

Farms and villas could be very productive. The main crop in Iron Age Britain was emmer (*triticum dicoccum*). Spelt (*triticum spelta*), a hardier plant, was grown in the northern regions. These had a high food value but were difficult to thresh so that often they were replaced by club wheat (*triticum aestivum*) and bread wheat (*triticum compactum*). These continued as the main crops in Roman Britain. In addition, six-row barley (*hordeum vuldare*), oats (*averna*) and rye (*secale cereale*) were cultivated; much of the yield was used as fodder crops, but could be ground to provide bread and pottage. Rye and millet were usually grown in the eastern areas; oats and barley were prominent in the north.

Grain had to be harvested. Diodorus Siculus mentioned that the British harvested grain by cutting off the ears of corn and storing them in covered barns. Strabo also mentioned threshing grain in barns. Corn-drying ovens were used to parch the grain before threshing and also to prepare barley for beer-making. During Caesar's first invasion he noted that his troops brought in corn daily from the fields, which implied that the Britons had adequate supplies of grain. Rotary quern stones, found in farms and settlements, indicate their inhabitants ground grain, probably daily to provide the bread needed for the household.

Better breeding of sheep and cattle can be noted in the increasing size of animal bones in Roman Britain. Possibly some animals may have been imported to achieve this, but more luscious pasture and better quality fodder would have produced a similar result. This would not only mean a higher quality of meat but improved quality and quantity of wool. By the fourth century, according to Diocletian's edict, British cloaks were being appreciated as they could command a high price.

Other improvements came in the form of more efficient farming equipment. The Celts had used a wooden ard, which scuffed out a shallow furrow. The Romans first introduced iron tips to the ards and then created an iron ploughshare with a mouldboard capable of turning the sod. A small model plough-share found in a barrow at an unidentified site in Sussex has a share shaped at the end like an arrow with pairs of wrests or boards. These would have piled up the earth between the furrows; a keel allowed the share to be tilted to turn over the sod covering seeds scattered by hand and thereby reducing their loss. A more efficient plough also meant that greater areas could be ploughed deeper and more quickly, and needed only to be ploughed once, thus avoiding cross ploughing. This resulted in Celtic square fields being replaced by long, rectangular fields, which would have allowed the growing of a more productive crop as waste land was only at the two narrow ends of the field.

Manuring was essential. Clay and marl could be used and scatterings of pottery in fields are assumed to be the result of mixing domestic refuse with animal and possibly human manure. Oxen, which pulled ploughs and carts, provided traction.

Tools introduced included mattocks, adzes and turf-cutters. Hoes were of both the two-tined and the spud or blade type. Part of a wooden hay rake and a complete wooden hayfork created from a naturally formed piece of ash were found at Stonea Grange; tiny iron prongs of a rake were found in the Walbrook area of London. Other sites have produced pointed iron tips and heads of pitchforks. Wooden spades had an iron sheath fitting to improve the cutting edge and this allowed digging to a greater depth. A complete spade, found at Stonea Grange, was made from a single piece of ash. The right shoulder of the digging part was worn where a right-footed person would have depressed it.

A machine for cutting grain used in Gaul, mentioned by Pliny the Elder, is depicted on a relief now in the Institute Archéologique du Luxembourg, Arlon. No evidence for this has been found in Britain but given the Roman capacity for efficiency it may have been used on some large estates. What is known is that scythes could replace the tiresome reaping of corn with a sickle and cut large areas of hay. Scythes have been found at the forts of Bar Hill, Brampton and Newstead and the villas of Barnsley Park (Gloucestershire) and Farmoor (Oxfordshire). Huge scythes, 2.13 m (7 ft) long, were found in a blacksmith's shop at Great Chesterford. Many have been found in fourth-century ironwork hoards. These could be sharpened or have their dents and bends hammered out in the fields on mowers' anvils. Axes were useful for coppicing, for cutting wood for fuel or to make charcoal and for clearing land ready for planting. A great deal of wattle would have been needed for fences, basketry and reeds for thatching. Iron shears also meant that wool could be clipped more evenly.

Some farms would most certainly have had orchards; small square enclosures revealed by aerial photography at the Ditchley villa (Oxfordshire) are indicative of only one of many in Britain. The Celts had collected wild fruits and vegetables but the Romans domesticated many of these and also imported new varieties. Some villas may have laid out areas for viticulture. Fruit, especially apples, would have provided a useful cash crop. Excavation of a pit on the Frenchgate site, Doncaster, produced a total of 1,400 apple pips, which might have been the residue from the making of cider. Possibly the apples came from a local orchard. Another useful activity would be the keeping of bees for honey. Hives were made of straw, pottery or wood. Wood and straw would have left no trace and pottery ones were, according to Columella, 'burnt by the heat of the summers and frozen by the winter's cold'.

These improvements were necessary because one result of the conquest was the presence of a large army and the development of urban areas, thus increasing the number of consumers rather than producers. The urban population may have grown vegetables and fruit and kept some animals; it may have bought grain to be ground in individual households but these households would have preferred to buy bread from a baker or fast food from a street seller. The army would have demanded constant supplies. Meat, vegetable and grain supplies would need to be increased and it was the duty of country villas and estates to provide these as well as contributing to the taxation imposed upon them.

12

RELIGION AND BELIEF

Before the Roman invasion Celtic Britain had its own well-established forms of religion. These had impressed Caesar: 'The whole Celtic race', he wrote, 'is imbued with religious observances.' Many aspects of Celtic religion are known through comments by classical authors; others can be deduced from excavated artefacts and structures or by making comparisons with other religious practices. The Romans, with their tolerance and acceptance of foreign deities, did not suppress Celtic religious practices except in one area. The priesthood of the Druids presented both a political challenge to Roman authority and an affront to their civilized society by its encouragement of human sacrifice.

Celtic religion seems to have centred on the worship of natural phenomena. This required certain practices and observances in order to prevent disaster or to ensure the goodwill of a deity – offerings of food and drink, erecting an altar which could be a stone or a piece of wood. Yet if the Celts believed their deities could grant favours or avert disasters, they must have been envisaged in human form and thus given names. A spoken name could therefore be engraved on an altar or a votive object. These names, syncretized with those of Roman deities who had similar functions (the *interpretatio Romana*), reveal the names of Celtic deities.

Celtic belief is elusive. Animals and birds were believed to have divine powers. Some Celtic tribes believed in totemism, that their original ancestor was some creature or had its powers, which may lie behind Caesar's comments that the Celts did not eat hare, fowl or goose. Even if this comment has been disproved by evidence of food debris there is some lingering survival of a respect due to an ancestor.

The three greatest gods of the Celts were Esus, Taranis and Toutates. Esus is not known in Britain. Toutates or Teutates, a warrior god, is linked with Mars, the Roman god of war. The inscription TOT, found on rings, often in East Anglia, may indicate a desire for protection by this deity. Taranis is often linked with Jupiter, the greatest of the Roman gods. Taranis's most important attribute was the wheel, portraying both the powers of the gods and the sun. Amulets in the form of wheels provided a wearer with protection against evil forces.

Many Celtic deities were located in one place, possibly their cult centres, and their names are revealed by inscriptions. Dea Arnomecta, named on an altar found at Brough-on-Noe, was probably associated with the spring waters at Buxton; Mars Rigonemetos, mentioned on an arch, was worshipped in a grove at Nettleham (Lincolnshire). Both have names derived from *nemeton* (Greek *temenos*), meaning a sacred place. Yet the latter god was worshipped by Q. Neratius Proximus, a Roman citizen who seemingly came from an area near Rome and was probably an important resident of nearby Lincoln. His linkage of the Celtic god with Mars was in connection with the Mars of the Italic woodlands. Lucan commented on a grove near Marseilles in southern Gaul where the gods were worshipped with sacred rites, altars piled with bloody offerings and trees drenched with blood. It was probably such a grove that Suetonius Paulinus destroyed in his invasion of Anglesey.

The Celtic goddess Sul or Sulis presided over hot springs at Bath, whose waters presumably relieved afflictions. She could easily be conflated with the Roman goddess Minerva, one of whose functions was healing. Sulis's humble grove was replaced with a huge classical temple dedicated to the goddess Sul-Minerva. In addition the complex included a series of baths, which took advantage of the hot, healing waters, and a theatre to provide suitable entertainment. The inscriptions carved on altars and votive offerings refer either to the joint name, Sul-Minerva, or to Sulis, indicating that worshippers chose their own form of address. The Celts might continue to address a Celtic healing deity but the Roman military would confidently seek the help of Minerva Medica, whose cult was venerated in Rome. The temple was efficiently organized with a priesthood – one priest, Gaius Calpurnius Receptus, lived to be seventy-five – and a haruspex who would consult the entrails of sacrificial victims.

Another large temple devoted to healing was erected in the late third or early fourth century at Lydney Park (Gloucestershire) to the Celtic god Nodens, probably of Irish origin, and conflated with Mars, who was associated with hunting, water and healing. His huge temple was based on the Celtic type with a cella, a tall inner chamber which rose above the ambulatory, but oblong in shape, more on basilican lines. Various buildings in the *temenos* were hospices for those seeking cures and treatment. One of these, a long building, could have been an *abaton* where worshippers might sleep; Victorinus, an interpreter of dreams mentioned on a mosaic, would assist in their interpretation. A number of dog figurines may also indicate that the cult was similar to that at Epidaurus in Greece where wounds were treated by dogs licking them.

Priestly regalia has been found at Hockwold-cum-Wilton in Norfolk. One headdress is in the form of a circular band with strips crossing over each other and a moulded point at the top. Depictions of severed heads on attached small bronze plaques suggests that the belief, if not the actual practice, had been incorporated into the religion there. An elaborate sceptre from Willingham Fen has a nude deity with his foot placed on a grotesque figure, a clear reference to the cult of Jupiter Taranis. References to other cults are indicated by a wheel, an eagle, a dolphin and a three-horned bull. Other sceptres had busts of deities on the top: Jupiter at Amersham (Buckinghamshire) and Mars at Brough-on-Humber; a fine bronze head from Worlington (Cambridgeshire) portrayed Hadrian. These sceptres continued an Iron Age custom; human heads had traditionally been carried on poles.

Pans, possibly used in religious ceremonies, have been found on the Staffordshire Moorlands and at Winterton (Lincolnshire). The Staffordshire one had stylized enamelled vine patterns, while the Winterton one, closely matched by one found at Bingen (Germany), had a grid of enamelled squares in four colours arranged in diagonal lines. The Staffordshire pan and a bronze vessel from the Rudge villa (Wiltshire) bear the names of forts on Hadrian's wall and were probably imported by the army.

Temples built by the Roman authorities in Britain on the whole followed a classical style with a high podium reached by a flight of steps. At the front was a narthex or porch surrounded by columns. A central door opened on a cella in which were placed the cult figure of the god and objects dedicated and relating to its divine power. The Uley temple contained a statue of Mercury; the Bath temple would have contained a statue of Minerva; only her head survives. The Bath temple was 9 m (29.5 ft) wide and 14 m (46 ft) long. Its columns were 7 m (23 ft) high and overall the temple towered 13 m (43 ft) to the roof. Over the narthex of a temple would be a pediment carved with figures of the gods and statues might be placed on the roof. Decoration on the fantastically decorated, sculptured Bath pediment conflated Celtic and Roman belief. Flying Victories hold up a large shield on which is a central boss with a Medusa head. This head, however, is male with flowing Celticized moustaches. Male and female serpents, the former with crested heads, are intertwined, thereby symbolizing healing. Rising from the head are wings, which may also be flames. Below are two helmets; one has an owl as a crest, companion of Minerva as goddess of wisdom; the other is in the form of a dolphin mask, implying a Sea-Medusa linking her with the water deity, Sul. Tritons blowing conches fit into the spandrels. When this pediment was painted, it must have blazed forth proclaiming the power of the goddess.

Evidence of another early classical temple comes from Chichester where Cogidubnus, King of the Atrebates, authorized the college of smiths to build a temple to Neptune and Minerva. Others would certainly have been erected in the four *coloniae* of Britain and probably in some of the *civitas* capitals. Three temples were constructed in the forum at Verulamium during the first century AD; one of these may have been a capitolium (a temple dedicated to the divine triad of Jupiter, Juno and Minerva).

The so-called Romano-Celtic temple took a variety of forms. The design probably originated in Gaul or the Rhineland, deriving from local tradition. The usual form was of a square building with a tall sanctuary (cella), surrounded by a veranda with its roof reaching halfway up the cella. Sometimes the veranda was enclosed creating an ambulatory or a series of rooms. Other temples might be circular or polygonal (usually octagonal). There are two surviving structures in France indicating the heights of the cella. A square one at Autun (Saone-et-Loire), known as the Temple of Janus, rises to a height of 13 m (43 ft); a round one at Périgueux (Dordogne) survives to a height of 21 m (70 ft).

Sometimes, as at Hayling Island, an Iron Age circular temple was replaced by a square one, which in turn was succeeded by a Roman stone one of a hybrid form. Temples were surrounded by a *temenos*, the sacred area where the priest could have his residence and the public might congregate. Religious ceremonies might have taken place here or stalls erected selling votive objects. This would explain the large number of these objects found in the *temenos* at the Woodstock temple (Oxfordshire).

Sacrifice to the gods was an essential part of both Celtic and Roman religion. Where once the Celts had practised human sacrifice they now followed animal sacrifice. Heifers were sacrificed at Bath following the Roman custom of sacrificing female animals to female deities. The temple site at Uley produced a huge number of animal remains, the majority being goats, an animal sacred to Mercury, and therefore almost certainly sacrificed to the god. After they were butchered the worshippers at the temple presumably ate the meat. Elsewhere slaughtered animals were ritually deposited in pits.

Celtic thought also emphasized the symbolic numbers three, seven and twelve, but the triad dominated, expressing itself in the attributes of a god or a god-animal. The three-horned bull symbolized powers of virility and potency. What could be regarded as monstrosity is symbolic of supernatural power. A bronze bull at Maiden Castle has three females on its back, one of which seems to be a harpy linked with the Underworld and death; another representing Diana is connected with childbirth and thus with the bringing of life. This is indicative of the Celtic belief in shape-changing, whereby one form can merge into the shape of another; here it assumes concrete form.

On a relief at Housesteads three hooded figures gaze impassively at the spectator. The Genii Cucullati, identified by the *cucullus* or hooded cloak, were so well known in Celtic religion that they could be sketched in outline on a relief from

Cirencester. As single figures they hold scrolls, moneybags and eggs as symbols of fertility, and are symbolic themselves, having a phallic shape. At Daglingworth (Gloucestershire) they stand beside a Mother Goddess, the earth mother, who appears alone or in the power of the triad, which seems to have continued from Celtic to Roman Britain.

The cult of the Matres or Mother Goddesses originating in northern Europe became popular throughout the Roman world and they appeared in a variety of guises. A dedication to the Lamiae Triades (three witches) at Benwell probably refers to them, although, given the wildness in that part of Britain, the dedicators may have invoked local goddesses. Two reliefs at Cirencester provide different interpretations of the Matres. One shows three stiff, hieratic figures, faces framed with braided hair, holding fruit, loaves and, in one case, a child, the ultimate symbol of fertility; the other is of a relaxed group of mothers indulging their children. Both are intended to indicate a fertility cult. Elsewhere dedications to the Matres included a variety of roles: *campestres* (the parade ground), *omnium gentium* (all races), *transmarinae* (overseas) and *communes* (widespread).

Another deity brought from the continent was Epona, whom the Celts worshipped in Gaul and the Rhineland as the goddess who cared for horses. Not surprisingly her followers occurred amongst the military on Hadrian's Wall and the Antonine Wall, but there are also two fragmentary statuettes found at Caerleon and Colchester and a charming copper-alloy figure, found in Wiltshire, shows her seated while two ponies nuzzle her garments.

These gods were entirely Celtic but elsewhere, as in northern areas, other gods became syncretized with Roman ones. The Celtic warrior gods, Belatucadrus and Cocidius, became syncretized with Mars, but Cocidius was also syncretized with Silvanus, the Roman woodland deity. Mars was linked to Lenus, a god known in the Rhineland, to Condates, the Celtic god of confluence of rivers, and to Barrax, possibly a reference to kingship. The functions of Celtic deities could easily be accommodated with those of the Romans.

Roman deities were celebrated in festivals, many based on a pastoral and agricultural heritage associated with the seasons of the year, a cycle that was constant and demanding. These could easily be aligned to Celtic festivals, which were fewer but equally important. In the Roman religious calendar each deity had his or her own separate festival extending throughout the months of the year. The Celts confined their festivals to the four great ones. Imbolc (1 February), dedicated to the god Brigit, marked the renewal of spring and the coming of the first ewe's milk. Hence it was a festival dedicated to fertility. Beltain (1 May), linked to the Celtic god Belenos, was a cleansing festival when fires were lit or renewed in houses. Fires were lighted in the fields so that cattle could walk through them and be cleansed. All grass and rush bedding was burned, so that household tasks started afresh. This, although possibly the Celts did not realize it, was the best way to stop infection as pests were burned with the straw. Lughnasa (1 August) lasting for almost forty days was a welcome festival when food and drink flowed in abundance. It was concerned with the harvesting of the crops and was dedicated to the god Lugh (Ireland) or Lugnos (Gaul). It was also held to propitiate the gods of the Otherworld to ensure that the harvest would ripen. The last festival of the year and the greatest, although it was the first in the Celtic calendar, was Samain (1 November), a sober and dangerous time. It marked the end of the old year and the beginning of the new and thus allowed the spirits of the dead to become visible to the human world.

These festivals were probably presided over by a priesthood, which might have been the Druids. Most of the evidence for these priests comes from classical authors. Caesar said that the Druidic doctrine began in Britain and was then taken to Gaul, adding that those who wanted to study the purest form would go to Britain. Pliny the Elder thought that on the contrary the

Druidic cult started in Gaul and from there moved to Britain. Whatever the case, the Roman authority decided to eliminate these opponents to their power. Pliny remarked that Tiberius had dispersed the Druids and Suetonius commented that Claudius had entirely abolished the religion of the Druids. Pomponius Mela, writing in the first century AD, implied that they had been put down in Gaul, but Suetonius Paulinus met them in his attack on Anglesey. Yet Druidism seems to have survived. Lampridius, in his *Life of Alexander Severus*, a third-century AD emperor, says that a Druidess, thus implying a female priestess, predicted Alexander's death.

One reason for the Roman abhorrence of the Druids was that they supervised human sacrifice. A result of this seems to have been the veneration of the cult of the human head. The Celts practised headhunting and from this developed the worship of the head, regarded as symbolic of human and divine power. When struck off a head could have a life of its own, as did that of Bran who continued to prophesy to his followers. Decapitated human heads were found in wells, thus indicating an association with a water cult, or were placed in shrines like those skulls found in niches in the shrine at Roquepertuse in southern Gaul. When the Romans proscribed headhunting the symbolism of the head came to be depicted in stone and bronze. Bronze heads ornament buckets found at Aylesford, Baldock and Marlborough, probably used for feasting or in religious ceremonies. Stone heads are found frequently. These have not been struck off statues but may have stood on a stone base. One, now in the Corbridge museum, has an indentation on the head surrounded by a ring that may indicate its use as an altar for receiving votive offerings.

Some heads have horns at the side, incorporated with hair. The horned god of the Celts was Cernunos, and his depiction as a horned human, sitting cross-legged accompanied by female goddesses, though frequent in Gaul, is not found in Britain. His worship was probably brought to Britain by Celts arriving from Gaul. This horned deity was associated with hunting and fertility powers. The horns might be bull's or ram's horns, although on the Gundestrup cauldron, dated to the first century BC and found in a bog in Denmark, the god sports antlers. A relief at Cirencester shows a god with antlers in the traditional squatting position, the more usual interpretation.

Antenociticus or Anociticus, recorded on inscriptions at Benwell, was worshipped by a centurion of Legion XX Valeria Victrix and by soldiers of *Cohors I Vangionum*. A small temple with an apse at one end, built by the military outside the south-east corner of the fort, probably replaced a local shrine dedicated to this local god. One of these dedications can be dated to *c.*177–80 when the army recommissioned Hadrian's Wall after its withdrawal from the Antonine Wall. A small head surviving from the statue, which was placed in the temple, has a distinct pair of horns on it linking it to Cernunos. Yet the troops at Benwell did not confine their worship to this deity. Other inscriptions reveal dedications to Mars Victrix (the Victorious) and the Matres Campestres (Mother Goddesses of the Parade Ground).

As previously indicated, Celtic gods may not be native to Britain. Coventina, whose shrine lay outside the Carrawburgh fort on Hadrian's Wall, was close to a spring into which her devoted followers threw their offerings, including at least 14,000 coins, indicating that worship of the goddess continued from the second to the fourth centuries AD, a lengthy period of time. On one altar, she is associated with the nymphs, whom the Romans associated with healing waters. An altar, found in a nearby shrine, consisting merely of a semi-circular seat, dedicated to the nymphs and the Genius Loci (the god of a particular place), indicates the veneration given to this site. Yet Coventina was also worshipped in northern Spain and merchants coming from Spain to Britain may have dedicated the Carrawburgh shrine. Troops from the nearby fort then continued her worship.

Coventina was only one of many deities who presided over water. Verbeia, a name inscribed on an altar found at Ilkley, was the goddess of the nearby River Wharfe. Votive offerings were cast into rivers, wells and springs, emphasizing their sacred nature. Sometimes these might be just one object like the shield found in the Thames at Battersea. It could be argued that this defensive weapon might have been lost or discarded but the large number of objects found in the Thames in the vicinity of London Bridge, which included several figurines of deities, suggests that these were cast deliberately into the river, probably by travellers who wished to express gratitude on ending a journey or for help as they set forth.

Deposits found in lakes and bogs may also have been made to placate deities. The large number of deposits found at Llyn Fawr (South Glamorgan) included two cauldrons, horse harness and vehicle fittings. A lake at Llyn Cerrig Bach in Anglesey contained slave chains, ironworking tools, parts of chariots and trumpets deposited over a period of time from the second century BC to the first century AD. These could have been cast into the lake from a cliff 3.35 m (11 ft) high, a natural point from which to throw these offerings.

The ease with which Celtic religious beliefs could be accommodated to Roman ones was because of Roman tolerance towards other faiths and the fact that the gods could be syncretized or conflated with each other under the *interpretatio Romana*. Roman religion was based on a pantheon of deities, which was derived from or allied to those of the Greeks and whose deities were envisaged in human forms. Overall was Jupiter, the greatest of the gods, who was worshipped as protector of the empire and of the army. Each year military units were expected to dedicate themselves as a corporate act anew to his service and thus of the state, a practice which was revealed by a calendar and roster of religious observances, the so-called *Feriale Duranum*, which was found written on a papyrus in an auxiliary fort at Dura Europos in Syria. These observances were certainly observed in what had been a temple to the god outside the fort of Maryport where a large number of altars were discovered.

An extension of the powers of this god, and again indicative of the Roman powers of assimilation came in the worship of Jupiter Dolichenus. Dolichenus was a military god of the Hittites, especially worshipped by the officer class for his warrior powers. As such he was often associated with worship of the Sun God as on an inscription found at Corbridge and with the Imperial Cult. Dedications to Jupiter Optimus Maximus, the greatest of the gods, are frequent on military sites and especially on Hadrian's Wall. A variation of this is on an altar at Old Carlisle where a dedication to Jupiter Optimus Conservator might suggest the need for greater protection in that area.

Jupiter's consort was Juno, who was worshipped by women, especially those who sought protection in childbirth. There are few inscriptions to her as Celtic women had their own deities to whom they could appeal for protection. At Chesters a statue of the Empress Julia Mammaea, mother of the third-century emperor Alexander Severus, depicts her as Juno Regina standing on a heifer, indicating political correctness in conflating the empress with this goddess. The fact that the statue is headless may be the result of some destruction after the murder of the emperor and his mother in AD 235. An inscription to Juno Regina (dedicated at Carlisle by a military tribune whose last name Syrio suggests an eastern origin) to ensure divine protection also includes Jupiter Optimus Maximus, Minerva, Mars and Victoria on the altar.

Dedications on altars and personifications of deities, often in the form of bronze figurines, indicate worship of other members of the divine pantheon, as well as their syncretization with Celtic deities. Dedications by soldiers to Mars, the warrior god, are frequent. Travellers and merchants worshipped Mercury who protected them. The Romano-Celtic temple at Uley contained an over life-size statue of the god, carved out of Cotswold limestone, but based on the work of the Greek sculptor Praxiteles. Apollo was also a protector of travellers, a healer god and a sun god. This would explain his conflation with Grannus, the Celtic healing and sun god, on a lost altar from Inveresk. The worship of Grannus has been noted in Gaul, Trier and in Hungary. On an altar at Nettleton (Wiltshire) he was linked with Cunomaglus (the hound prince). There was a shrine to him from the first century, but in the mid third century this had developed into a site of major importance with a polygonal temple, a hostel and a priest's house. As a youthful god Apollo was associated with the Celtic Maponus, the 'divine youth' on altars at Corbridge, by officers of Legion VI Victrix. His exploits are also portrayed in other ways as on a mosaic at the Lenthay Green villa (Dorset) where he is engaged in contest with Marsyas. A dedication was set up at Housesteads by the *Cohors I Tungria*, 'according to the interpretation of the Clarian Apollo', an oracle with its centre in Ionia.

Hercules, a human elevated to divine status, was especially worshipped by soldiers who wished to invoke his protection. This is apparent in the many altars dedicated to him in the northern forts, where he is also referred to as Hercules Victor and Hercules Invictus. He certainly came to the aid of Publius Sextanius, prefect of *Ala Augusta*, who erected an arched slab found at Carlisle celebrating the slaughter of a band of barbarians. If dated to AD 192, as has been suggested, the prefect was also associating Hercules with the Emperor Commodus, who believed he was the reincarnation of Hercules. An altar at Old Carlisle records Sigilius Emeritus dividing his spoils with the god, no doubt in an effort to ensure the god's favour.

Diana was the goddess of hunting, an activity beloved by Romans and Celts. Reliefs and statues of her holding a bow are found; one is preserved at Housesteads. She was also goddess of woodlands as was Silvanus, who was worshipped by farmers for Virgil described him as god of flocks and field. The many inscriptions to him on Hadrian's Wall are possibly because of the wild situation in that area, as well as the opportunities for hunting. Gaius Tetius Veturius Micianus, prefect in charge of the *Ala Sebosiana*, dedicated an altar to Silvanus Invictus at Bollihope Common, Stanhope (County Durham), boasting of taking 'a wild boar of remarkable fitness which many of his predecessors had failed to catch'. Silvanus's conflation with a local Celtic hunter-god, Vinotonus, on altars at Scargill Moor (North Yorkshire) by Julius Secundus, centurion of *Cohors I Thracum*, and T. Orbius Primianus, prefect of the same unit, may also be thankful testimonies to the enjoyment of the chase.

Sometimes syncretization was complex. Minerva was not only a warrior goddess but was also the goddess of crafts and trades. Her conflation with the Celtic Sul has already been noted. As a warrior goddess she was conflated with Brigantia, tribal goddess of the Brigantes. A relief at Birrens (Dumfries and Galloway), dedicated by Amandus, a military engineer, portrayed a winged female figure, symbolic of Minerva Victrix, whose official portrayal was at Corbridge. She carried Minerva's weapons of spear and shield and wore her usual plumed helmet but a turreted crown encircled this. She also held a globe and to her right was an omphaloid stone indicative of Juno Caelestis, consort of Jupiter Dolichenus, and thus a tutelary goddess in Syria and Africa. Seemingly the relief paid homage to the African Emperor Septimius Severus and his consort Julia Domna. G. Julius Apolinaris, a centurion of Legion VI Victrix, who also included the Eternal Jupiter of Doliche and Salus, dedicated an altar at Corbridge to Caelestis Brigantia. It would appear that in the north the Celtic Brigantia took precedence over that of the Roman Minerva, just as in the south the Celtic goddess Sulis took precedence.

Other deities were representative of personified virtues which soldiers were expected to show and which were linked to the power of the state. Virtus was personified in a relief at Chesters as a female wearing a helmet and tunic; Disciplina and Discipulina Augusti (Discipline of the Emperors) were necessary forces in the Roman army. Concordia, mentioned on an altar at Corbridge dedicated by Legion VI and Legion II Augusta, was obviously intended to promote good relations between those two legions. Dedications made to Victoria, an understandably popular deity, depicted her as a winged victory holding a palm and a wreath, and specifically to a Victory of Legion VI Victrix, the latter on a silver plate found in a quarry and possibly looted from the legionary fortress of York. Dedications to Signa, the goddess of the Standards, appear regularly. A tribune and the propraetorian legate of *Cohors I Vardullorum* dedicated separate altars to her at High Rochester; *Cohors I Aelia* at Birdoswald dedicated a statue of which the base survives. These would have been erected in the *sacellum*, where the standards were kept.

Dedications to the goddess Fortuna appeared frequently on inscriptions at forts. These included Fortuna Conservatrix (the Preserver), Fortuna Populi Romani (of the Roman people), Fortuna Redux (the Home Bringer), possibly erected by soldiers who longed to return to warmer climes, and Fortuna Balnearis (of the Baths). During the empire, Fortuna, who was originally conceived as a bringer of prosperity, became increasingly associated with perversity of fate, so that she was perceived as bringing both good and ill luck. The cult was also popular in forts where baths were provided because naked men were particularly vulnerable to evil and required protection. At Bowes, Virius Lupus, governor of Britain in AD 197–202, ordered the bathhouse to be restored after a fire and dedicated it to Fortuna. Records from Vindolanda include the accounts of Privatus, presumably a household slave, who noted quantities of food and the impressive amount of drink needed for the prefect's private dinner parties. These included 46 litres (10 gallons) of vintage wine, 68 litres (15 gallons) of Celtic beer and 15 litres (3.3 gallons) of indifferent wine for a festival on 24 June, presumably that of the goddess Fors Fortuna. Her protection was sought elsewhere: Sosia Juncina, wife of Quintus Antonius Isauricus, the legionary legate, erected an altar to her at York. Statues of the goddess show her carrying her attributes of a rudder and wheel to signify the vacillations of life and a cornucopia for prosperity.

Nemesis, the goddess of vengeance, punished impiety but rewarded virtue and thus extracted vengeance on enemies. She was thus a goddess whose powers demanded respect. Apollonius, a priest, erected an altar to her, which was found in the vicinity of Hadrian's Wall. An altar dedicated to her by the centurion Sextius Marcianus, 'as a result of a vision', was found at the back of a small room at the Chester amphitheatre. Small wonder that a shrine to this goddess, often implored to defeat opponents, was included in amphitheatres and her vengeance was sought on curse tablets.

Most important was the Imperial Cult based on the worship of the emperor and through him the empire. Emperor, empire and religious observance were therefore entwined in a deliberate attempt to weld together disparate provinces and ensure total loyalty to the state. Emperors were not worshipped in their lifetime but were deified after death. The Emperor Vespasian cynically summed this up on his deathbed: 'Alas I am becoming a god.' Some identified themselves with a deity during their lifetime, as Commodus did with Hercules. Ceremonies had to be performed to the Imperial Cult and presumably the Provincial Council performed one each year in Britain. One council in London dedicated a tablet to the Deity of the Emperor.

The temple dedicated to the Imperial Cult erected at Colchester and dedicated to Claudius after his death was a deliberate attempt to make Britons loyal to Rome. Only the massive base remains but the temple was certainly built in the classical style with Corinthian columns. In front of the temple was a huge altar and courtyard where sacrifices could be performed. That the Britons took this to symbolize Roman power was obvious in the fury with which it was destroyed in the Boudiccan rebellion. It was quickly rebuilt after the revolt but later the cult moved to London where a well-cut inscription to Numen Caesaris Augusti by the Province of Britain has been found. Elsewhere there is evidence of the advancement of loyalty to the Imperial Cult. This cult was served by *seviri Augustales*, groups of six freedmen, elected by decurions and organized in colleges, who sacrificed in the emperor's name. They needed to have considerable wealth, as not only were they required to pay for games and festivals, but also to pay for some amenity to the town in the form of a public building or an entertainment. Two examples are known in Britain: Marcus Aurelius Lunaris, who traded between Bordeaux, Lincoln and York, and Marcus Verecundius Diogenes, who identifies himself on the sarcophagus at York to his wife Julia Fortunata as being from the Bituriges Cubi tribe from Bourges in Gaul.

There was an additional factor to the Imperial Cult. The emperor also had his numen, his or his family's guiding spirit. That this worship or obedience was imposed as an obligation of loyalty on the army is seen in the dedications to the Numen Augusti (the Numen of Augustus), the Numen Domini Nostri (the Numen of Our Lord) on altars set up by the army at numerous forts, some by officers, some by military units. Many of these are by auxiliary units, seemingly desirous of expressing their loyalty.

The emperor also had his *genius*, a guardian spirit, as did every man. The Roman poet Horace believed the *genius* was a companion 'who rules our birth, our human needs and accompanies each mortal for his whole life'. The spirit of the genius could rule over places and objects. Some dedications were specific. The Genius Eboraci, together with the Numen Augusti, was invoked at York; the Genius Collegii Apollinis protected a college dedicated to Apollo at Burrow in Lonsdale. The Genius Loci (god of the place), often found inscribed on altars, many erected in lonely places, may have been worshipped by Romans who were not sure if a Celtic god already inhabited that place.

The Roman army recognized the *genius* in multiple ways. The *genius* of the century was invoked at Carlisle and Chester; the *genius* of *Ala I Hispanorum Asturum* was invoked at Benwell and the *genius* of Legion II Augusta at Caerleon. Buildings could be also protected. The *genius* of the *praetorium* (the commandant's house) was invoked at Lanchester and Vindolanda. Soldiers of Legion II Augusta dedicated an altar to the Genius Huius Loci, Jupiter Optimus Maximus and Cocidius at Housesteads. An altar dedicated by Marcus Cocceius Firmus, a centurion of Legion II Augusta based at Audendavy, covered a wide area when he dedicated an altar to the Genius Terrae Britannicae (the god of the Land of Britain). Statues and figurines of the *genius* display him carrying a cornucopia, symbol of prosperity and fertility. One relief at Tockenham (Wiltshire) depicts him dressed in a toga.

Other cults were brought from Gaul and Germany and the Danube regions, many of them by auxiliaries. At Housesteads these included soldiers from Twenthe in the province of Over-Yssel in Holland, who worshipped the Alaisiagae, Bede and Fimmilena, and soldiers of the unit of Hnaudifridus, who worshipped Baudihilla and Frigabis. Some of these deities may be connected with the Matres, as were the Matres Alatervae, goddesses known from the Lower Rhine who were worshipped by *Cohors I Tungri* at Cramond.

From the Rhineland came the Jupiter column, a tall column crowned by a Corinthian capital on which was placed a statue of Jupiter either standing or on horseback and which incorporated homage to the Celtic god Taranis, the Roman Jupiter and the emperor. Evidence for this is found at Chichester where a large block forming the base of a column had an inscription dedicating it to Jupiter Optimus Maximus in honour of the Divine House. Lucius Septimius, governor of Britannia Prima, dedicated a statue and column base at Cirencester, thus dating it to the Diocletian reorganization of AD 296. The Bacchic Corinthian capital mentioned below may be part of this column or the remains of another.

Soldiers and traders brought many deities from the Near East and North Africa into Britain. A popular one was the healing god Aesculapius, often worshipped by doctors, such as a cavalry doctor at Binchester, or grateful patients, including a legate at Chester and a tribune at Lanchester. On the Chester altar Aesculapius was accompanied by Salus, the goddess of health, and on an altar from the fort of Overborough (Lancashire) by his daughter Hygiaea. The Egyptian goddess Isis was worshipped in London as evidenced by an altar recording the rebuilding of a temple to her by M. Martiannius Pulcher in the third century AD, who identifies himself as the Imperial Governor. A flagon found in a separate area, inscribed *Ad fanum Isidis* (at the temple of Isis) and dated to the first century AD, may imply an earlier date for the cult. The goddess's appeal was universal, being associated with fertility and the protector of women in marriage and in childbirth. Her son was Hippocrates and figurines of the child have been found in London. The fact that the London temple was rebuilt on the order of a governor of Britain indicates that there was some official approval for the cult. Another Egyptian god worshipped in London was Serapis, a fertility deity: a head broken from a statue has been found in London; another head was found at Silchester. At York Claudius Hieronymianus, Legate of Legion VI, dedicated a temple to this god sometime in the late second or early third century AD.

A popular deity in Rome was the Phrygian Magna Mater. In 204 BC, when Rome was menaced by the invasion by Hannibal, the Sibylline Books decreed that he could only be defeated if the Idaean Mother known as Cybele was brought to Rome. During the empire Claudius admitted her to the Roman pantheon for her powers of fertility equated with those of Juno and Ceres. Cybele's lover was Atys who became unfaithful to her. Remorseful at his lapse he castrated himself. This action was copied by faithful adherents of the goddess, in particular her priests – the Galli. Castration clamps have been found in the Thames at London, at Chichester and at Silchester. The London clamp was decorated with busts of deities including one of Diana for she and Cybele were protectors of wild beasts. Figurines of Atys have been found in Britain, one in London wearing trousers open at the front. A so-called triangular temple at Verulamium was suggested to have been dedicated to Cybele on the basis that carbonized pine cones were found there. An inscription on a funerary urn found at Dunstable, but probably from Verulamium, mentions the *dendrophori*, priests of her cult.

Bacchus, a popular god, appears in many works of art and even on a Corinthian capital, which probably crowned a Jupiter column at Cirencester. This capital also includes a carving of his adversary Lycurgus and his followers Silenus and a maenad. One of the maenads, Ambrosia, pursued by Lycurgus, implored Bacchus for help. He turned her into a vine that strangled Lycurgus. Vines are therefore common to Bacchic sculpture. Bacchus was not only the rescuer of Ambrosia; he also rescued Ariadne who had been deserted by Theseus on the island of Naxos. This scene is shown on an altar at Bath. He was therefore a saviour god riding in triumph on a tiger or panther as depicted on a mosaic found in London. A silver patera (a shallow drinking dish) found at Capheaton (Northumberland) includes Bacchus and Ariadne. An elaborate marble statuette found in the London Walbrook mithraeum (a small building for worshippers of

Mithras) included Bacchus with his thyrsus (a staff topped with a pine cone, a phallic symbol of fertility), accompanied by Pan, a satyr, a maenad and Silenus, riding on a donkey. An inscription acclaimed the god as a giver of eternal life to wandering men, probably travellers, merchants and the military. This, together with two marble torsos of Bacchus, a silver bowl and a lidded casket identified as a *cista mystica* that held narcotic substances placed in wine drunk during ceremonies, suggested that the mithraeum was later dedicated to Bacchus.

An eastern cult, popular with the military and especially the officers, was that of the Persian god Mithras, who represented the victory of the soul after death; merchants also worshipped him as the god of fair-trading. His birth, represented on a relief at Rudchester, showed him springing from a rock, but at Housesteads he emerged from a cosmic egg, symbol of resurrection. The egg-shaped frame depicted the signs of the zodiac; lamps placed behind the sculpture surrounded Mithras with awe-inspiring light, an effect deliberately conflating him, as inscribed on another altar, with the Invincible Sun. Mithras was worshipped in a mithraeum, which indicated the elite nature of the cult, often built partly underground with little or no natural light. At the end of the building could be the *tauroctony*, portraying the slaying of the wild bull. From the body sprang plants useful to man, from the blood came the vine of life and from the spinal cord and the tail came wheat. A dog and a serpent, symbolizing the Underworld, lapped the blood, while a scorpion tried to prevent the act of creation.

Cautes, whose upturned torch indicated life and light, and Cautopates, casting his torch downwards to signify darkness and death, often accompanied Mithras. Their statues were found at Housesteads and Carrawburgh. As Mithraism was practised in secrecy many of the details are obscure but, according to St Jerome, writing in the fourth or fifth century, devotees had to progress through seven grades, including

The Mithraeum at Carrawburgh, Hadrian's Wall. On either side are the benches on which the devotees would recline. At the far end are replicas of three altars, all dedicated to the Invincible God Mithras

ordeals of fire and water, representing a spiritual journey from darkness to light and from earth to the afterlife. Some were symbolic, such as hands being covered in honey, which countered evil. Others were more unpleasant. To the left of the entrance to the Carrawburgh mithraeum was a pit, which, when covered with stones on which a fire might be lit, would give any man suffering from claustrophobia a terrifying experience. In the fourth century many of the ceremonies, including a sacred meal (which initiates believed was indicative of a better life beyond this world), the ritual use of wine and water and the celebration of 25 December as the birthday of Mithras, roused the wrath of the Christians. Violent attacks on mithraea in Britain may have been initiated by the visit of the Emperor Constantine in AD 312. Mithras's followers buried objects and altars to save them but impious hands smashed sculptures. In

London the mithraeum was destroyed but Mithras's followers buried the statuary.

Christianity was brought to Britain from Gaul. Tertullian, writing in the third century, said that Christianity was practised in parts of Britain outside Roman settlements. It progressed so much that about forty years later Origen could refer to Christianity as 'a unifying force'. It had been first regarded as an eastern cult, but it soon aroused the wrath of the Roman state. Christians were regarded as being antagonistic, even treacherous towards the empire because of their refusal to acknowledge the divine nature of the emperor. Christianity claimed domination over all other faiths on this earth and in the world beyond. It also actively proselytized for adherents and was hostile to other cults, believing that they mocked the Christian faith. The Bacchic and Mithraic cults held sacred meals which included bread and wine. Mithras was created out of a cosmic egg and his birthday was given as 25 December. Death and resurrection was also a feature of other cults: Bacchus had been born from the ashes of Semele; Atys died under a pine tree and the carrying of a pine log commemorated his resurrection. Isis suckling Harpocrates was akin to the Virgin suckling the Christ child. Even Orpheus who charmed the beasts, a frequent theme on mosaics, could be associated with Christ the Good Shepherd.

In spite of persecution, or perhaps because it strengthened the determination of its adherents, Christianity gained converts. Evidence of its gradual appearance in Britain is seen in a variety of ways. The central roundel of the Hinton St Mary (Dorset) mosaic has a head of Christ with the Chi-Rho monogram behind, symbolizing Christ, ruler of the world. The rays can be conflated to the rays of the sun, thus associating him with Sol Invictus, universal symbol of energy and light. In turn this linked him with Mithras, Hercules and Silvanus, whose altars incorporated that symbol. More definite evidence is the appearance of acrostics – ROTAS OPERA TENET AREPO

SATOR – found in Manchester and Cirencester indicating loyalty to Christ. Archaeological evidence for Christian worship is seen in a number of hoards. Christ's followers were expected to follow a moral code and to partake of bread and wine as blessed by Christ in the Last Supper. This ritual needed sacred vessels, such as those discovered in a buried hoard at Water Newton composed of silver bowls, cups, spoons, flagons and wine stoups. The majority of the twenty-eight silver items bear the Christian monogram or have inscriptions that can be interpreted in a Christian fashion. Decoration and motifs, however, found on spoons and other objects in other hoards, like that discovered at Thetford (Norfolk), may indicate that for some people belief in Christianity and pagan cults fused.

There is no firm evidence for churches in these places. Worship was not at first in obvious buildings. Churches may not have survived if they were built of wood and wattle-and-daub. A reference in a *Life of St Wilfred* mentions Christians worshipping in sacred places (*loca sancta*). Worshippers met in a house church as at Lullingstone where the owners either were Christians or were sympathetic to them. The first recognizable Christian church is at Colchester, dated to AD 320–30. Others dating to the same period are suggested at Water Newton, Ancaster and Witham (Essex) and at more important sites: Silchester, Lincoln and London. Bede in his *Ecclesiastical History of the English Nation* refers to a church dedicated to St Martin at Canterbury *dum adhuc Romani Brittaniam incolerent* (while the Romans were still inhabiting Britain). Burials in the Christian tradition have been noted at Winchester and Poundbury. Persecution is indicated in Britain by the martyrdoms of Aaron, Julian and Alban.

In AD 312 the conversion of the Emperor Constantine, together with his proclamation of the Edict of Milan, ensured toleration to Christians throughout the empire. In AD 314 at least three bishops from London, York and *Londiniensium* are reported to have attended the Council of Arles and later, in AD 359, the Council of Rimini, on both occasions being so poor that they had to have monetary support. This may suggest an organized church, especially as in AD 325 at the Council of Nicaea Christianity became the *de facto* religion of the empire.

There were still eras of persecution, notably in AD 361–3 when the Emperor Julian revived pagan faiths, but the eventual triumph of the Christian faith was assured, spreading throughout the empire. In Britain pagan shrines were destroyed but worship of pagan deities continued in more remote places, so that Christianity and paganism coexisted until well beyond the fifth century AD. Pagan temples might have been destroyed or their buildings reclaimed with holy water, but that pagan worship continued beyond the Celtic era is evidenced by the instructions of the Christian Church. Clause 23 of the Second Council of Arles in AD 453 ordered Bishops to take steps to oppose the worship of trees, springs and stones, and as late as the seventh century AD the Councils of Rouen and Toledo continued to urge prohibition of the worship of natural phenomena. The Christian Church dealt with pagan deities by metamorphosing them into Christian saints, so that St Triduana's well, at Restalrig near Edinburgh, ostensibly dedicated to the saint who tore out her eyes rather than suffer the attentions of Nechtan, King of the Picts, very probably owed its origin to a Celtic water deity renowned for curing eye diseases.

The apparent success of the Pelagian heresy argues for the strong presence of Christianity in the province; the fact that St Germanus was sent from Gaul to suppress this heresy indicates that the continued organization of the church was considered essential. In the late fifth century St Patrick, then aged fifteen, was captured by pirates and taken to Ireland. He stated in his *Confessio* that he was the son of Calpurnius, a decurion and son of the presbyter Potitus, who lived near Bannavem Taberniae. The place has not been identified but it is presumed to be in the north-west of Britain, which may indicate that Christianity by then had become established in the northern parts of the province.

Bronze figurine of Mars, found at the Foss Dyke, Lincolnshire and displaying great competence in the casting even though the limbs are somewhat out of proportion. The inscription recorded that Celatus made this figure of Mars for two brothers, Bruccius and Caratius who had Latinised their surname to Colasunius, and who had paid 100 *sesterces* for this figurine from their own purse. Celatus, not to be outdone, stated that he had given a pound of bronze prepared for the casting.

Small bronze figurines such as these were placed on *lararia*. These were altars in a household where deities relevant to that household were worshipped. The main ones were the larus and penates who cared personally for the inhabitants of the house and ensured their prosperity

13

FOOD AND DIET

The main evidence for food products in Roman Britain comes from archaeological remains, especially animal bones and plant remains. Much of this evidence has been discovered and analysed within the last few decades as their importance has been recognized. It reveals a wide range of eating habits and preferences not only between civilians and the military but also between town and country and north and south of the province. Personal and local preferences and availability of food also dictated what people ate, and the wide range of imported goods enabled some people to alter their eating habits and their diet.

This is not to say that before the conquest the Celtic population did not have a reasonable diet. Grains were very important. The main wheat crop was einkorn, a spring-sown wheat, and this was supplemented with emmer. Spelt, a hardier crop, was grown in the northern areas and was sown as a winter crop in southern Britain. Grain was ground with the rotary quern, a method producing nearly 80 per cent stone-ground flour, with at least two grindings and siftings being necessary to ensure the elimination of grit. Flour, mixed with water and salt, was baked on a hot flat stone producing a kind of bannock. Vegetables and fruit were gathered from the wild or cultivated; these plants included what might be considered as weeds, such as nettles, dandelions, charlock, silverweed, sheep's sorrel and Good King Henry, but all gave nutritional value. In addition, there were ample supplies of meat, milk and cheese from the cattle, sheep, goats and pigs kept on farms and settlements. Classical writers provide details of the amount of meat eaten at Celtic feasts and the contests, which took place over the right to the champion's portion.

The main wheat crop of Roman Britain was emmer, which had a high protein value, and this was supplemented by bread wheat. Rye continued to be grown in the northern areas where it was suited to poor or shallow-cultivated soils. Oats were useful for pottage and barley, although issued to the troops in case of hardship or personal preference, was used in times of emergency, as a fodder crop and as a basis for making light barley ale. Dioscorides in the late first century BC, as well as mentioning drinks made from wheat in Britain, identified a drink called *curmi*, probably a light barley ale. Grain was also imported into Britain from the Mediterranean, judging by the remains in London of carbonized einkorn, lentils and bitter vetch. Imports at Caerleon in the second century AD imply not only a shortage of grain in Britain but also the importance of maritime links with the continent. Barley in a huge granary in York became so infested with grain beetle, probably brought in from abroad, that the flour had to be sealed and the building dismantled.

Flour would not keep over long periods so households needed to grind it daily or at least every two or three days. Milling would be done by rotary querns, many of which were imported from the Andernach region of the Rhineland. In the Trentholme Drive cemetery at York the skeletons of several women had squatting facets on their legs indicated long periods of squatting to use a saddle or rotary quern set into the floor. In India a skilled grinder will produce 1.8 kg (4 lb) an hour; in Algeria a grinder can produce 3 kg (6.6 lb) in one-and-a-half hours. The flour was kneaded with water and salt, and baked in a pan or on a hearthstone. The dough could also be covered with a conical pot (*testa*) over which hot ashes were placed to provide all-round heat. The heat drew up the dough so that it cooked by a steaming process, which gave the bread a leavened appearance.

In towns it would be far more convenient to buy bread daily from a competent baker, who could also grind grain on his premises. A donkey mill, which the Romans introduced into Britain, would do this more efficiently and quickly. The mill consisted of an hourglass-shaped hopper supported on a spindle above a cone-shaped base. Grain, poured into the hopper which was turned by means of a wooden framework either by donkeys or slaves, was ground as it passed between the upper and lower millstones; the resulting flour was collected around the circular base. The output of flour has been estimated as the equivalent of 0.127 cu. m (4.5 bushels) of wheat a day rising to 0.543 (15 bushels) if a horse was used to turn the mill. Pieces of this type of hopper have been found at Corfe Mullen (Dorset), Hamworthy (Devon), Clyro fort (Powys) and London.

The army on Hadrian's Wall sensibly used watermills to grind grain and large millstones, more than 3 m (9 ft) in diameter, at the Gloucestershire villas of Chedworth, Frocester and Kingscote may have been turned by waterpower. Substantial remains of a late first- and second-century AD watermill and two storage barns at Redlands near Stanwick (Northamptonshire) on the floodplain near the River Nene show that civilian watermills were not uncommon. A newly discovered site close to the fort at Healam Bridge (North Yorkshire) had large timber buildings at the side of a beck that powered a watermill. This could have supplied the fort with flour, probably during the third century.

Commercial bakers baked bread in ovens by the dry-heat method. The oven would be heated by wood or charcoal packed into it, the ashes raked out and the dough put in. When baked, the loaves were drawn out with a peel; one was found at Verulamium. Bread could be flavoured with coriander, baked on celery leaves and sprinkled with poppy seeds. At the Bearsden fort, where the latrines had debouched into the fort ditch, the faecal remains were examined. They revealed quantities of spelt and emmer pericarp, seeds of celery, figs and opium poppies, and minute quantities of lentils and peas. These may indicate that the soldiers had eaten a pottage of these ingredients or a bread of the *panis militaris* type, sprinkled with poppy seeds and rich in the B vitamins.

The Celts had bred animals for meat and milk, and animals also had other purposes. Oxen were used for ploughing and traction. Sheep provided wool and goats provided hair. Cattle and goat skins provided different types of leather. Goats bred easily; they could be corralled or allowed to roam freely and had the advantage that they would eat most organic products including undesirable plants. Goat manure was also extremely useful. If required a goat could provide meat for a household for two or three days, even if the meat was rather dry. Kids produced more tender meat but their killing could deprive a household of future milk products. Pigs alone were kept solely for meat. Animal bones were shaped into implements such as needles and spindle whorls. Other parts were boiled down to produce a form of adhesive.

In pre-Roman Britain, the main cattle are believed to have been Bos Longifrons, akin to Highland cattle, and Bos Taurus, a short-horned variety. Dexter cattle, noted for their milk and meat, Kerry cattle in Ireland and Welsh black cattle, both bred for their meat, may be the nearest equivalents. The nearest equivalents to Celtic sheep are Welsh Black Mountain and Soay sheep. The last are a unique breed preserved by their isolation on the St Kilda group of islands, 65 km (40 miles) west of the Outer Hebrides. Their wool needs to be plucked, as they are not shorn. John Wild, however, suggested that a Roman breeding programme produced a sheep more akin to the Orkney sheep of South Ronaldsay that produced a thicker fleece, which could have been a factor in the making of the *birrus* (cloaks), highly priced in Diocletian's price edict of AD 301. The Romans probably introduced more selective breeding of native stock, which resulted in larger animals giving a greater amount of meat. If there were difficulties in bringing these animals across the Channel arrangements could be made for such select groups to be kept as breeding stock.

Much of the beef consumed in Britain probably came from animals that had a hard working life. The meat would therefore be tough and would need slow, lengthy cooking or being made into sausages or hash. Sheep were eaten when younger, in most cases less than two years old. In some areas, one being Wroxeter, examination of bones has indicated that butchers were selling meat from older sheep, which probably until then had been kept mainly for their wool.

The proportion of cattle and pig bones found on sites seems to have been higher on military, urban and villa sites, less so on rural native sites. Those of sheep were higher on rural native sites, while pig bones tended to dominate on the more Romanized sites. Pigs were the easiest animals to keep, being allowed to roam freely in woodland or kept in sties in a back yard in a town, even in the most confined conditions. Large assemblages of bones in Southwark, London, may be evidence that pigs were kept under these conditions or that they were brought into the town for slaughtering. These pigs were mature pigs, whereas those killed in Silchester were killed when young, suggesting a liking for sucking pig. The high percentage of pigs killed in the *coloniae* may be the result of veterans eating more beef and pork than lamb or mutton.

One advantage of pigs is that they are prolific breeders. They were regarded as most economical animals, probably because they can produce a litter of up to twelve piglets a year or even, with a young pig, twice a year. Pliny the Elder said a sow could produce a litter of twenty piglets. Pork was a status symbol in Celtic Britain where it was one of the main foods in feasting. A joint of pork was awarded as the champion's portion and pork joints were buried with warriors in their graves to sustain them either in their journey to the Otherworld or beyond it. At Vindolanda pork, pork fat and ham were bought on several occasions for the commanding officer's household. Bone evidence from Fishbourne indicated that pork was the most common meat consumed in that luxurious building.

Beef cattle were the next prolific animals. Specialist slaughterers and butchers ensured that the carcasses were expertly divided, each limb being removed as a whole before being further divided. Examination of bones at Winchester, where cattle formed half the meat supply of the town, has revealed how expertly this was carried out, being done with cleavers rather than knives. A recent study by Maltby of bones in Hampshire suggests that different butchery techniques were used in town and country. In the towns, heavy cleavers were used to split carcasses; in villages, the limbs were disjointed with knives, a technique perfected in the Iron Age. The cleaver would also be used to shear meat from the bones and then to chop the bones into small pieces to obtain the marrow and grease for cooking. Marrow was highly prized both for its nutritional value and for its cosmetic and medicinal qualities. The bones could be used for producing glue. Waste was deposited in pits outside towns or in abandoned areas in towns.

At Portchester, skull evidence has suggested that slaughtering was carried out by poleaxing, which either killed the animal outright or stunned it so that it could be hung up and bled. Cheek meat and the tongue were then boned out. Holes punched into scapulas at Lincoln and York indicate that these joints were probably hung up to smoke or cure meat. Cato said that meat should be smoked for two days before being rubbed with salt or vinegar to keep out worms. Salting meat, however, would act as a better preservative.

Lincoln seemed to have had intensive and systematic slaughter, with butchery of carcasses and processing of meat taking place on a large commercial scale on the fourth-century waterfront. The carcasses had been systematically reduced to smaller joints of meat, and then the bones were chopped longitudinally and split to get at the marrow. Breaking of jaws allowed the butchers to get at the tongue. The carcass components of the animals were sent to tanneries, horn-workers, cosmetic-makers and other craftsmen in the town and they then sent back their waste, which was dumped along the waterfront, building it up and stabilizing the river frontage. This suggests that fourth-century Lincoln had a highly organized system of preparing and distributing food and its associated products, and of collecting and disposing the resultant waste.

One source of meat may have been from sacrificial animals. The large number of sheep and goat bones found at the temple site of Uley, in addition to those of domestic fowls, indicate that those animals were sacrificed especially as goats and chickens were companions of Mercury, who was worshipped at the site. The devotees could have partaken in feasts dedicated to the god. Fowls were also sacrificed in the worship of Mithras. Evidence from his temple at the fort of Carrawburgh on Hadrian's Wall indicate that young pigs and lambs were consumed as part of a ritual meal. At a mithraeum at Tienen in Belgium cocks seem to have been consumed, possibly because cocks are associated with crowing at dawn and Mithras was a god linked to the sun.

Bulls and oxen were sacrificed to Jupiter and Mars; cows to Venus and Juno. An average ox weighs 363 kg (800 lb) and provides 180–225 kg (400–500 lb) of beef as well as copious

A reconstructed granary at Baginton Roman fort. The grain could have been kept in bins but the building would also contain other food stuffs. Meat could have been hung from the roof or preserved in barrels. At each end of the granary was a loading platform

quantities of blood, which could be made into blood puddings, a favourite Roman food. Some meat would go to magistrates, town officials and those who officiated in temples but most would be sold to butchers or given to the populace. On country sites such as Uley, Woodeaton (Oxfordshire) and Springhead (Kent) numerous worshippers might have expected to be fed. The army would also have been expected to partake of ritual meals. A *lustratio* performed before a battle or an important military event included a *suovetaurilia*. The scene on the dedication at Bridgeness, presumed to commemorate the beginning of the building of the Antonine Wall, shows such an event with a ram, a boar and a bull waiting to be sacrificed. Soldiers would have eaten this dedicated meat and other meat after sacrifices or on festive days.

Game was eaten, although perhaps not in large quantities. Strabo mentioned that hunting dogs were exported from Iron Age Britain and hunting scenes are found on mosaics, pottery and silver plate. Inscriptions imply a love of hunting but probably more for sport than to collect meat. It would be unlikely, however, that the hunter allowed a kill to go to waste and country people would wish to extend their food supplies. Wild boar bones were found at the military sites of Caerwent, Exeter, Lincoln, Wroxeter and York. Bones of roe and red deer are common. Roe deer and venison are noted in at least one account at Vindolanda, possibly being eaten by the officers. The excavators at Poundbury (Dorset) suggested that some were killed because they were a menace to crops. Bones of deer found in London and Caister-on-Sea (Norfolk) indicate that meat was sold in the towns and antlers were used from which to fashion tools.

Caesar said that the Britons did not eat hares but this taboo does not seem to have existed into Roman Britain. Hares supplemented the diet at the forts of Vindolanda and Brancaster, and at Poundbury. A hunter has caught a hare on a relief at Piercebridge (County Durham) and 'Winter' is represented on part of a mosaic at the Chedworth villa as stumping along, a hare dangling from his right hand, ready for the pot.

More exotic tastes are represented at Caister-on-Sea where the carcass of a badger seems to have been jointed as if being prepared for the pot. Badger was eaten in Ireland where it was cured like bacon. Dormice bones found at York indicate that garden dormice were available for gourmet meals. Apicius said that they should be stuffed with minced pork, pine kernels and liquamen. At Trimalchio's feast they were sprinkled with honey and poppy seeds. The taste is like that of rabbit, but they have little meat on them. Frog bones found at York and Silchester suggested that the edible frog was available. Snails were deliberately fattened on a diet of milk before being poached or simmered. The edible snail (*helix aspersa*) was found at Silchester and Dorchester (Dorset) and the escargot (*helix pomatia*) at the Shakenoak villa (Oxfordshire). Edible snails at the fort of Papcastle (Cumbria) may have been introduced to the area by auxiliary troops. Disarticulated bones of dogs with cut marks on some sites suggest their occasional consumption.

Caesar also commented that the Britons reared fowl and geese for pleasure but had a taboo about eating them. However, bones indicating jointing before eating are a common find on sites. Geese and ducks included wild and domesticated species kept in large numbers and probably loosely penned. The Vindolanda garrison had nets for catching ducks. Geese could be bred in captivity providing they had plenty of water and fresh grass; they were also useful as an alarm system against intruders. Few Romans would not know the story of how the geese had saved the Capitol of Rome against an attack by the Gauls.

Chickens were easy to rear and were a cheap source of protein. The Romans kept cocks for cock-fighting as well as finding them an easy form of meat. The species of birds would be something like the old English gamecock and the Indian red jungle fowl. The Vindolanda accounts often mention chickens, some seemingly served to visiting officers or the provincial governor. One mentioned 20 chickens and 100 eggs in the list of foodstuffs. Eggs of both wild and tame birds provided a welcome and nutritious addition to the diet. Eggs were a vital part of Apicius's recipes, including custards and omelettes. They have also been found in graves but whether these were to provide food for the journey to the Otherworld or were part of religious ritual is uncertain.

Doves could be kept in *columbaria* (compartmentalized dovecotes) and would be a useful source of food in winter. In addition there would have been wild birds and Parker lists ninety-four species from British sites. Bones of wild birds are frequently found on urban and rural sites and they would have provided a valuable addition to the food supply. These included golden plover and snipe, both of which were found at Dorchester, woodcock and pheasant. A large quantity of pheasant bones were found at the Barnsley Park villa (Gloucestershire) and the excavators speculated that these might have been kept for the food chain. Black grouse found in some Hadrian's Wall forts suggest these had supplemented the military diet. Crane bones have been found on several sites including Dragonby, Dorchester, Lincoln and Caerleon. Apicius gave instructions about cooking a crane: boil the bird with its head dangling over the side of the pot; when cooked, twist the head and pull. The head will come out, drawing with it the sinews. A cook at Caerleon had no idea of this as he had cut off the rear of the head.

Saltwater and freshwater fish do not seem to have been an appreciable part of the diet but there are problems on excavations, as fish bones are not preserved so easily as meat bones. There would have been difficulties in transporting fish but preservation could be done by drying, salting and placing in brine. Fish bones are mainly found on urban sites where there could be a quick sale in the market. Flounder and herring eaten in Winchester were probably prepared elsewhere, possibly on the coast at Bitterne. Herring bones from Leicester must indicate that saltwater fish were preserved before being brought there. Saltwater fish were mostly from estuarine waters. Deep sea fish, such as cod, were very rare. Bones of cod and sturgeon found in London may indicate purchases for an elite household. Other unusual fish were the firm-fleshed meagre at Bishopstone (East Sussex), the giant wrasse at Waddon Hill fort (Dorset) and the red sea bream at the religious site of Uley (Gloucestershire), where the large fish may have been offered as a gift to the gods. Other unusual finds were at the fort of Brancaster, where the First Cohort of Aquitanians was stationed, and at Caister-on-Sea, where whalebones had chop marks on them. These probably came from whales washed up on the shore but, curiously, whalebones were also found at Southwark and Leicester.

London, as is only to be expected with its large community based within easy reach of the tidal water of the Thames, has produced evidence of saltwater fish including mackerel, herring, smelt, plaice, flounder and dace, and river fish – perch, pike and roach. Bones of saltwater fish were found at Colchester and Dorchester. Cesspits at Dorchester also produced bones of sea bream, conger eel, red and grey mullet and garfish. At Skeleton Green (Hertfordshire), believed to be an early trading post, bones of plaice, flounder and Spanish mackerel found in a well may be evidence of long-distance trade. Some villa sites like Gorhambury received supplies of herring, mackerel, plaice and salmon, probably bought in the market at Verulamium; trout could be caught locally.

River fish would have been easier to catch and eels and salmon seem to have been caught and eaten in a variety of places. Mature eels, captured between July and November, provided an ample food supply: they were especially common at Colchester and Winchester. At Lynch Farm near Water Newton and at Shakenoak there were a series of ponds with feeder streams going through them. These might have been used for fish farming with separation for spawning, young fish and adult fish.

If the remains of fish were rare, remains of shellfish were much more common. These included mussels, cockles, whelks, periwinkles, scallops and oysters. People in Colchester ate carpet shellfish and those in York had the benefit of eating crab. Oysters were the most prolific and they were certainly not a luxury food. The excavators at Caister-on-Sea began to count the shells but gave up when the number passed 10,000. So prolific were the oysters that, according to Juvenal, British ones were sent to, and appreciated, in Rome.

The main oyster beds are along the south coast and on the Kent–north Essex coast. Those on the south coast could be infested with the worm *polydura hoplura*, which causes blisters on the inner part of the shell; those on the other coast were infected with the worm *polydura ciliate*, which bores holes in the shell. It is therefore possibly sometimes to identify from where the oysters were taken. Thus people at Silchester ate oysters from the south coast whereas those at Leicester had them from the Kent–north Essex coast. Oysters can be transported in barrels or jars; if they are kept cool they can survive without water for a week. They may have been taken on the decks of barges and other ships and kept fresh with seawater for as long as possible before being sent on by land transport. Oysters found on Hadrian's Wall and the Antonine Wall were probably conveyed by sea to the north.

Dairy products were very important. Sheep and goats' milk were regarded as more important than cows' milk and goats gave a greater yield, five times as much as their body weight. As raw milk can go sour very quickly, it was often better to convert it into butter or cheese. The Romans preferred olive oil to butter but the Celts had always eaten butter, so much so that Pliny the Elder said that they considered it their choicest food. Cheese was particularly popular. It is a nutritious food with a high protein value; 100 gm (3.5 oz) of cheese could contain 400 calories. Cheese-making probably was part of the tasks on most farms; any surplus could be sold in nearby markets. Cheese presses have been found in many places including Lower Halstow (Kent), Silchester, Leicester and the forts of Bainbridge, Corbridge, Holt and Usk. Residue of milk products has been found in strainers; possibly strainers were brought into Britain by the army for they have been found in kilns at Holt, Longthorpe and York. The Celts may have used equally effective ones made from organic materials. Cheese needs to have rennet to encourage the separation of curds from the whey. Columella regarded lambs' rennet as the best; Varro favoured that of kid. The juice of some plants – nettle, thistle and fig – was equally effective.

The Romans introduced new plants or domesticated those in the wild. New plants included herbs (aniseed, mint, dill, rosemary, parsley and thyme) and vegetables (fennel, cabbage, beets, onions, broad beans, leeks, lentils and turnips). They brought new varieties of carrots and parsnips as well as cultivating those brought from the wild into the garden. These carrots were white in colour; the Dutch developed the orange carrot in the seventeenth-century. A slave at Vindolanda was ordered to provide radishes, seemingly to eat at the feast of Saturnalia. New fruits included domesticated plums and damsons. A peach stone found at London indicates that this fruit was imported and Pliny the Elder said that the cherry tree had been taken to Britain as early as AD 47, a statement confirmed by cherry stones found in Colchester, London and Silchester. This would be the sour cherry (*prunus cerasus*); there was also the native cherry (*prunus avium*) that had been enjoyed in pre-Roman Britain. Medlar stones were also found in these three towns. The fruit does not travel well so the Romans first imported it and then began to cultivate the trees in Britain.

Figs were probably dried before being imported in large quantities. Their seeds have been found on many urban sites and their presence at Colchester implies that they were eaten in Britain soon after the conquest or even before, if the evidence in a cesspit at the Gorhambury villa can be dated to before AD 43. They were especially popular both as a staple meal for the poor and an after-dinner gourmet delicacy. Dates were also imported. Remains of these, carbonized from the burning by Boudicca's forces, have been found at Colchester. Both of these fruits would have been imported in amphorae.

A staple addition to Roman food was fish sauces akin to those used today in the Far East: Vietnamese *nuoc-mam* and Thai *nahm pla*. The Romans manufactured their sauces from a large number of fish: mackerel, herrings, mullet, tuna, oysters, sea urchins and small fry such as sardines, anchovies and sprats. These were placed in troughs or pits, mixed with salt or brine and left to ferment for one to six months through the actions of enzymes in the viscera. The enzymes convert the solid proteins of the fish into water-soluble amino acids and peptides as they dissolve the flesh, giving a highly nutritious product. The product could be made in any quantity provided that a precise ratio of salt to fish was observed – anything between 1:1 and 1:7. This gave each production area its distinctive taste and there could be other factors such as the addition of wine, herbs and spices, the freshness of the fish, the length of preparation time and the temperature. The resulting mixture was then transferred to amphorae ready for conveyance throughout the empire. Although on their own these sauces were pungent, when used in cookery and combined with other products their flavours meld with others and become unobtrusive.

There were four main fish-sauce products, although it cannot be certain which and how much was conveyed to Britain. Garum, the finest and most expensive, seems to have been a blackish blood and viscera sauce, made mainly from mackerel. Liquamen, a brownish-yellow sauce made from a large variety of fish, was the usual sauce, mentioned often in Apicius's cookery book and probably used in everyday cooking. Muria was the brine derived from the salted fish, probably used by poorer people. Once these liquids had been drained off a fish paste was left. This was allec, which was often sieved to get rid of the bones. These terms are often loosely used in literary texts and some modern writers use garum as the generic term in the early Roman period and liquamen in the later empire.

Whatever the term, fish products became a standard item in Roman Britain judging by the number of amphorae identified by their shapes as coming from liquamen production regions. Colchester imported fish sauces soon after the conquest, with one inscription on an amphora identifying the contents as the product of Proculus and Urbicus, who were known to be supplying the sauce to Pompeii before AD 79; York imported the sauce of Postumus; Chester favoured a sauce from Baetica. An inscription on an amphora from the Poultry excavations in London precisely contained, '80 measures of fermented fish sauce matured two years from tunny of the best quality, the product of Gaius Asicius Probus'. The name of Asicius is known from Cadiz and the main importation of this sauce, according to amphorae shapes, was the Iberian peninsula. Yet another amphora from Southwark, London, indicated the contents were Lucius Tettius Africanus's finest fish sauce from Antinopolis (Antibes) in Gaul.

Importation of this product seems to have declined after the second century AD and possibly it was popular mainly on urban sites and or rural sites occupied by those who had adapted their taste to Roman ones. Nevertheless excavations on the waterfronts of London, Lincoln and York from the mid third century into the fourth have revealed wooden troughs whose contents suggest that they could have been preparing fish sauce for local markets.

Olives and olive oil were also regarded as vital additions to the diet. As mentioned, the Romans were not lovers of butter; they regarded this as food for barbarians although it was probably a staple food in pre-Roman Britain. An amphora filled with at least 6,000 olives imported from Tarraconensis in Spain was found in the Thames. An inscription on the top of another amphora found in London indicated that it contained green olives transported by Gaius A— L— under the control of Avernus. Olive stones are found on civilian and military sites until the early fourth century when the imports seem to have declined. Until then olives had been eaten and enjoyed and olive oil had been used in great quantities not only for culinary purposes but also for lighting, sealing wood, lubrication and for rubbing into limbs in the belief that it made them supple. Pliny the Elder said that a happy life was one that used wine inside and olive oil outside but he cautioned that the oil should be used within a year.

Wine was vital to the Romans and the Celts had developed a taste for it before the conquest. Amphorae fragments dating to AD 5 were found at the pre-Roman site of Sheepen, Colchester, and at least 40 vessels, which had contained imported wine, were excavated at the Iron Age fort of Hengistbury Head (Dorset). Amphorae in the Welwyn site tombs reveal the desire of the Celtic aristocracy for wine either at their funerary feast or to sustain themselves in the Otherworld. The Lexden tumulus had 17 amphorae, one of which contained wine from Pompeii. The total liquid wine contents would have been about 460 litres (10 gallons).

Wine from Gaul, Spain and all the Mediterranean provinces was mainly imported in amphorae or glass vessels. London received wine in barrels of silver fir, cedar and larch, which also had a secondary use in lining wells. Wine for Silchester arrived in barrels from Aquitania and the Rhineland. These barrels had a capacity from 550 litres (120 gallons) to 1,000 litres (220 gallons) but were not suitable for the preservation and aging of wine as they were not airtight. Their contents must have been decanted soon after arrival. Details of the types of wine can be obtained from the wooden writing tablets at Vindolanda and these types may be applicable to elsewhere in Britain. One account at Verulamium gives the name of a wine called Massic from the Falernian region and there were also orders for sour wine (*acetus*). Another sour wine was *posca*, almost akin to vinegar, a type of wine antiscorbutic, which can help to prevent scurvy. It was the wine offered to Jesus on the cross and was not intended as an insult but was the usual wine drunk by soldiers.

Other identified wines are *mulsum* (a mixture of wine and honey), Aminean wine at Caerleon and Falernian wine at Colchester and London. At Carpow, Legion VI was supplied with medicated wine. The inscription on one amphora had part of the Greek word *prasion* (horehound) written on it, no doubt a drink to alleviate the coughs of the soldiers. Wine was also spiced and flavoured. Reducing grape must, depending on the amount of boiling, produced a variety of sweet syrups (*defrutum* and *caroenum*). Imports of wines seem to have been prolific from the first century AD, possibly much of it for the army, but by the third century they had begun to decline and seemingly were no longer a major trading commodity.

There were attempts to grow vines. One vineyard has been postulated at North Thoresby (Lincolnshire) but the arrangement of trenches might have equally have been an orchard. Whatever the position the attempt was abandoned by AD 285. Another vineyard may have existed in the Verulamium region with the resulting wine bottled in amphorae from pottery supplied from Brockley Hill. If so, the amphorae from this site were coated internally with a sealing of resin. More secure evidence came from Wollaston (Northamptonshire) in the Nene Valley. Pollen found in ditches indicated that vines had been grown there, probably held up by wooden supports. The ditches covered over 6 km (3.7 miles), which could accommodate over 4,000 vines. If the grapes flourished the yield could be as much as 10,000 litres (2,200 gallons). More vines could have trebled these quantities but would still only produce a small amount compared with what could have been imported. Amphorae in the shipwreck of the *Madrague de Giens* off the coast of Gaul may have totalled at least 6,000. If each amphora held 24 litres (5.2 gallons) this would give an overall total of 144,000 litres (31,680 gallons) and such a ship arriving in Roman London would have been extremely welcome.

The Celts drank beer (*cervesia*) and this beverage was also drunk by auxilia troops in Britain, many of whom were recruited in the northern provinces. Hops were not used at this time and so the beer was probably a light ale. Hops also act as a preservative so that Roman beer would have to be drunk soon after brewing. The Vindolanda tablets refer to Atrectus, a brewer (*cervesarius*), and Optatus, a maltster (*braciarius*). These trades would have been welcomed elsewhere, especially in the towns, although rural households could have brewed their own beer. Surviving evidence about brewing is slight as the process took place in wooden vats and the liquid was transported in barrels. One site where malting might have taken place is Fordington Bottom, about 2 km (1.2 miles) from Dorchester (Dorset). The brew could have been drunk on the estate or transported for sale in the town. Corn-driers, identified elsewhere, might also have been used for malting grain. Probably beer was also imported from the northern provinces in the previously mentioned barrels.

Herbs and spices were natural to the Romans for flavouring food and their use increased after the conquest. The Romans had access to a vast emporium of spices, many of which came from the East. Pliny mentioned that both black and white pepper were necessary condiments. Pepper grinders were part of the fourth-century Hoxne (Norfolk) hoard and carbonized peppercorns were found in Southwark. Black pepper worth two denarii was mentioned at Vindolanda. Black and white mustard seeds were found in Silchester and London. Salt was easily obtainable either from the brine springs of Droitwich and Cheshire or from the numerous salt-making areas in the Fenlands or along the Essex coast.

Honey was used as a sweetener or for medical purposes. Honey is a source of instant energy as it contains liquid glucose. Spread over meat or fish it helped in the cooking process and also acted as a preservative. The Romans mixed it with wine and the Celts had used it as part of the production of mead. It was purchased at Vindolanda in large quantities. One account referred to the purchase of at least one *modius* (8.6 litres, 1.9 gallons). An inscription on an amphora from Southwark stated that the contents were 24 *librae* (8.4 litres, 1.85 gallons).

It can be seen that given reasonable quantities of food the diet in Roman Britain could be an adequate and varied one.

Much, however, depended on circumstances. If food was unavailable, as it could be in winter, quantity not quality is a priority. In pre-conquest Britain people prepared as well as they could during the summer months, collecting food and preserving it, while relying on their own ingenuity and the cooperation of others. Some cattle had to be killed but most would be brought into enclosures for survival. Sheep, as now, could be left to fend for themselves, only being brought nearer to settlements when the weather was at its worst. In the more hilly regions, people would move their animals between summer and winter pasturage.

After the conquest food supplies needed to be increased to supply an expanding consumer market. In consequence, there would have been a greater variety of food and this probably affected people's taste and habits, especially with the number of soldiers stationed in the province and the large number of traders who quickly began to import their wares. The four *coloniae* and those towns that housed administrators or whose inhabitants were prepared to adopt Roman ways would be the most likely to welcome and experiment with the newer varieties of food. Administrators sent to the province might bring cooks amongst their entourage who had the advantage of knowing the many cookery books known in Rome and whose skills could be passed to Britons willing to have a new career.

Settlements and villas with surpluses could take their goods to markets along newly laid out roads, making transportation of perishable goods easier. Most towns had a market of some kind, often handsomely built. The large variety of shops made it easier to buy food. Buying bread from commercial bakers reduced the tedium of grinding grain and baking bread for the household. Fast food was obtainable in taverns and *popinae* (low-class wine bars) or from vendors who hawked their wares along the streets.

One excavated site in Dorchester (Dorset) produced abundant bones of cattle, sheep, goats and pigs, evidence of the large-scale processing of carcasses and that meat formed a large part of the diet. Amphorae remains from North Africa, Spain, Gaul and elsewhere in the Mediterranean showed that wine, liquamen, olive oil and probably dried goods had been imported. Shellfish remains, especially oysters, were common, the latter possibly from oyster beds in Poole Harbour.

Rubbish used to fill a disused well at Great Holt villa, Boreham (Essex), included cherry, plum and olive stones, walnuts, pine kernels, bones of cattle, geese, chickens, ducks, woodcock, salt- and freshwater fish bones, including those of eels, and oyster shells. Grain products and vegetables would supplement this food. Sparrowhawk bones may be evidence that someone had practised hawking. Amphorae sherds from Campania, Baetica and Gaul indicated that wine, olive oil and possibly liquamen had been ordered. The buildings included the villa, an adjoining house, a bathhouse, corn-drying oven and workshops; these, together with the food assemblages, suggest that the owners enjoyed a prosperous style of living lasting from the early second century until the mid fourth century AD. The collapse of the villa's economy was probably due to the loss of the Romanized infrastructure on which it depended.

Taken as a whole, if people in Roman Britain had access to sufficient food they were able to have a reasonable diet of protein and carbohydrates, allowing for the lesser amount of food in the winter months for people in the northern areas. Stored grain could be turned into pottage and bread; salting, drying and steeping in brine could preserve meat. Over the year there might be other problems: a lack of vitamins and a threat of scurvy. Iron deficiency, which causes the haemoglobin levels to fall, resulting in anaemia, could be avoided if iron pans were used for cooking. If lead pans were used for food preparation there was a danger of lead poisoning, as was clearly indicated in some skeletons at the Poundbury cemetery.

Greater variety of food would be available in the summer although fruit and vegetables needed to be transported quickly before they lost flavour and nutritional value. Berry fruits and rose hips provided vitamin C. Calcium intake would have been higher because of the availability of green vegetables and more fresh milk and cheese. Vitamin A content was also greater in summer milk. Care needed to be taken as milk can carry disease-causing organisms, especially brucellosis and tuberculosis. Three examples of the latter found in skeletons at Poundbury may have been the result of infected milk. Vitamins A, B1 and B12 are obtained from eating liver and offal and the Romans excelled in using all parts of the animals.

A mainly cereal diet of stone-ground bread was excellent for providing fibre and the B vitamins but one problem was that it also contained phytate. Its consumption interfered with the absorption of calcium, thus predisposing individuals to osteo-malacia, a disease found in skeletons in Romano-British ceme-teries. This could be countered with vitamin D obtained from egg yolks, liver and fish oils, but most vitamin D is created by the action of sunlight on the skin.

Fish also needed to be eaten quickly. Pliny the Elder and Columella had warned against eating tainted fish and Roy Davies drew attention to a case of fish poisoning amongst soldiers in a fort at Alexandria. Food poisoning, however, can occur with any food and that people can survive infection and infestations is revealed by analysis of the faecal remains from a cesspit at Carlisle and from the York sewers. Whipworms and round worms, which both live in intestines, were present in large numbers. Lack of hygiene, especially with regard to food-stuffs, could result in anything from mild food poisoning to death and the streets of Roman Britain, in spite of instructions to keep them clean, were probably as filthy as any other province in the empire.

The Romans often preferred sour, spicy and bitter tastes to bland ones and these could have been followed with regard to food in Britain. Olive oil, liquamen, herbs and spices livened up the food. The oil blunted bitter phytonutrients and had the added advantage of containing some vitamin E. Excessive drinking of wine and gorging of food resulted in liver disease and bad breath. A wall painting at Pompeii shows another result of overindulgence. At first glance this appears to be a lively dinner party but closer inspection reveals a woman so drunk she has to be held up and a man, equally intoxicated, has passed out. A similar warning of excessive hedonism may yet be found in Roman Britain.

This account of the evidence for diet and nutrition in Roman Britain is very general and people may have changed their diet for a variety of reasons. When the olive oil trade dried up more attention would have been paid to butter. The decline of the international trade in liquamen led to the development of a home-produced product that was enjoyed in the area where it was produced for as long as possible. Religious beliefs may have played a part in dietary changes. Sacrificial meat, as indicated previously, probably was sold in the market place but as Christianity was adopted by more of the population sacrifices would have ceased. Christians were urged to be charitable to their neighbours. In the medieval period the monasteries distributed food to the poor. Possibly early Christian communities did the same. Hilary Cool has suggested that the disproportionate number of young women, who died between the ages of thirteen and fifteen, excavated at the cemetery at Poundbury may have been because they obeyed the Christian decree of fasting to extremes, even to death.

The population of Britain changed throughout the years of occupation. People from many parts of the empire came to Britain and settled here. These included military veterans who had married or formed relationships and, on discharge, decided to settle in the province. These men, especially those from the eastern regions and North Africa, brought with them their own dietary preferences and their own cooking vessels, which they may have kept or adjusted for use according to the foods that were available. In the late fourth and early fifth centuries mercenaries from the Germanic regions who settled on the east coast and were absorbed into garrisons would have had their own particular eating habits. There would also be variations in the diets of the elite groups and poorer people. In the fifth century, as the supply lines ceased, people probably reverted to the situation as it had been in pre-Roman Britain with food being more available in country areas where it would be easier to grow or gather from the wild.

14

INDUSTRY, CRAFTS AND TRADE

As soon as the Romans established themselves in Britain, they needed to construct a road system similar to that built throughout the empire. Roads were made for and by the military. Before the system was created, the army would have advanced along existing trackways such as the Jurassic Way and the Icknield Way. Temporary roads at first were probably cleared strips of land 8.6 m (28 ft) wide, flanked by two ditches. The road from Richborough to London may have been constructed over a period of 15 weeks using a labour force of 1,000 men. Later, more permanent roads were laid out, overlying the earlier roads. Sections of Watling Street at Springhead (Kent) and Southwark have revealed earlier light metalled road surfaces from the early first century AD.

Roads were intended to support an economic infrastructure as part of a land-based supply system and an imperial postal system to link up urban settlements and ports. They also gave an impetus for small and large estates to convey goods to towns. These were not only agricultural producers but also those who made industrial goods on the premises, such as pottery and agricultural implements. They also encouraged the growth of settlements. Roads were laid out with layers of earth, clay and stone creating an *agger*, cambered to allow drainage, 13.4–15.2 m (44–49.8 ft) wide. Some roads were laid out on natural ground. Roads mainly had two layers, a foundation layer made of carefully rammed down gravel and sand to spread the load imposed by the upper layer. The cambered top surface could be of stones, cobbles, granite and flint depending on what was available. A few – Dean Road in the Forest of Dean and Blackstone Edge (Greater Manchester) – were paved with flagstones. Curbstones and two drainage ditches might be placed parallel to the road.

Land transport would be by mules with panniers and two- or four-wheeled carts pulled by oxen, mules and horses. Horses were often shod with a hypposandal, a flat plate with a back rim and handle so that it could be fastened on to a hoof. Transport of heavier goods could be by canal or river. Boats could go from the Humber estuary through the Fenlands and the rivers Don, Trent and Idle. The Foss Dyke between the Rivers Trent and Ouse probably carried military supplies to York, but the Car Dyke system in Lincolnshire, once believed to be for transport, is now thought to be a catchwater drain for the Fens.

Many heavier goods would be transported by sea and from the nearest port conveyed onward by land. There was probably intensive coastal trade. Lancaster had a river frontage and a company of bargemen. Archaeological evidence from Chester and Caerleon suggests than these places had inland ports with wooden revetted quays running alongside a waterfront. From these a series of jetties extended, allowing shipping to dock. At Chester the quay, about 350 m (383 yd) long, was constructed of oak planking laid on heavy cross beams secured to tall oak piles. Later this quay collapsed and was replaced by a stone one. A port was established in London as early as AD 50 and by the second century a river frontage extended to the east for 2 km

(1.25 miles). Deep water quays were found on the sites of the former County Hall and east of the Walbrook, accommodating both river and sea-going vessels. The ship found on the County Hall site in 1910, 13 m (42.6 ft.) long and 5.5.m (18 ft.) wide, was constructed of oak in classical Mediterranean tradition.

According to Tacitus, one of the main reasons for the invasion of Britain in AD 43 was the mining of gold, silver and other metals – the prize of victory. Gold might have been the great objective but Cicero disparaged this, stating that there was no trace of gold and silver in Britain. The only known Roman gold mine in Britain is at Dolaucothi (Wales), where sufficient gold was extracted to justify the building of an aqueduct 11 km (6.8 miles) long and capable of carrying 13.6 million litres (3 million gallons) daily in order to wash the crushed ore and break down the softer beds of rock, much of it obtained from opencast mining. The main Ogofau pit descended to 44 m (144 ft) below the present surface, involving the removal of 500,000 tonnes of rock. Waterwheels, similar to those found in Spanish mines, drained these deep workings. Whether this effort was worth it for the Roman authorities is a moot point. It has been estimated that if one-third of the tonnage of rock extracted contained gold mineralization at 5 gm per tonne this would have yielded 830 kg (1830 lb) of gold. The gold would have been sold to goldsmiths in Britain or sent to Rome.

A goldsmith's shop has been found at Verulamium and another in the forum at Cirencester, both identified by the discovery of crucibles used for heating gold. At Norton, near Malton (North Yorkshire), a slave gave thanks to the Genius Loci (the god of a place) for allowing him the opportunity to manage a goldsmith's shop, probably being given the chance by an indulgent master. Gold was also refined in London where on the Cannon Street site two large gold-impregnated crucibles were found. A large number of gold items have been found in Britain. Some would have been imported; others could have been made in the province. Rings, bracelets, chains and necklaces were popular. The pre-Roman Celts had decked themselves with gold jewellery and it was unlikely that jewellery-making techniques had been lost. Celtic ornamentation has been found on a bracelet from Rhayader (Powys).

Pottery found at the fort and bathhouse at Pumsaint, near to Dolaucothi, suggests that the fort was founded in the mid AD 70s and the soldiers would have guarded the workforce. The mines would have been run by slave labour, many of them prisoners captured in warfare against the Romans, enslaved and given the sentence *damnatio ad metalla* (condemned to the mines). Tacitus, in the speech he gave to the Caledonian chieftain Calgacus in the *Agricola*, said that one of the consequences of a Roman victory was working in the mines as slaves. Even though Pumsaint was small, 1.9 hectares (4.75 acres), it would have held six barracks, sufficient for an auxiliary *cohors peditata quingenaria*. The fort was reduced in size, if not abandoned, by AD 120, which indicated either that it was becoming increasingly difficult to extract the gold or that the mine was of less importance after the development of the Dacian gold mines. By that time a *vicus* had grown up around the fort and until at least the third century private contractors worked the area.

The Romans had hoped to find silver mines in Britain. In this they were to be disappointed, although some silver might be obtained from lead by the process of cupellation where the lead was smelted at a temperature of 1,000–1,100°C (1,800–2,000°F) in a strong current of air on a porous substance such as bone ash. This converted the lead to oxides, which could be skimmed off, leaving the pure silver. Silver items are known in Britain although it is not certain whether they were made in the province or imported. The Mildenhall Treasure and the late Roman silver hoard found at Water Newton were obviously imported. The great dish found at Mildenhall, 600 mm (23.5 in.) in diameter and weighing 8.28 kg (18 lb) had in the centre the head of

Neptune and round it mythological figures. The Water Newton hoard contained objects decorated with the Chi-Rho monogram indicating a Christian significance. Silversmiths in Britain probably confined themselves to minor pieces of jewellery – rings, earrings and brooches.

It was probably this desire for silver that led the Romans to exploit lead mining in Derbyshire, Flintshire, the Mendips and Somerset. Later lead was extracted in Yorkshire. Pliny the Elder reported that, although in Spain and Gaul lead was extracted with considerable labour, in Britain it was found in the surface stratum with so much abundance that there was a law prohibiting the production of more than a certain amount. Augustus had arranged that the state would maintain control over the exploitation of all minerals by a *procurator metallarum*. These men were either equites or freedmen appointed by the emperor and given considerable power over their area. They could lease mines to individuals or companies (*societates*), who often followed in the wake of the army to exploit the minerals. An iron punch bearing the initials *M(etalla) P(rovinciae) B(ritanniae)*, found in London, suggests that the British procurator was based there.

The ore was smelted and the resultant metal was cast into trough-shaped moulds called pigs, weighing about 80–90 kg (175–200 lb), which were stamped on the bottom with the name of the emperor or sometimes the contractor's name. Lead-mining in the Mendips began as early as AD 49, as indicated by a pig bearing the title of Claudius. Other pigs found in the area of Charterhouse-on-Mendip, which soon grew into a small town provided with an amphitheatre but under the control of a nearby fort, were stamped with the name of Legion II Augusta. This mining area seems to have consisted of small narrow trenches exploiting local outcrops, which justifies Pliny's statement.

Although the Mendip mines continued into production until the third century, pigs, stamped with the names of C. Nipius

Ascanius and Tiberius Claudius Triferna and dated to the reigns of Nero and Vespasian, may indicate that some mines had passed into the hands of these procurators or entrepreneurs. Other pigs bear the name of Vespasian and the tribal name of the Deceangli. Ascanius's name also appears on a lead pig at Carmel (Flintshire), indicating that he had taken a lease in that area, probably later in his career. In Derbyshire pigs bearing the inscription *Soc(iorum) Novaec*— and *metal(li) Lutud(arensis)* suggest that cooperatives worked the mines. Lutudarum was presumably the administrative centre for the area. Other lead mining areas in Yorkshire were exploited in Domitian's reign. Much of the lead was exported. Pigs stamped with the names of legions stationed in Britain have been found in France at St-Valéry-sur-Somme, Sassenay near Chalon-sur-Saône and Alouettes.

Lead was used for pipes, roofing, water tanks, weights, seals, labels and the ubiquitous curse tables. It lined the floor of the Great Bath at Bath and could also be used in the making of coffins and cremation urns. It might also be used for the making of pans but this could be dangerous for those who consumed the food cooked in them. It was extremely useful when alloyed with tin to make pewter.

The Greeks had known in the sixth century BC that tin was obtained from an area in the west from a group of islands known as the Cassiterides. Caesar mentioned that tin was found inland, probably deliberately misled by merchants who wished to keep their source of supply secret. Diodorus, who gave a description of quarrying the ore, obtaining the metal and cleansing it from its impurities, provided more definite information. The metal was then conveyed to Ictis (almost certainly St Michael's Mount, Cornwall) where merchants could obtain it.

The ore was probably obtained from streambeds where water-concentrated deposits could be found and made into ingots; two, each weighing 3 kg (6.5 lb), were found in the Bath spring. During the early part of the occupation the Romans had neglected the Cornish tin mines as they could obtain more tin from the Spanish mines. Most of the tin was used for the production of pewter vessels. There were some early finds of pewter ware in London. A large deposit of vessels including canisters, plates, spoons and finger rings, dating to the early second century, was retrieved from the Walbrook streambed. Others dating to the second century were found in the area of the Tower of London. A group of pans from the spring at Bath may also be dated to the second century.

Later, by the third century, when production in the Spanish mines waned, interest in the Cornish mines revived. In addition, during the third and fourth centuries rising standards of living, especially amongst wealthy villa owners, encouraged them to demand pewter table vessels to rival the silver ones of the very rich. Manufacturing seems to have centred on the area round Bath, which would allow the concentration of tin from Cornwall, lead from the Mendips and limestone for the moulds from the surrounding areas.

Most of the finds of pewter come from the areas of the Fens and the Mendips; finds in the north are relatively rare. Many were deposited as grave goods like those found at the Winchester Lankhills cemetery; other finds at Richborough and Springhead may have been buried as a form of safekeeping. Pewter objects were found in wells, rivers and ponds. Some may have been discarded but given that pewter was relatively expensive to produce and the objects would have had a certain value, these may have been deposited with a ritual purpose, which could have been the intention behind the pans deposited at Bath. A group of ten pewter ingots have been found in the Thames at Battersea. Several bear the Chi-Rho monogram and the name, Syagrius, presumably the maker, but whether these were a ritual deposit or a lost riverboat cargo is uncertain.

Bronze-working had been one of the most productive industries in pre-Roman Britain and the Romans continued to exploit this metal. Bronze is a mixture of copper and tin, and copper was mined by the Romans in Shropshire and Wales, especially in Anglesey where it was cast into bun-shaped ingots. Impressed stamps on these carry the names of the lessees of the mines. One from Anglesey bears the name of the *Sociorum Romae* (partners resident in Rome). These ingots were worked in towns; excavation of a pit at Silchester provided crucibles, snippets of bronze, slag and filings from a bronze-worker's furnace. The crucible would be heated on a charcoal hearth and the metal contents poured into larger moulds. Many bronze objects were smelted and reused so that metalworkers had a constant supply of material. One of the largest bronze vessels found in Britain was a corn measure (*modius*) found at the fort of Carvoran on Hadrian's Wall, which exceeded the stated capacity inscribed on it by almost 20 per cent. This was suspected of being a device for defrauding Britons who came to pay their dues in grain. Bronze was used for practical objects, jewellery and for large and small figurines. It could be decorated by various techniques including enamelling used on rings, brooches, studs and seal boxes. There was a ready market in the army, which made great use of bronze for body armour, helmets, scabbard fittings, shield bosses, diplomas (military documents inscribed in bronze) and *phalerae* (discs worn on breastplates). Surgeons' implements were also made of bronze.

The most practical metal was iron and the Romans soon exploited the extensive deposits of iron ore in the Sussex and Kent Weald areas, and the Forest of Dean. Two Late Iron Age sites in Snowdonia have produced evidence of large-scale Roman iron smelting. Ample evidence of iron-ore working in the third century AD has been found at Lydney Park. A shaft 1 m (3.3 ft) wide was open for 5.5 m (18 ft), then enclosed, forming a tunnel. The ore seems to have been hacked out with a small pick hammer judging by the marks left on the walls of the mine.

In the Weald the main workings were from the first to the mid third centuries AD with a major output of 700–750 tonnes of iron between AD 100 and 250. The fleet, *Classis Britannica*, seems to have been involved on some sites such as a large lead mining area at Beauport Park near Hastings, in production between the second and mid third century, either in supervising the extraction of the ore or in arranging for shipments of the iron across the English Channel. A large number of tiles from a large military-style bathhouse are stamped *CL.BR* and huge mounds of the slag produced were used for road-metalling in the nineteenth century.

Iron ore needs to be smelted at a high temperature. It was heated with charcoal in a shaft furnace and at about 1,300°C (2,400°F) much of the ore became fluid and could be tapped off, leaving a spongy residue. This was constantly reheated until white-hot and hammered into a bloom weighing about 2 kg (4.4 lb). The reheating in charcoal meant that some of the carbon remained ingrained in the metal, turning some iron into mild steel. The bloom was then sent to smiths who, like the one depicted on a tombstone at York, produced tools for the household, the farm and, if required, for the army. Such a man could combine the tasks of wheelwright, farrier, locksmith, wheel-maker and probably several others.

Iron slag found in forts indicates that the army had its own smiths and other craftsmen. Vegetius gave a list of those in a legion, which covered most of the trades necessary to support the army, not only those relating to the production and repair of armour and weapons but carpenters, blacksmiths, wood-workers, masons and builders. The army was seemingly almost self-sufficient and, if required, could give support to the civilian population. The work provided by the army smiths is indicated by the huge number of nails needed for a legionary fort. When the fort of Inchtuthil was demolished nearly 10 tonnes of nails, estimated to be over a million in number, were buried rather than be removed from the site. Shirley has estimated that for fixing the roof tiles, shingles and cladding 1.5 million nails would have been needed.

Much of the heating for smelting was done by charcoal for which at first there was ample timber available. This industry, together with the demands made by urban areas, must have put a strain on local resources and depleted the forests. Pliny had described the different types of wood needed to produce charcoal and indicated their best industrial and domestic uses. The only classical reference to coal in Britain was by Solinus (*Collectanea rerum memorabilium*) who described, in the third century AD, the novelty of fuel which burned on an altar to Minerva, presumed to be at Bath, where the eternal flames of a substance never whitened into ash but when the fire had died away turned into rocky, round masses.

During the last ten years, excavations in Britain have indicated that coal was used for domestic and industrial purposes more than had been expected, often being transported by road for long distances. Coal mined in the Nottinghamshire area was conveyed 83 km (52 miles) to Holbeach in the Fenlands. Analysis of coal at Vindolanda found that it came from the West Durham coalfields; coal found at Doncaster originated in Castleford. Coal was not merely used as ballast on ships returning from supplying forts in the northern areas but was shipped as a valuable commodity for industrial and domestic use. Travis has argued that given the amount of coal found on Romano-British sites the level of coal extraction in Britain 'was substantial and can no longer be viewed as a minimal, marginal activity'. He estimated that when a smithy used coal the minimum amount used on a hearth in one day could be 50.8 kg (1 cwt) and over a full year averaging six days a week could be 15.25 tonnes.

An average open fire in a villa might consume at least 2.5 tonnes of coal, which could be used for both cooking and heating in the stokehold of a hypocaust. It was found in numerous places – the public baths at Wroxeter, the *mansio* at Lancaster, the forts of Vindolanda, Melandra Castle

(Derbyshire), Templeborough and Castleshaw (North Yorkshire), and agricultural sites where it could be used in corn-drying kilns; in industry one of its uses was for drying pottery prior to firing. Large piles of coal were found on the industrial premises at Wilderspool (Cheshire) and Little Chester (Derbyshire). It was used in a ritual capacity on the altars found at the shrines of Nettleton (Wiltshire). At the Trentholme Drive cemetery in York it helped in cremations. One of the problems with coal is that it requires constant removal of the waste ash, in contrast to charcoal, but there would be no difficulty in doing this with an economy using slave labour.

One industry that developed during the second century AD was jet. Not only jet but coal, coal shale and even burnt bone could be fashioned into objects, probably admired for their black shiny finish. Solinus, in his *Collectanea rerum memorabilium*, written soon after AD 200, noted that jet was found in Britain, 'in great abundance and of very fine quality. If you wish to know what it looks like, it has the appearance of a black jewel . . . it burns with water and is extinguished with oil; when warmed by rubbing it holds on to things in contact with it like amber.' Pliny the Elder, who also described jet as being black, smooth and bright, confirmed his comments. Polishing was done with linseed or olive oil and the addition of lamp black would give a darker shade. Final rubbing with a cloth or soft leather gave the material a high shine so that it was extremely popular for jewellery.

Jet is found in Yorkshire, near Whitby, and in Dorset where it was gathered by beachcombing or searching after cliff falls. Sometimes a tunnel was dug into the cliff to extract jet or promote a fall. The smaller fragments were suitable to make jewellery, amulets and other little objects. Excavations at York have produced rough-outs, which may have been the work of apprentices. Craftsmen would then complete the finished objects – beads, finger rings, bracelets, beads and necklaces.

Amulets, some of the most popular being pendants, like those found at York and London shaped into a Medusa head to ward off evil, were made on a lathe probably worked on a treadle, with the centrepiece cut out to form a disc. In the nineteenth century, antiquarians called these 'Kimmeridge shale money' because of the large numbers found at Kimmeridge (Dorset), where mention is made in 1859 of 600–800 pieces being found in two small excavation trenches.

Cutting a rod of jet into sections, then drilling a hole through each section, made beads. Examples from York reveal an hourglass-shape indicating that the hole was made from one side and then the other. Pins could easily be whittled into shape or turned on the lathe. Large slabs of jet from Dorset were crafted into table legs and tops; tabletops were found at Caerwent and Silchester. Craftsmen working in Wroxeter, Silchester and London seemingly sent finished objects to other parts of the empire.

The only literary evidence for glass being made in Britain comes from Strabo, who lists glass vessels being imported together with other objects from Gaul during Augustus's reign. Glass production, however, had developed in Britain soon after AD 43, first being situated in forts, where the most important work was to make and repair windows, and in towns, where more artistic goods would be displayed. Glass production sites in Britain include Caistor-by-Norwich, Mancetter (Warwickshire), Leicester, Silchester and Water Newton. The industrial settlement of Wilderspool (Cheshire) also produced evidence of circular flues and furnaces while York had at least three glass workshops. The Coppergate site had crucibles, melted glass and vessel fragments dating from the late second to early third centuries AD, probably indicating a large glass-working site making bowls and jars. Glass waste has been found in other towns. In London one site produced a large second-century AD deposit of blown and worked glass, weighing about

50 kg (110 lb), which suggests glass was worked there on a large scale. Glass could also be recycled, thus increasing production.

Glass production took two forms. There was a primary production where raw materials – silica (sand), soda and lime – were heated to drive out impurities. Then the mixture was heated to about 1,100–1,200°C (2,000–2,200°F) to produce glass in a molten state. This could be used to make vessels in a mould or be used for glass-blowing. Much of the process was the same as used today in glassworks, even using the same tools – long tubes measuring 1.2 m (4 ft) and pincers. Most of the vessels found in Britain were blown.

Glass was used extensively for a wide variety of vessels to contain liquids, foods and medicines, and for jewellery, especially necklaces and bangles. Green or blue glass vessels were popular. These might have been used for purposes other than domestic; a glass jar found at Caerleon contained a person's ashes. Window glass, found on some sites, may have been made by casting glass on a sanded surface or blowing glass into a bottle form, which was then cut open and rolled out flat.

Production of pottery soon became important in Britain. When the Romans arrived they found many local pottery industries already established and potteries in Kent, Essex and Hertfordshire were importing wheel-thrown pottery on a large scale. Mainly, however, the pottery produced was handmade and used or sold locally where it was made. Some areas had no pottery but relied on leather, skin and wooden vessels.

Once pottery was produced on a commercial scale, it was made in kilns. A large circular hole or furnace chamber was dug into the ground with a stokehole to one side through which heat could be provided. Pots were stacked on an internal floor, supported on piles, with vents in it to allow the heat to rise. The sides of the kiln were built of turf or brick blocks and the roof was either thatched or made of turf. This was provided with a hole, closed if grey or black wares were made or left open if pots were to be oxidized. It was most important to keep a steady temperature as much of the work would be wasted if this was not done. Individual households produced their pottery in a bonfire or clamp kiln where a covering of turfs was plastered over with clay. This method fired pots cheaply and easily although there would always be a great deal of waste.

The Roman army needed pottery in large quantities and at first had to rely on its own potters or use goods brought in by merchants. Soon native potters were encouraged to increase production, especially as they saw this as a lucrative market. To obtain a military contract meant development from local status to commercial and industrial enterprise. At first, these contracts were overseen, if not enacted, by the military, as seems to have been the case at the forts of Longthorpe, Holt and Usk. At Usk, potters from the Rhineland and Danube provinces influenced production. Establishment of towns and large villas also provided lucrative markets. At first, many products continued the Iron Age designs but the importation of handsome wares meant that models were available to influence pottery development for both the kitchen and the dining room.

Some pottery had a specialized use. Mortaria, introduced by the army, became common after AD 43. This pottery had a heavy rim for lifting with a poring lip. Grits were included in the interior to help with the pulverization of vegetables and herbs. At first mortaria was imported but by AD 70 potteries near to Verulamium, including Brockley Hill and Radlett (Hertfordshire), and at Colchester, were supplying mortaria in a cream and buff fabric. Some potters stamped their name on the rim. Q. Valerius Veranius worked at Bavai in Gallia Belgica before he moved to Britain. Doinus, known at Brockley Hill, may have been a local potter but Gaius Attius Marinus, whose name indicates his Roman status, worked at Brockley Hill in the AD 90s, then at Radlett between 100 and 110 before moving to Hartshill and Mancetter between 110 and 130. As the army moved north, more potteries were established and mortaria produced at Mancetter and Hartshill (Warwickshire) dominated the northern and midland market for the next three centuries. Other potteries near Corbridge, Doncaster and Lincoln seem to have served garrison areas. Mortaria in a pale cream fabric was produced in the second century AD from kilns round Oxford. So productive were all these kilns that little mortaria was imported after the early first century except for huge ones found near Verulamium, marked by Verecundus from Soller (Germany), possibly for use as kneading troughs for bakers.

Another specialized form of pottery was amphorae, vital for transporting wine, olive oil, liquamen and bulk goods. One found in the Thames estuary contained 6,000 olive stones, the remains of excellent Posean olives. Amphorae had already entered Britain before the conquest, being found at Sheepen, Oswaldbury (Hampshire), Prae Wood (Hertfordshire) and Hengistbury Head (Dorset) in a variety of forms depending where they were made. North African cylindrical amphorae, with a large bulbous body, brought in olive oil; Spain produced a globular variety, which could hold up to 80 litres (17.6 gallons). This was in use until the third century AD when it was replaced by a smaller version. Their shape made for easy transportation and stacking, while the cylindrical base could be inserted into the ground or put through holes in wooden planks. Bungs or wax sealed in the contents. Olive oil was imported on a regular basis from Spain, especially from Tarraconensis and Baetica, reputed to be the best oil available, then from North Africa. The army imported it in great quantities and its versatility as a cooking agent was obvious and acceptable. It was also used for lighting, lubrication and sealing wood. Spanish supplies declined in the third century but replacements came from the North African trade. The only known British site making amphorae was at Brockley Hill, presumably for the local wine industry.

Roman pottery coarse ware. On the left is a mortaria

Pottery had a variety of uses. Pots could be containers to hold ashes; small incense cups were used in ritual practices and two pedestal incense burners made and dedicated by Saturninus Augusta were found at Coventina's shrine. Pots acted as storage vessels for burying coins in times of crisis. Potsherds were trimmed to provide spindle whorls, gaming counters and tesserae for mosaics. Pottery could be ground down and mixed with lime as a foundation for floors and pavements. It was cheap and would be discarded once broken, as illustrated by the huge amounts found on archaeological sites. In London, pottery broken on a voyage seemed to have been tipped into the Thames in front of the Roman wharves, or used as ballast in their construction.

Kitchenware included flagons for pouring liquids; some produced in the Verulamium region had moulded faces on the necks and these found a ready market in London. The main kitchen items – bowls, platters and dishes – were probably black-burnished wares. In the Dorset region this was developed from black, gritty pottery made by the Durotriges, but soon after the mid first century a grey, fine and silkier ware was being produced in Canterbury and north-west Kent. Potters round Poole Harbour managed to get contracts to supply the army on Hadrian's Wall and may have transported their goods by sea to the north. Other kitchen- and dining-ware – beakers, bowls, storage vessels and tankards – consisted of orange ware from the Severn valley, and shell-tempered ware from north Kent included large storage vessels with their interior sealed with pitch, probably intended to hold salt. Wessex potters produced a range of vessels finished by tempering with crushed pottery (grog), making the outside burnished but with the inside left distinctly rough.

Lamps were at first imported from Gaul, Germany, Italy and North Africa. Most were of fired clay made with or without a handle. Oil was poured into the lamp through a hole in the lid, which also allowed air to enter. Lids were decorated with plant life, animals and mythological scenes. A wick, possibly a twisted piece of cloth impregnated with oil, would burn for about two hours, although this would be expensive if imported olive oil was used. This gave a small, orangey light and plenty of smoke. Oil would seep through the pottery fabric so bronze lamps were preferred, although these could be expensive. A bronze one found in the Thornborough Barrow (Buckinghamshire) had a removable lid with a chain attached to prevent it getting lost. A particularly splendid one found in the Thames at Greenwich, probably imported, had two nozzles and a curved rear handle ending in a ram's head.

More expensive pottery was Samian ware, so called after the pottery industry of the island of Samos from which comes the Latin *samiare* (to polish). The term refers to the red-slip polished tableware imported at first from the Arezzo region of Italy and later from its imitators in Gaul, especially from La Graufesenque and Lezoux. The potter Cinnamus, who had a business in central Gaul, between AD 140 and 160 exported much of his wares to Britain. So valued was this pottery that it was often placed in graves to accompany the deceased to the Otherworld. It was in great demand not only for its high shine but also because of rouletted, appliquéd and incised designs illustrating abstract, mythological or natural world scenes.

Given such a popular commodity it was inevitable that British potters would try to imitate it. One group at Colchester about AD 160 began making pottery, copying designs from eastern Gaul. They could not, however, achieve the same form of clay or produce the same handsome designs, although some of their bowls reveal a liking for animal chases. Another industry in the Nene Valley between AD 160 and 200 was similarly unsuccessful as the potters were unused to firing their wares correctly. One pottery at Staines managed to produce a passable imitation of the ware.

Pottery imported into Britain included items made of terra rubra in varieties of orange and red, terra nigra made in grey and black from the Trier region, African red-slip ware and Rhenish beakers in black and red fabrics with white trailed motifs making abstract or hunting designs and words such as *BIBE* (drink). Potters in the New Forest and the Nene Valley eagerly copied these designs. Between the first and third centuries AD, the so-called Castor-ware industry produced pottery with hunting scenes, dogs chasing hares and deer, and phallic designs believed to bring good luck or avert evil.

Clay was also used for a variety of manufactures, especially tiles and decorative antefixes for roofs, hypocaust pillars and box tiles used in heating walls. Primus stamped his name on box tiles in Leicester, as did Clementinus at Silchester. Those made on military sites were stamped with the name of the legion; others were made for official groups such as the *Classis*

Britannica at Beauport Park (East Sussex) or the procurator's office. Legion XX had its own pottery and tile-making factory at Holt that was used mainly to supply their fort at Chester.

Salt was an important industry organized by a procurator, although extraction and distribution could be leased to private contractors. Distribution was carefully regulated, and a regular supply might have been difficult to obtain without access to official sources. Sodium chloride is one of the minerals essential to human and animal life. Part of a man's pay could be made in salt, hence the term *salarium* or salt money, and buying salt at times became part of the taxation system. Diocletian's edict in AD 301 gave a price of 100 denarii for a *castrensis modius* (about eight pints), which was the amount that Cato suggested should serve one person for a year.

In Britain salt was obtained from evaporation methods along the coast and from inland brine springs. The former method would provide sea salt, which included the trace element iodine. Saltern sites identifying salt production extend from Lincolnshire around the coast to Dorset. These were normally associated with settlement sites where workers were housed and the majority of the Lincolnshire ones seem to have been most active during the first two centuries AD. Saltern sites, called 'Red Hills', are prolific in Essex. Seawater was run into flat, clay-lined tanks and allowed to evaporate into a more concentrated brine which was then placed in iron pans. These were put on firebars over beds of glowing charcoal and kept simmering to crystallize the salt, which was scooped out periodically. Packing into containers provided cakes of salt. Salt was also transported in pots sealed with pitch or clay, in barrels or in leather sacks.

Excavation of the saltern sites on the Lincolnshire fen edge indicated that kiln-type structures were built of tiers of evaporating dishes supported on briquetage stands. At Denver (Norfolk) feeder channels led into ditches where the water was naturally evaporated to become a concentrated brine; this could be heated on surface hearths. Slow heating produces crystals; fast heating, followed by rapid cooling, produces fine grains.

Inland, salt was produced at Droitwich and Middlewich, which are both called *Salinae* in the *Ravenna Cosmography*. A salt industry had been established at Middlewich in the late Iron Age and the Romans quickly took advantage of this. During the late first and early second centuries, the *Ala Classiana Civium Romanorum* guarded the industry and controlled native salt exploitation of the industry. Recent excavation has revealed that different types of kilns and hearths were in use from AD 80 until the fourth century. Experimental archaeology has revealed that some kilns could reach temperatures of 800 to 1,000°C (1,832°F), well above the 150°C (302°F) needed to produce clear crystals. One salt workshop, dating from AD 100–160, seems to have had brine pits, kilns for salt evaporation and a supply of amphorae. These could have been used as packaging, but one amphora had the graffito *amurco* ('waste from brine') scrawled on it, which the excavators suggested referred to the storage of brine or the liquid left over from the salt-boiling process. The jar had originally contained wine imported from southern Spain.

Salt pans have been found at Nantwich and Northwich. Fragments of one found at Shavington (Cheshire) measured 100 cm (39 in.) by 96 cm (38 in.) by 14 cm (5.5 in.) when restored and weighed about 118 kg (260 lb). Marks on it indicate attempts to remove pan-scale – deposits of calcium and magnesium sulphates. Failure to remove these would lead to 'furring up' of the pans and over-heating. The salt industry was well organized and seemingly spread into the surrounding river valleys. From Middlewich salt ways crossed the Pennines, going north and east, part of a series of trackways known to have been used by packhorses bearing salt until the nineteenth century.

Other industries included building, painting and flooring. Roman administrators, retired veterans and other members of society accustomed to a civilized way of life expected to have comfortable houses. Some houses had marble on the walls; in London Purbeck marble, slate and limestone were used, but it was obviously cheaper to employ wall painters. Before the 1950s little was known about wall paintings but the discovery of those at the Lullingstone villa and at Verulamium changed the situation and further excavations indicate that many houses had rooms with decorated painted walls. Wall paintings reveal convergence of taste. Many followed classical designs, understandably as their interpreters were used to working in fresco where the plasterer carefully prepared the surface with coats of slaked lime and gypsum. Powdered brick could make the plaster watertight. Each layer was applied to the next while it was still wet. Vitruvius had recommended at least six layers of plaster but in Britain the average appears to be two. Paint was applied to the final wet layer and this was often done in sections. The finished result was polished with stone. Redecoration might be frequent, after a fire or a change of taste. One house at Catterick had a room repainted three times, not perhaps an unusual occurrence if the occupants became bored or irritated by a design; new owners would also wish to impose their own tastes. Soldiers in the fort at Lancaster painted a wall five times in eighty years. If a wall was to be repainted the original surface was pecked to give purchase to a new layer of plaster.

Pigments were made from a variety of sources: black came from charcoal or lampblack, while white from white lime was mixed with other colours for subtle shades. Red composed of oxides of iron was used extensively on the walls of some houses in Verulamium. Vermilion was produced from mineral cinnabar by heating and washing the ore to remove impurities. Woad provided blue, as did basic copper carbonate and imported lapis lazuli. Blue frit, artificially prepared from copper silica and calcium by firing in crucibles, was found at Woodeaton, as if ready to be sold. Purple, made from a Tyrian species of sea mollusc, was expensive. Vitruvius suggests using the juice of whortleberries mixed in milk; bilberries would be easier to obtain in Britain. A little gold leaf has been found at Lincoln, London and Colchester, where wealthy patrons would appreciate the value of such work.

Quality varied according to the wealth and status of the owner. Walls were normally divided into three zones, the dado at the bottom, the middle zone and the frieze at the top. In the simplest form the dado was splashed with colour to imitate marble or, as at the Sparsholt, Bignor and Lufton villas, has imitation guilloche decoration. The middle zone was usually plain at first but later was coloured red, occasionally with figurative or naturalistic decoration, and sometimes with a *trompe l'oeil* effect. The frieze might be plain or have a scroll decoration.

The villa owners at Winterton decorated eleven of the sixteen rooms as well as the bathhouse. Three wall areas from the peristyle of a courtyard house at Leicester indicate elaborate decoration. The red coloured main zone of the west wall was decorated with human figures and masks and a centrally placed painted niche or aedicule with columns on either side. The central column was entwined with tendrils and perched on a side branch was a delicately painted bird. This painting resembles those found in houses at Pompeii and evidence from elsewhere in Britain shows that simpler designs in red and black schemes were popular in the Flavian–Trajanic period. Whoever painted the north wall was completely confident in his craft, using delicate brushwork and a masterly hand in creating his design.

Painting reflected the taste of the owner. One house at Colchester, not surprisingly, was painted with gladiatorial scenes. Fragments of a wall painting at a villa at Otford (Kent), dated to the late first century, had the words *bina manu lato cripans hastilia ferro* (grasping in hand two shafts, tipped with broad steel), which could refer to lines in Virgil's poem *Aeneid*, either concerning Aeneus circling round Carthage or Turnus coming in his chariot to fight Aeneas. Either way they indicate that the owner had some classical taste.

Ceilings were also painted, usually in white with a rosette or striped garlands. At Wroxeter the *caldarium* of the baths had a vault decoration resembling coffering while the corridor of a house at Verulamium was decorated with barley ears and panels of floral decoration. These have been described as 'jobwash rather than art' but elsewhere in the house a frieze showed delicately painted birds set within scrolls.

Wall paintings did not necessarily complement floor mosaics. Mosaics were being laid in houses in Britain soon after AD 43 as they were essential for both Roman administrators and those Britons aspiring to hierarchical status, and they were demanded by the military. Mosaics in the bathhouse of the legionary fortress at Exeter, dated to AD 55–60, indicate that officials and administrators desired the same level of comfort as they had experienced on their last posting. Mosaics were both a permanent floor covering and an indication of personal taste, and over the next three centuries distinctive schools of design emerged in Britain. Although the designs remained classical some elements of Celtic artistic tradition crept into them, not in the patterning but in figurative interpretation.

Mosaics need a firm bedding. Few in Britain followed Vitruvius's elaborate instructions as to the laying of mosaics but most were soundly laid. Usually tesserae were laid on to a fine bed of sand, the central part of the design being made first, then the outer areas. This was usual for plain tessellated pavements and geometrical designs. For more complicated designs the tesserae were placed on a bed of sand on to which the design lines had been sketched. Once the design had been completed a linen sheet was glued to the tesserae which was lifted from their bed, the undersides were coated with fine mortar and the panel, then upturned, was placed into position on a prepared damp mortar bed. The cloth was softened and peeled off. The mosaic was hammered or rubbed into position with wooden blocks, so hard that the mortar would be forced up between the tesserae and then wiped down.

Occasionally these methods led to problems. Sometimes a circular panel was laid out of position as happened at the Bignor and Brading villas or there was a lack of symmetry in the spandrels. Some mosaics were laid in prefabricated sections as at the Rudston villa but borders were usually laid directly. Once a pavement had been completed the plasterer would seal the junction between the pavement and the wall plaster. The pavement would be cleaned by washing it with water and rubbing it, if needs be, with an abrasive such as sand, taking care not to scratch the design or patterning. Oiling or waxing would heighten the colours.

Mosaic workers used various materials to create their designs. The earliest ones were created in black and white tesserae with repetitive motifs. Later more complicated and figurative designs were preferred. Materials would be obtained locally where possible with large slabs of stone being cut into sticks by iron saws, using sand and water to reduce friction. The sticks were then cut with a chisel and a pincer into tesserae. On site, knapping was usual. Heaps of tesserae, sorted into piles by colour, found at the Rudston and Gadebridge villas seem to have been left by the mosaicist in case running repairs were necessary.

White and pink tesserae were provided by chalk and limestone, red and orange by chopped brick and tile and red pottery, and blues by shale and Purbeck marble. Black came from shale or burnt interiors of tile; purple, grey, brown and green were from sandstones and marble; brown came from ironstone. Imported marble gave a greater variety visible in tesserae used in mosaics at London and Cirencester. Glass tesserae were used to highlight particular details such as the gladiators' outfits at Bignor. Red glass created vivid blood on the wounded Actaeon's thigh at Cirencester.

Commissioning of mosaics in Britain might be purely on artistic grounds. They may subtly indicate solidarity with the new regime or provide an indication of the patron's status. Mythological scenes were extremely popular, not only familiar ones portraying Bacchus, Venus and Neptune, but more obscure stories of Lysurgus and the nymph Ambrosia, and Ceres and Triptolemus. Yet it is not clear if the villa owners at Lullingstone and Keynsham commissioned the story of Bellerophon and the chimaera for its attractive device or because it could have Christian iconography. Many mosaics were probably chosen for their colourful displays and visual designs. But the owners of the Low Ham villa (Somerset) probably deliberately requested scenes from the story of Dido and Aeneas and villa owners round Cirencester appreciated designs of Orpheus surrounded by animals.

Mosaic from the Low Ham Roman villa depicting the story of Dido and Aeneas, possibly commissioned by someone with an appreciation of classical learning. Somerset County Museum, Taunton

Geometrical designs, such as the one found in a second-century house at Aldborough (North Yorkshire), might be enjoyed by families used to the abstract patterning of Celtic art. Running pelta patterns and guilloche borders from Roman artistic tradition were popular as they were reminiscent of Celtic abstract design. Mosaic pavements had a utilitarian function, providing an easily cleaned, bright floor covering, although, as they were set in a bed of mortar and both costly and immovable, their subject matter might require some thought before they were commissioned. Professor Toynbee has suggested that pattern books were available to aid choice. Mosaics could be replaced by laying one on top of another as happened at Fishbourne, where a new owner may have been tempted by the scene depicting sea-panthers and an admirable roundel of the boy on the dolphin.

Mosaics in Britain have been the especial study of David Neal who has identified schools of craftsmen. Some workshops identified are the Corinian centred on Cirencester and the Durnovarian at Dorchester, which specialized in the design of Orpheus charming prowling animals. The magnificent mosaic at Woodchester is the largest known north of the Alps. A Durobrivan workshop may have been at Water Newton, specializing in abstract patterning, and in the north a Petuarian one was possibly based at Aldborough. There may have been one in the south working on the Chichester and Silchester mosaics.

Sometimes an owner wanting something exceptional may have commissioned an outstanding worker. The superb series of Bignor mosaics were laid about AD 300. These, revealing cupids acting as gladiators and a head of Venus, whose nimbus glitters with green glass tesserae, were created by a master craftsman possibly from Gaul, who signed his work with the abbreviation TER (possibly Terentius, Tertius or Tutullius). One villa owner insisted that his name should be incorporated in his floor. The inscription *Quintus Natalius Natalinus et Bodeni* indicates that Quintus commissioned this mosaic at his villa at Thruxton (Hampshire) and included on the inscription his friends, clients or tenants of his estate.

Leather was produced in large quantities, much of it demanded by the army. Leather is a versatile material – flexible, durable and easily worked. Hides and skins, the by-product of butchery, were easily obtainable, as were those from religious sites; the large number of goats sacrificed to Mercury at the Uley temple site probably provided a wealth of material for local butcheries. After the conquest the Romans may have found some difficulty in procuring leather as the Celts had cured skins by smoking and oiling rather than tanning, which the Romans did to a high degree. Evidence from forts reveals a careful reuse of leather; boots at Vindolanda had often been resoled and dumped leather at York indicated that tents had been patched and repaired several times.

Goods were acquired from traders. At Vindolanda Octavius provided 170 hides – possibly from Catterick, a collecting point for hides and skins – which had been tanned in civilian tanneries. This might have been part of a regular military contract, which Octavius knew provided a ready market. Some soldiers in the army would specialize in making standardized equipment such as tents, shields and body armour. Shoemakers supplied units with a variety of footwear; amongst a list of men who were fit at Vindolanda were twelve shoemakers. Some pieces of leather found had an official stamp on them – an eagle was found on footwear in London and Vindolanda. Army shoemakers might pass on their knowledge of the trade to civilians or set up their own establishment on their retirement. Fellow soldiers would always seek a good shoemaker and sons of army shoemakers could learn their father's trade, which would give them superior status if they joined the army. As shoes were a fashionable item and one which could indicate a person's status in society, shoemakers could be in great demand in towns and make a good living. On rural sites someone in the settlement or on a farm would make shoes or they would be bought from travelling peddlers.

Sheep rearing had been a major occupation in pre-Roman Britain and it continued its importance after the conquest. Textiles from Britain are mentioned twice in Diocletian's price edict of AD 301. A *birrus Britannicus*, seemingly a woollen hooded cloak, was sold at the high price of 6,000 denarii. For comparison, the price a tailor could charge for cutting and finishing a cloak of the highest quality was 60 denarii. A second text of the edict, found at Tolmeita (ancient Ptolemais) in Cyrenaica, mentioned British *tapete* or woollen rugs costing 5,000 denarii for the first quality and 4,000 denarii for the second quality. These were probably used under horse saddles or as an item to be thrown over furniture. These prices indicate that textile industries in Britain could produce high-quality garments although pieces of wool found at Vindolanda, dated to about AD 100, do not seem to have been finely made. This wool may have come from the feral variety of sheep resembling the modern Soay sheep found on St Kilda, which has a brown fleece, but later selective breeding led to an improvement in quality and to whiter fleeces.

Shears for sheering sheep and cropping cloth have been found on many sites together with combs, a vital tool needed to untangle the fibres and ensure they were parallel with each other. A wall painting at Pompeii shows three men sitting beside upright posts with the combs set vertically on the top and pulling the wool through the combs. When the wool had been combed, it was ready for spinning although wool can be spun directly from the fleece. Spinning was woman's work. They were expected to do it or to supervise their slaves. A tombstone at Chester to Marcus Aurelius Nepos and his wife shows her carrying a distaff and weaving comb to indicate her duty. Once the wool was spun, it could be woven on looms. Baked clay loomweights, indicating a warp weighted look, were common. If wool was not spun on an estate or in a household – and numerous spinning bone and pottery whorls found on sites shows that this was a household occupation – the fleeces would be sent to market. Fleeces were valuable. A curse tablet at Uley begs Mercury to curse a thief who stole a fleece.

Undyed wool is a yellowish white to brown colour and many garments would have been made from washed undyed wool. In Roman times wool was dyed in the fleece using materials found in Britain or imported. A mordant of alum or salts of iron was needed to make the dye take. Madder roots produced red, woad a blue colour and some lichens a purple colour. Weld was introduced into Britain for a yellow colour and deep purple, obtained from a Mediterranean whelk, would be pricey and exotic. Green was obtained by over-dyeing yellow cloth. Textile fragments include plain weave, herringbone and diamond twills and a half basket weave.

Flax seeds have been found on a number of sites but little is known about its production. The plant needs tanks for retting the fibres and these have been tentatively identified at settlements at Standlake (Oxfordshire) and Lower Caldecote (Cambridgeshire).

There was some imported silk. Some was found in a grave at Butt Road, Colchester. Fragments of damask silk were found in London and in a child's grave at Holborough. Spun gold thread has been found in graves at Lexden, London and Poundbury; cotton was very rare: a piece came from a well at Chew Stoke (Somerset).

The Romans demanded clean cloth, free from grease and neatly trimmed. Finishing and laundering was done by fullers treading cloth in tanks of water and urine or fuller's earth. It might have been bleached with sulphur or by the sun. The army would have required large quantities of wool for their garments.

Each soldier might have received a tunic, cloak and blanket either yearly or every two years. When the army was at its greatest strength this could be as many as 45,000 garments and probably this was the biggest market for cloth merchants, as many civilians would recycle or patch their clothes. Supplying the army in wool, clothes and other products was probably a task for over half the households in Britain.

15

SOCIETY: LIFE AND DEATH

It would be impossible to provide an accurate description of life in Roman Britain during a period which lasted over 400 years. Over that time, the lives of the inhabitants changed constantly as they raised their status or fell into decline and as fashions and lifestyles altered. People came into Britain from all parts of the empire, bringing with them their tastes, ideas and fashions. Britain could not be immune from these changes, as has been the case in our lifetime. Teeth and bone evidence from towns such as Silchester has indicated that at least a quarter of the population of Roman towns came from other areas – Scandinavia, North Africa and central Europe. The Roman Empire allowed complete freedom for those within its boundaries to settle where they wished and it is clear that many people – especially traders – took advantage of this. Britain was also a land of contrasts. People in one class of society had a lifestyle far removed from that of another. The wife of a legate accompanying her husband to this distant province had little in common with the woman who shared a hut with a man on a bleak northern hillside, with a woman who helped her man in a shop and certainly not with a slave. She might have made a personal slave a confident but that slave was never entirely sure of her mistress's loyalty.

All one can do is to attempt to describe what life may have been like for some families who lived in houses and villas in Roman Britain. When the Romans occupied Britain they brought with them a very different lifestyle to what had previously been lived by the Celtic Britons. Rome, as a conquering nation, deliberately imposed its laws, financial decrees and administration on the defeated enemy, expecting them to conform. It might also assume that many of its customs would be adopted, especially if they were superior or more convenient. The *coloniae* and the *civitas* capitals would be expected to provide examples of the benefits of Roman civilization.

After the conquest Britain was expected to conform to Latin, the official written language of the empire: the language of the army and administrators. Celtic civilization had encouraged learning by oral means. Caesar said that the Druids taught their students for twenty years and that oral education encouraged the mind. People who rely on oral tradition have a facility for retaining knowledge even if it is in a mechanical form. This could make them quick to learn and progress was achieved soon after the conquest, starting with the elite. Tacitus reported that Agricola trained chieftains' sons in a liberal education, which might mean they were inducted into classical literature through the medium of Latin. Possibly trained teachers such as Demetrius of Tarsus, who is known to have been in Britain in the first century AD, found ready employment, although Demetrius was more concerned with his official duties.

It was vital to learn Latin to progress and trade in society. Traders and merchants would have needed to pick up a smattering of Latin fairly quickly although those coming from Gaul would still convey their meaning in the Celtic language. How far Latin was well spoken and written was a different matter and one not easily solved. Auxiliaries would have had their own language while responding to official commands in Latin. In some areas of Britain Celtic dialects would have remained a first language and probably most areas might speak a kind of patois while using a form of Latin when dealing with officials. Gildas in the sixth century AD spoke of Latin as 'our language' but Latin was usually the language of the religious orders.

Writing tablets were common. Messages were written on wax with the pointed end of a stylus, which often penetrated the wax to leave any writing on the wood, much of it being in Latin cursive script. A blunt end to the stylus acted as an eraser on the wax. Most of the tablets have been found at Vindolanda, obviously written by the military, but others found in London and elsewhere are connected with administration and trade. Graffiti written on walls, scratched on pottery and produced elsewhere indicated that people wrote messages that they expected others to understand, and a number of writing exercises have been found. The lead curse tablets at Bath may have been the work of professional scribes. Professional sculptors inscribed tombstones and could achieve high quality of work on monumental inscriptions. Not all sculptors were accurate in their spelling, especially ones working along Hadrian's Wall. A few mosaics and wall paintings have Latin inscriptions on them, mostly implying some form of good luck. That at Lullingstone is more erudite, having a quotation from the *Aeneid*. The implication might be that villa owners wished to show that at least they had some understanding of a classical education and an appreciation of the Latin language.

In addition to a new language people had to get to grips with a new system of weights and measures and coinage. Coinage had been used in pre-Roman Britain, although some areas had used metal bars and people also relied on barter. Bartering would continue but the coinage and weights in use throughout the empire would now become common: the Roman pound (*libra*) of 327.45 grams (11.5 oz) and the ounce (*uncial*) of 27.288 grams (0.96 oz). In addition, balances and steelyards would be in used. The balance had two scale pans dangling by chains from opposite ends of a rod. Goods were put into one pan and lead, bronze or stone weights into the other. Correct weight meant that the two should balance. The other system was the steelyard where goods to be weighed were placed in one pan or attached by a hook linked by chains to one horizontal arm. A weight was moved along this arm until it balanced the other arm. The weight of the goods was measured by marks on the horizontal arm. People in Britain would expect to get used to this new system.

The population of Roman Britain is difficult to estimate. Collingwood in 1936 suggested 'half a million and at most a million'. Frere in 1974 raised this to a population of about 3 million at the end of the second century AD. Salway in 1993 postulated 4–6 million, probably too high, while Fulford in 1984 lowered it to 2.8 million. Millett in 1990 made a serious attempt to calculate a reasonable figure, suggesting 3.6 million at the beginning of the fourth century. He calculated that the military and their families and dependants would have been about 125,000 and the urban population about 240,000.

The urban population would possibly be the easiest to calculate given a rough estimate of the size of a town and allowing about 150 people per hectare, which would be a typical number applying to a medieval town. In theory Cirencester's 170 hectares (264 acres) could have had a population of 16,000, assuming that all sites in the town were developed. This was unlikely so the population might have been a half or a third of this. Tacitus had given the number of people killed in the sacking of the towns of London, Verulamium and Colchester as 70,000. The London amphitheatre has been estimated to hold between 7,000 to 11,000 people, which could mean that London had a population of between 15,000 and 20,000. Frere suggested that as the three aforementioned towns were the largest in the province they may have supported a population of 20,000 each, with the proviso that London's might have been higher. The smaller *civitas* capitals could support between 5,000 and 3,000, and smaller towns even fewer.

Roman Britain was essentially rural so the country population would have been much higher and Millett estimated this could be about 3.3 million. Collingwood suggested that there might have been about fifty inhabitants living and working in a villa but, given the number of people required to work the land, this figure might be higher. The nuclear family is usually estimated as four to five people (two adults and two to three children) but, given that Celtic families often formed a kinship group that could have been carried over to Roman Britain, and allowing for the number of workers and slaves on an estate, the figure for the larger villas would be much higher. This must certainly have been the case with the large fourth-century villas. These figures also do not take into account slaves working on imperial estates, mines and quarries, and inhabitants of isolated settlements in the northern and western areas.

In the Roman Empire status in society mattered not only according to wealth but also according to whether a person was free, a freedman or a slave. Only free men could achieve Roman citizenship. Some people in Britain, tribal leaders for example, would have been given this. Others could obtain it through military service. Eventually, in AD 212, citizenship was granted to all free adults. The term 'free' might not apply to most women who for all their lives remained under the control of a father, brother, husband or nearest male relative. A woman could not vote or take any public office. Celtic women in Britain, however, previously had considerable freedom. Two, at least, were tribal leaders and some compromise might have to have been made. A lead curse tablet at Bath gives the names of families, one of which is *Veloriga et famili(am) (s)uam*, a definite reference to this woman being the head of a family and of equal status with the other names mentioned.

In Celtic Britain, polygamy had been practised: Caesar remarked that 'wives were shared in common between groups of ten to twelve men, especially between brothers, and fathers and sons'. The offspring of the women were counted as the children of the man with whom the woman first cohabited. Reliefs on tombstones in Britain give the impression that the family unit was a man, wife (or partner) and one or two children, as was the practice in Rome, although there was nothing to prevent a man having a concubine or a lover. Under Roman law children could be betrothed at any age although it was usual for girls not to be married before the age of twelve. Cemetery evidence suggests that not only did most women gave birth in their twenties but many died in their late twenties, probably from the effects of childbirth.

Children are under-represented in all cemeteries. Infanticide was not a crime in Roman law, as children were not considered to be real persons until they could walk and talk so exposure or killing was one way of getting rid of unwanted births. Females, in particular, were often unwanted by poorer people because of having to pay a dowry. Nevertheless native British families may have kept all their children. Dio Cassius commented that the Scottish tribes reared all their children.

Marriage was a civil contract in Rome, merely a matter of exchanging vows, and divorce could be equally easy. If a wife was adulterous the man was automatically expected to divorce her. Cartimandua is said to have divorced her husband Venutius but this might have been the Roman interpretation of his being sent away from her immediate circle. Celtic society seems to have given women a higher status than Roman society.

A woman could make a will and had to be certain that her husband had made a will as she could not get the property if he died intestate. This did not stop the state claiming a property, as happened in the case of Prasutagus's two daughters, although a daughter if an heiress could have a claim to a share of the estate in intestacy. A tombstone at Chester to Titinius Felix, a *beneficiarius* of the legate of Legion XX, was set up by his wife and heiress (*coniux et heres*) Julia Similina; the fact that this is the wife of a serving soldier suggests a third-century date. Women could better themselves as happened in the case of a former slave girl Regina from the Celtic Catuvellaunian tribe who married a merchant, Barates from Palmyra. When she died at South Shields, aged only thirty, he erected a handsome tombstone to her with words in Palmyrene which restrainedly express his grief: 'Regina, the freedwoman of Barates, alas.'

Slavery was an economic fact of Roman life, without which the state could not have functioned. The system also absorbed the huge number of captives acquired once the Romans expanded their territory. Enemies defeated in battle were routinely reduced to slavery and this was one of the principal mechanisms by which the Romans acquired slaves. When Carthage was destroyed in the third century BC, 55,000 people were enslaved. In 25 BC, 44,000 members of the Salassi, an Alpine tribe, were reduced to slavery. Britain was not spared. Tacitus put this feeling into the speech he gave to the Caledonian chieftain Calgacus before the Battle of Mons Graupius when he warned his followers about the perils of being enslaved: 'Our goods and chattels go for tribute, our lands and harvests are requisitioned for grain . . . Slaves born to slavery are sold once and for all.' Calgacus may have forgotten that the Britons themselves had slaves and, according to Strabo, they were part of the export trade.

Celtic tribes continually fought to protect or extend their territories and often for the sheer pleasure of fighting. Strabo had declared that the whole race 'is war-mad, high-spirited and quick to battle'. It was not surprising that defeated enemies lost their right to freedom. Iron Age slave chains have been found in a hoard of metalwork from Llyn Cerrig Bach, Anglesey and at Lord's Bridge (Cambridgeshire). Roman slave chains were found at Caister-by-Norwich. Slaves could also be confined by thick ropes as indicated by two small bronze figurines from London depicting seated slaves with rope tied round their necks and binding their hands and their feet. A bronze *balsamarium* found at Aldborough (North Yorkshire) summarized the condition of all slaves as he sits, weary and pathetic, waiting for his master.

The number of slaves owned by families varied: a small household might have up to ten; Pliny the younger provided in his will for a hundred slaves. Cato suggested at least twenty-four slaves for a farm; Columella lists duties for thirty-seven and any large rural estate might have twice that number. Those who worked on the land would need to be prepared for hard work. Columella treated slaves as part of the chattels of a farm regulating age, strength and ability to work: 'See that they have useful clothing against wind, cold and rain, all of which can be warded off with long-sleeved garments of patchwork or hooded cloaks.' The small figurine of a ploughman from Piercebridge wearing this form of cloak might be considered such a slave. Varro considered them equally dispassionately. They should be neither cowed nor high-spirited. They might keep animals if this would make them more diligent to work. They must mate from amongst fellow slaves to bear children because this means that they become more attached to the place.

Slavery also perpetuated itself. Slaves born of slaves took their slave status from their mother and a legal structure was created to cover the problems posed by the offspring of slave women. According to law women should have been rewarded for bearing children and might have special privileges if they bore three children and even be granted their freedom if they bore more. Judging by the finds of infant burials at the

Hambledon villa, however, slaves might not have been allowed to keep unwanted offspring.

Imperial estates required slaves and many worked in the mines and quarries. They also served in official capacities as Anencletus, the slave of the Provincial Council, did in London. Military men had slaves as personal servants. Victor, a Moorish tribesman, seems to have had a close personal, possibly homosexual, relationship with Numerianus, a trooper in the First Ala of Asturians. He had been given his freedom, possibly through Numerianus's will and thus 'most devotedly conducted him to his tomb'. Slaves could be freed by manumission in a variety of ways – by payment, disinterested altruism, will or written agreement. Marcus Aufidius Lemnus was probably given his freedom by Aufidius Maximus, a centurion of Legion VI, in gratitude for his services, which included dedicating his tombstone at Bath.

The Romans' legalized system of slavery was brought into all their provinces and this ensured that anyone enslaved had no legal rights except those provided within the empire. A hint of these laws is given by several cases in Britain. The first is on a first-century AD wooden writing tablet found in London. A woman called Fortunata 'or by whatever her name is' had been brought from Gaul and sold for 600 denarii by Albicianus to a slave Vegetus, assistant to an imperial slave Montanus and a former assistant slave of Iucundus. The buyer was assured that the girl was in good health and was guaranteed not to run away. The transaction was done by a Roman legal document indicating the precision with which buying of slaves was conducted as the contract guaranteed the purchase of the girl to the buyer. A second writing tablet, also from London, was addressed to Epillicus from Rufus, who asked him to 'do everything carefully so as to extract the last coin from the girl' – implying that a slave girl could be turned into cash.

The third case comes from Scotland. Sextus Pomponius, a second-century jurist, quotes a case from Britain in the forty-ninth book of Justinian's *Digest of Roman Law*. Pirates captured a woman working in the salt mines somewhere in Britain and sold her to Marcus Cocceius Firmus, whose centurion service in Legion II Augusta is recorded on inscriptions at Auchendavy, Strathclyde. When the authorities found out, they insisted she should be returned to the mines, leaving the centurion to sue the imperial treasury for refund of her purchase price. She might have preferred the colder air of the Antonine Wall region to the toil of the mines, but neither her wishes, nor those of her new master, were of any importance. The law prevailed.

The duty of household slaves was to make life more comfortable for their owners and household conditions certainly became more comfortable in Roman Britain. Mosaic floors and painted walls contributed to this, as did the furnishings, although little survives in Britain of the actual objects. Evidence mainly comes from reliefs on tombstones and one of the most frequent chairs seems to have been a basket chair. A good example can be seen on Regina's tombstone at South Shields and Julia Velva's daughter sits on one on her tombstone at York. A full-sized one, carved in stone, was found in a tomb at Weiden near Cologne and the lady on the Murrell Hill (Cumbria) tombstone sits in a wooden one of similar shape. Small pipe-clay figurines imported from Gaul of nursing Mother Goddesses show them sitting in these chairs.

Remains of stools have been found in burials at Bartlow (Essex) and Holborough (Kent). A reconstruction of the latter shows that it opened with crossed iron legs and had a seat, probably made of leather, fixed to two bars, one for some inexplicable reason being split into two, which were supported on the main frame by two brackets. The stool was burnt with its owner, probably on the assumption that it was needed in the afterlife, and traces of vegetable matter and bronze threads indicate that a cushion gave added comfort. Soft furnishings included drapery, curtains, rugs and wall hangings. A wooden tablet found at Verulamium gave the cost of what appears to have been a set of complete curtains. These included 54.5 denarii for a scarlet one, 64.5 for a green one and over 55. 5 denarii for a yellow one.

Beds and couches had substantial mattresses and cushions judging by those depicted on the tombstones of Julia Velva at York and Victor at South Shields. Other tombstones show mattresses decorated with tassels and strips of materials. Not all would be pristine. Petronius mentioned one filled with bedbugs. Usually the couches had headrests and footrests with, occasionally, high backs as seen on Aelia Aeliana's tombstone at Chester. The couches would be made of carved wood decorated with bronze ornaments. They were provided with a wooden seat or a lattice made of leather, both covered with a cushion. Footstools seen on tombstones would have kept bare feet off mosaic floors. Stone benches were also provided. The Chesters bathhouse seems to have had one running the whole length of the changing room; others were provided in bathhouses at the forts of Mumrills on the Antonine Wall and Wallsend.

Three-legged tables were common: Julia Velva had one with straight legs; Aelia Aeliana's table had curved legs. In Britain there was a fashion for tables made of Kimmeridge shale judging by the several fine legs found mainly in Dorset. One from Colliton Park, Dorchester, had its top carved in the shape of a griffin's head and a foot in the shape of a lion's claw. Fragments of circular tabletops have been found at Caerwent and Silchester. Rectangular tables can be noted on tombstones and one top from a small table found at Castleford had four holes drilled in it to accommodate the legs. There would also have been side tables on which to display such splendid silverware as the Mildenhall Treasure.

One feature in the south of Britain was stone tabletops. These are usually found on both urban and villa sites dating from the late third and fourth centuries and are decorated on three sides, suggesting that the fourth was fixed to a wall. The decoration was of beading while one top at the Rockbourne (Hampshire) villa had floral patterns and sections of circles. There were probably also two-legged and four-legged stone tables like those that can still be seen at Pompeii.

Cupboards and chests were essential for storage. These were displayed on the inner sides of the sarcophagus of a woman found at Simpleveldt, the Netherlands. Remains of a fourth-century cupboard door found in a villa at Hayton (East Yorkshire) were decorated with geometrical designs inlaid with wood and bone. A small box by Regina's foot may have held jewellery or her work tools. Large chests would have held clothes, bed linen and draperies. Martial refers to sets of dining cloths being kept in a small chest. These could also be used to store food: Columella recommended storing apples in beech or lime chests like those for storing clothes. A house at Silchester had a cavity in the floor into which a strong box could be placed. Covered with a rug it could have provided a secure place for valuables. Evidence from elsewhere in the empire indicated that homes were provided with bookcases and desks.

Furniture would have been polished with cedar oil, beeswax and rose oil. Cato said that if lees of olive oil (*amurca*) were rubbed over furniture, this would prevent decay and give a high polish. He also recommended this for polishing copper vessels. Furniture might have been sparse in poorer houses. Juvenal said Codrus had a bed, cupboard, pitcher and chest. Martial's Vacerra took his bed, table, lantern and wooden bowl with him when he moved. Obviously wealthier people, especially those in the large villas, needed more furniture, and locks and keys indicate that they made their possessions secure. Key handles in the form of sleeping lions are frequently found.

Rooms were lit by single- or double-wick pottery lamps. A bronze one found in a barrow at Thornborough (Buckinghamshire) had a removable lid with a chain attached to it to prevent it getting lost. A twisted piece of cloth impregnated with oil formed a wick. An iron candlestick at Great Chesterford had three crudely made animal legs, but a more splendid one found in London had three well-carved paws. A tallow candle might be stuck on a spike set into a wall. Such methods of lighting might give off a strong smell and their flickering light could easily tire the eyes. Romano-British people worked mainly during daylight hours. Fragments of a lantern were found at Richborough and a near-complete, cylindrical, copper-alloy lantern, probably surrounded by horn, with a domed lid attached by two chains, and dating to the first to third centuries AD, has recently been found at Glemsford (Suffolk).

Heating was usually done with portable braziers and dark patches on floors indicate where these had stood. In some villas, especially in Hampshire and the Isle of Wight, there seems to be evidence for fireplaces. Usually the hearths were made of brick projecting into the room with a recessed fireplace in the walls. At the Star villa (Somerset) the fireplace burned coal; at Combley (Isle of Wight) charcoal was used. Charcoal fireplaces must have a hood, as the fumes can be dangerous. The Star villa had a masonry hood, while Newport (Isle of Wight) had a plaster and stucco one. Some probably had chimneys like houses in Pompeii.

The weather in Britain and the lack of heating meant that clothing needed to be warm. The most usual garment was the Gallic coat worn by men, women and children from the first to the fourth centuries AD and frequently depicted on tombstones. On the tombstone of his wife Flavia Augustina at York, the family of Gaius Aeresius, a veteran of Legion VI, wears thick Gallic coats, sleeves down to the wrists with a wide slit neckline or voluminous folds forming a stylish V-shape in front. A seated Mother Goddess on a relief at Bewcastle is depicted wearing an even thicker, heavier garment with voluminous sleeves. The coat was made from two rectangular pieces of cloth with two other pieces sewn on to form sleeves. Evidence from tomb-stones indicates that women wore the garment to the ground, men to their knees. In the cold climate of Britain, men wore breeches or trousers as they had done in the Iron Age, and these were adopted by legionaries; some of the auxiliaries already wore them. The ploughman from Piecebridge wears leggings. On a relief at York a smith wears a belted, sleeveless tunic, fastened over the left shoulder and leaving his right arm bare.

Magistrates, senators and any man with pretensions to office wore a toga varying from beige to brown in colour. The toga was a difficult garment to wear being a huge semi-circular piece of material 5.6 m (18.5 ft) long and 2.13 m (7 ft) across at its widest point. Magistrates had a broad purple stripe along the straight edge; equestrians had a narrow one; mourners wore one of black or a dark colour. Arranging this garment was so compli-cated that some men would have a slave following them to rear-range a toga if, or more likely when, it slipped. Augustus had given instructions that every man should wear a toga in the forum but its use was dying out and most men wore it only occasionally. Martial envied Linus, living in the country, who wore his only twice a month; Juvenal said that some men only wore it on their funeral bier.

There is no direct evidence for its use in Roman Britain although it has been suggested some male skeletons found in graves in Britain, which had one arm placed against the waist and the other left free, seem as if they had been buried in a toga. Tacitus remarks that in the second winter of his governorship (AD 79), Agricola's policy of Romanization was so successful that the British determined to learn Latin and 'our national dress came into favour and the toga was everywhere to be seen', flaunted, no doubt, by young bloods determined to be in the new fashion. In Britain, its adoption in the first century would outwardly indicate enthusiasm for the new regime as well as presenting to the world a visible sign of sharing power with the elite.

Heavy cloaks would also be essential in Britain. For the military the cloak (*sagus*) was an essential garment. A lighter cloak (*lacerna*), made in several different colours, was worn in the third century. The *byrrus* was a long cloak with a hood, which was often worn when travelling; Philus from Cirencester seems to be wearing one on his tombstone at Gloucester. Probably one or both sides were flung over the shoulders to leave the arms free. The quality of this cloak is evident from the prices quoted in Diocletian's price edict. Another hooded cloak was the *cucullus*, a Celtic item, made of wool impregnated with lanoline or of leather and worn by agricultural workers. This garment also had cult status in the godlings, the Genii Cucullati, and their representation at Housesteads shows them wearing cloaks falling almost to their feet. No fastenings are apparent; generally, cloaks were probably fastened by brooches or sewn up and pulled over the head to give greater warmth. Cloaks were such necessary garments that if they were stolen their luckless owners had tablets made vehemently cursing the person who stole them, as particularly seems to have been the case at Bath.

Beneath the outerwear men wore tunics and a loincloth or underpants; a bather at Bath had his shirt stolen. Cato recommended a clothing allowance every other year of a blanket and a tunic 1.7 m (3.5 ft) long, and, once these had been issued, 'take up the old one to have a patchwork made of it'. Women might also have worn underpants and wound a long piece of linen or wool (*strophium*) round their breasts to act as a brassiere. Ovid said they were useful hiding places for love letters. Leather briefs, such as those found in a well at Shadwell (London), were probably worn by athletes and entertainers, especially if they performed before men at dinner parties. Martial mentions women wearing briefs in a bathhouse and a mosaic at Piazza Armerina in Sicily shows women exercising wearing breast bands and briefs. During menstruation women could pad themselves with a loincloth tied with cords; safety pins were not invented until the nineteenth century so strips of cloth or leather were used as ties.

As in later times, men were conservative but women preferred to follow fashion. The population of Britain included women from other parts of the empire. One item worn in the German provinces was a loose tunic over a tight-fitting bodice with the front and back probably fastened with a brooch. Wives of officials might have worn a loose, long tunic over which was draped a shawl (*palla*) and scarf (*focale*) round the neck. By the end of the third century, the fashion was for loose fitting tunics decorated down the front and back. One figure painted on a wall at the Lullingstone villa seems to be wearing a single garment, a tunic with long, tight sleeves, belted so that there was an overfold at the waist. There are bands of embroidery on the cuffs and on a sash running horizontally down the tunic, presenting a somewhat eastern look. Representations on tombstones show that children wore tunics and small Gallic coats.

Wealthier people would have colourful clothing. A piece of cloth found at Falkirk was in what might be called a tartan of yellow and brown, and another from Vindolanda was dyed deep purple. During the summer the sun could be kept off with a parasol; a woman buried at York took hers with her in her grave and another is depicted on the Mumrills tombstone.

Socks are mentioned on a writing tablet at Vindolanda and something like a woollen sock, made from two pieces of diamond twill roughly tacked together, was excavated there. There is a representation of a sock on a bronze leg found at Piercebridge, but pieces of cloth bound round a foot would serve equally well. In hot provinces open sandals were often preferred because they let the air circulate round the foot and if feet got wet they would dry quickly. The soles were of several layers of leather stitched together. Sandals might be made for each customer by tracing round the sole of the foot. If so, one of the earliest cases of bunions has come to light, as a sandal from London has revealed that the owner's toes were out of joint; two other shoes had been made for someone with a clubbed foot.

As well as sandals there were several varieties of footwear. The *calceus* was an enclosed boot with a pointed toe, which could be decorated and worn by the status conscious. It was open down the front, had a tongue and was fastened by two straps attached to the side of the shoe, which were crossed over and wrapped several times around the ankle. Some had openwork uppers. One, found in a burial at Southfleet (Kent), was of gilded purple leather. A shoe found in London had expensive gold-leaf decoration with a cork sole. In the third century women's styles became narrower and men's wider so that they were almost triangular, but by the fourth century ankle boots seem to have become the main fashion.

The *caliga* was a military boot of hard leather with an insole, outer sole and upper cut into lattice work. It was held together by iron nails hammered into the sole until they were bent round and soles found at Vindolanda show that these nails were arranged in patterns. Later a new style of boot was adopted with fully enclosed sides made of a single piece of leather sewn up the front. It has been estimated that a legion would need at least 36,000 boots a year. The boots were so useful that civilians wore them, especially for heavy work. A form of wooden clog (*sculponae*) with a thick wooden sole held on by a broad wooden strap was probably worn in hot bathhouses. This was probably the *balnearia* mentioned on a Vindolanda writing tablet. They could also be worn as protection against damp. Cato said that a slave should be given a stout pair every other year. Men changed out of their heavier boots into a softer shoe (*solea*) in the house. Martial mentioned that Menogenes, after he had bathed, was already waiting for dinner in his house shoes.

Both men and women were particular about their appearance. Men preferred to be clean-shaven during the early years of the empire. This was done either by a personal slave or a professional barber with a sharp knife or rough razor (*novacula*), which scraped across a well-softened face. Cuts were numerous. Pliny recommended staunching the blood with a mask made from spiders' webs mixed with oil and vinegar. Some men had their hairs plucked out, probably contributing to the cries that Seneca deplored. In the second century the Emperor Hadrian wore a beard and this fashion was quickly followed, no doubt with some relief. His visit to Britain in AD 122 may have encouraged the fashion there.

Women followed fashion regarding hairstyles. Celtic women had worn their hair long, either loose or in a plait. According to Diodorus, Boudicca had a 'great mane of red hair falling to her knees'. Venus, depicted on a relief at High Rochester, has her hair drawn back in two thick bunches. In the first century women pulled back the hair and fastened it in a bun, sometimes with a curl at the front of the head. By the second century women were wearing their hair with ridges of curls, often piled high at the front. After the Empress Julia Domna's visit to Britain in the third century, hairstyles followed her fashion of crimped waves down each side and a large roll at the back, often tied with a ribbon. Real hair may have been interlaced with false hair and some women sold their hair or had it forcibly taken from them if they were slaves. Some women in Rome wore blonde wigs taken from German captive women. Christian women often covered their hair and others did the same to protect their modesty. Numerous bone, ivory and bronze pins have been found, indicating how hair could be kept in place. An actual head of hair from a grave at York has a centrepiece, twisted and drawn back from the forehead and then wrapped around the head.

Accessories included bags and purses of various shapes. A leather purse was found in a tomb at Holborough (Kent) and a linen one at Husthwaite (North Yorkshire). A lady on a tombstone at Chester seems to be holding a clutch bag. Some bags were made of cloth pulled tight by another piece of cloth. Gloves were rare; hands were tucked into sleeves to keep warm. Docimedes, however, on a tablet at Bath, curses the thief who has stolen his gloves.

Many items were buried with the dead as if the deceased required them in the afterlife. Jewellery in particular was necessary. Torques had been worn by the Celts in order to depict status and as a religious token. This seems to have continued into Roman Britain. Regina wears one on her tombstone at South Shields but as she was a member of the Catuvellaunian tribe she might have been proud of her Celtic descent. Some jewellery was used as amulets, especially roundels on pendants. A swastika brooch found at Brough-on-Humber probably was for good luck.

Brooches were used to fasten cloaks; some were chained together in pairs. Mostly they were made of bronze decorated with enamelled patterns or in an animal form – tortoise, hare and dolphin. About AD 408, a hoard of over 15,000 gold coins and items of jewellery was buried at Hoxne (Suffolk) for safety in a wooden box, within which were smaller padlocked boxes. The hoard included necklaces, finger rings, bracelets of gold, silver and jet and gilded silver spoons, ladles and four pepper pots, one in the form of a bust of a late empress. A solid-cast figure of a leaping tigress was deduced to be a handle from a silver amphora. The hoard may have been buried during the upheavals of the early fifth century; the unfortunate owner never returned to retrieve it. Jewellery was brought into Britain from elsewhere either by traders or as part of the owner's personal collection. Two magnificent gold necklace torques found at Winchester, made in the Mediterranean region, may have been presented as a special gift, while a gold pendant in the form of the head of an emperor, possibly Tiberius, with a loop at the top, recently found at Alton (Hampshire), was made in Alexandria and probably brought into Britain by the wife of an administrator.

Earrings were always made for pierced ears, often with pendants of gold, glass or precious stones. Rings and bracelets were common. Women would wear numerous bracelets – gold, silver, bronze, jet and shale – and several finger rings. Many of the rings were set with precious stones or intaglios. Men might prefer Mars or Victory to use as a seal; women could select Venus or Cupid. A ring found near Bedford, inscribed *Eusebia Vita* (life to Eusebia), may be a love token.

Other items found in graves were scent and perfume bottles. Analysis of the contents of a bottle in a cemetery in the Hunsruck region in Germany revealed a mixture of animal fat, sandalwood and lavender, possibly a form of beauty cream. A wooden box found in London contained a mixture of tin oxide, cow fat and starch, probably from boiled roots and grain. This would form a stiff paste to be used as a foundation cream. Ovid recommended a facepack of honey, egg and oatmeal but also said bluntly that spots should be covered with patches. Some aids would have been lethal – white lead for cheeks, powdered antimony for eyebrows and red ochre for lips. Juvenal's suggestion for putting soot on the eyebrows was not practical for a rainy day in Britain.

Sets of toilet articles or *chatelaînes* consisting of polished metal ear-picks, scoops, scrapers and twisters have been found. Men and women would have regarded tweezers as necessary to remove unwanted hair. Polished bronze Iron Age mirrors as found at Desborough and Birdlip were polished at the front and decorated on the back with intricate incisions. These could be held by slaves so that their mistresses could admire themselves, blurred though the image may have been. Glass mirrors were found at York. The central figure on a mosaic from the Rudston (North Yorkshire) villa is so overcome with her image that she drops the mirror. A lady on a tombstone at Chester, holding a comb in one hand and a mirror in the other, is accompanied by her maid carrying a tray on which are other artefacts. They enact in death a scene that had often been repeated in life.

Life was followed by inevitable death. After death the body would be washed, prepared, clothed in garments suitable to status and laid out ready for mourners to pay their respects. The body would then be carried to the cemetery for the last rites. The law of the Twelve Tables was enacted throughout the empire to ensure that burials could not take place within town walls so that the dead did not pollute, physically and spiritually, the material world. Cemeteries were laid out along roads leading to a town; at Gloucester, cemeteries have been found alongside roads leading to the south and east gates, to ensure it would be easier to carry out rituals to the dead after burial. At Silchester evidence for cemeteries and mausolea extended well beyond the area of the walls, which were built about AD 200. The position of the dead after death seems to have been due to status consciousness. At the Trentholme Drive Cemetery, York, the poorer classes had fewer coffins and grave goods while burials further away were in stone coffins, wealthier burials being given a covering of gypsum either to preserve bodies for the afterlife or to prevent grave-robbing.

During the first century cremation was usual, but gradually during the second century AD inhumation became common. This is exemplified at Dorchester-on-Thames where cremations were practised until about AD 180, then cremation and inhumation together until AD 260, then inhumation alone. At the London Road cemetery, Gloucester, inhumation became the dominant burial rite during the second century. There were areas where cremation continued, as at the fourth-century cemetery at Lankhills, Winchester.

Cremation rites took two forms. A body might be burned at the place of burial (*bustum*) with a pit dug below the pyre to receive the remains. Alternatively, bodies could be burned at a communal location (*ustrinum*) with the ashes retrieved to be placed in a pottery or glass vessel before being buried in a grave. An *ustrinum* was found at the London Road cemetery, Gloucester; another was deduced at the Trentholme Drive cemetery, York. A considerable quantity of fuel would be needed to cremate the body. The colour of the bones noted at cremation sites indicates that a temperature of 600–700°C would be successful. Goods and animals might be cremated with the dead person; at Gloucester, complete pig carcasses had been consumed. The preference for pig is a reference to Celtic burial rites when joints of pork were buried with warriors. Alternatively, these animals may have been slaughtered as part of a funerary ritual.

Superstition played a part in burial. Some individuals had a coin to pay Charon to carry them across the river Styx to the afterlife. Bodies in graves should have been placed in a supine position; some were placed in a prone position or special precautions were taken to prevent the dead from returning. They could be covered with stones or beheaded with the head placed by the feet or the legs. Decapitation, however, was usually the lot of criminals, which may have been the fate of eleven bodies buried at Dunstable that had cuts at the neck. One man at Southwark had his legs bound and his ankles pierced through with a stake to make sure he did not walk. Cemeteries were also surrounded by high walls to keep the dead within their own precinct.

Goods buried in inhumations include miniature objects such as a shovel and tongs at Littleton (Cambridgeshire), which represented the actual objects. Charcoal placed in the grave is a symbol of change; lamps provided light for the dead and made them feel at home. At York one person insisted on having an elaborate candelabrum. Jewellery was common, as were perfume bottles whose contents may have been used to anoint the body. Melon beads were probably regarded as amulets. One individual in a grave at Winchester had a bag containing eight beads, a finger ring and a banded flint. These might have been *crepundia* (playthings), a feature of the burial of young girls and unmarried women. A magnificent glass dish found in a cemetery at Aldgate (London) was made using the millefiori technique in which coloured glass rods are arranged in bundles so that the cross-section forms a pattern. This had possibly been made in Egypt and was the proud possession of a man whose cremated remains were found beside it, together with other ceramic and glass vessels, two of which seem to have contained perfume. Children seemingly had their toys; a boy at York had his bronze pet mouse. But children who had died before adulthood would not be allowed to go to the afterlife unless they had achieved maturity. They would linger at the gates of Hades, so familiar objects, amulets and animals would help them on their journey. The bear, a nurturing animal, is often found in graves as a companion as happened in graves at York and Malton.

At Winchester, on a shale trencher placed to one side of a body were eating implements with half a pig's skull, a leg of pork and a drinking vessel: refreshment for the last journey. Often footwear accompanied the body, clearly indicating these were items deemed necessary for the journey to the afterlife. The dead were also provided with entertainment. At least twenty-six sets of gaming counters, many with boards, have been found either in graves or on cremation pyres, usually accompanying young people. Several have been found in graves of elite members of native society. A young man, buried at Pins Knoll (Dorset), lay in the crouched Durotrigian tradition with twenty counters, placed in a bag in the crook of his left arm, and an iron stylus. The excavators suggested that he was making a statement of being 'Roman'.

After burial the dead still needed to be commemorated at least once a year if not more frequently. Often money was left in wills to ensure this happened. The animal remains in graves may be evidence of the funerary feast as represented on some tombstones. At Caerleon and Chichester, the dead were nourished by pouring liquid through the neck of an amphora or a pipe. For poorer people these also served as a grave marker. The funerary banquet appeared pictorially in the iconography of the tombstone. At Chester and York the deceased is shown resting on a funerary bed. Tombstones often had symbols: pine-cones symbolized mourning, felicity and life after death, dolphins and tritons symbolized the journey, poppies, sleep and death, rosettes and stars, prosperity and apotheosis in the next world, and lions, devouring death. On the tombstone at Chester of the unfortunate *optio* who was shipwrecked off the Cheshire coast the doors of death carved on the tomb are merely symbolic.

Tombstone inscriptions observed a fairly conventional pattern. *Dis manibus* (to the spirits of the departed world) was followed by the person's name and age. An official or soldier might include details of his rank, status and career. The names of the person who erected the stone – a freedman, the heir or a sorrowing wife – were sometimes added. Some are precisely detailed. Lucius Vitellius Tancinus, son of Mantaius, a tribesman of Caurium in Spain, trooper of the cavalry regiment of Vettones and Roman citizen, had twenty-six years of service before he died at Bath aged forty-six, possibly while he was trying to regain his health. Some reliefs are stereotyped. Tombstones at Cirencester and Gloucester depicting cavalrymen riding over a prostrate enemy have their origins in Gaul and the Rhineland.

There are hints of personal tragedies. Tadia Exuperata, 'the devoted daughter', set up a tombstone at Caerleon 'beside her father's tomb' to her mother who had died aged sixty-five and her brother who had 'died on the German expedition'. At York Felicius Simplex, a soldier of Legion VI, mourned Simplicia Florentina, 'a most innocent soul who lived ten months', while one husband who had lost 'his most dutiful wife' asked, 'may the earth lie lightly on you'. An unknown father at Lincoln bewailed the fact that his 'sweetest child' of nine years had died, comparing her to Prosepina, 'torn away no less suddenly than the partner of Dis'.

Some bodies or cremations were placed in columbaria (sections for storing human remains, usually in urns). One is suggested to have been placed at Lincoln where a small gabled tombstone recorded briefly, 'Marcus Laetilius Maximus from the first cohort, soldier.' The name of the legion, presumably Legion IX, would have been placed on the main structure.

Death could come at any age and, although doctors and surgeons were available, most were attached to the army and good health depended on good luck. A grave at Stanway (Essex), dated to AD 40–60, contained a full set of surgical instruments and other objects which suggested that the person was a surgeon or even that he may have been some kind of Druidic healer. Other instruments found include a uterine sound at Hockwold and scalpels, probes, knives and spatulas on other sites. There is also firm evidence for a trepanning operation being performed on a skull in York.

Trachoma, an infectious eye disease caused by a virus prevalent in unhygienic conditions and carried by flies, would be common. Bath and Lydney have provided some of the examples of oculist stamps, small four-sided tablets on which are carved retrograde inscriptions. These could be pressed on to a dried ointment cake or stick or on to small pottery vessels, holding eye salve. At Cirencester, Tiberius Claudius recommended frankincense salve for all eye trouble and at Bath T. Junianus made a somewhat rash claim that his quince salve for clearing the vision was for *any* medical defect. Balsam (balm) can be any form of ointment but it also means opobalsamum, an exuded resin from trees in the Near East. As well as for eyes, it was used for wounds, arthritis or even internally. Lycium, an ointment from Asia Minor, was highly regarded in the treatment of eye disease. A substance similar to this was found in a pot in a grave at Weston Turville and Michael Faraday's analysis of a substance on basketwork in one of the Bartlow Hills barrows suggested that it was myrrh or frankincense.

Skeletal evidence produces a sobering picture. Excavators at Cirencester suggested that at least 80 per cent of the adult population had osteoarthritis; at Dorchester-on-Thames, almost everyone over the age of thirty had it in the spine. Cases of leprosy were identified at Poundbury and Cirencester, and evidence of spinal tuberculosis and poliomylitis has been found at Cirencester and Vindolanda. A fourth-century body found in the grounds of the University of York had its spine and pelvis deformed in a way consistent with tuberculosis. Some skeletons at Cirencester and Poundbury had a high lead content, probably caused by food, especially fruit, being cooked in lead pans. Many skeletons revealed evidence of diet deficiencies or vigorous wear on the spinal column caused by humping heavy loads. Wear and tear was noted on the joints or bone fractures caused by accidents at work, a misdirected hammer blow or a slip in ploughing. Bones seemingly broken deliberately with a fist or stick were common. A man at Cirencester, possibly an ill-treated slave, sustained sixteen fractured ribs.

People suffered tooth problems; the grinding surfaces of some teeth at Chichester had almost gone. At Cirencester, Ilchester and York most teeth were in good condition with little evidence of dental caries. This was not due to oral hygiene but to a lack of sweet foods in the diet, or perhaps due to fluoride occurring in the water. A high fibre diet also protected teeth because it adheres less than highly refined foods. Bread baked with stone-ground flour creates a problem because it wears down teeth. There would have been difficulties in cleaning teeth, leading to much halitosis, and citizens of Roman Britain may have been an oral menace to their neighbours. Pliny recommended a mixture of charcoal and oyster shells for cleaning teeth and henbane to alleviate toothache.

The average age of death was low. Keith Hopkins has calculated that life expectancy in Rome was fewer than thirty years, but this figure equals those in any pre-Industrial Revolution society. It was certainly the case in Roman Britain. At Gloucester almost half the burials were of people aged below thirty-five; only seven individuals were over forty-five. The average age of death at Ilchester was forty for men, thirty-six for women. Many women probably died in childbirth or from puerperal fever. Few people at Cirencester had lived beyond their fifties; at Dorchester on Thames only 50 per cent of the men and 30 per cent of the women survived the age of forty. This seems better than at Lankhills cemetery, Winchester, where only fifty-two of two hundred and forty-eight skeletons examined indicated survival beyond the age of thirty-six. According to the ages on tombstones, if these were correctly recorded, there were people who survived into their sixties and seventies and even longer: Claudia Crysis at Lincoln lived ninety years; Julia Secundina died at Caerleon aged seventy-five while her husband Julius Verens, a veteran of Legion II Augusta, reached the remarkable age of a hundred. Overall, however, the overwhelming picture is of a life of hard work, which caused accidents and often led to quarrels. The excavators of the Trentholme Drive cemetery at York noted that, 'there is compelling evidence that the majority of the denizens of second, third and fourth century York could not expect to long survive their fortieth year'. Very few in fact survived that age so that elderly in Roman Britain is middle-age in the twenty-first century.

Survival in life was probably a matter of luck. At York in the 1870s, a mass grave was found that may have been used for poor people who could not have afforded personal burial. They may have been buried hastily for another reason. A mass grave, excavated carefully at Gloucester between 2004 and 2006, contained the remains at least ninety-one people who had been flung in haphazardly. The skeletons were examined in detail, revealing that all had died during the late second to early third centuries, which would be consistent with the so-called plague of Galen. This spread throughout the empire during AD 165–6 and there were later outbreaks. Dio Cassius reported that in AD 189 Rome had suffered at least 2,000 deaths a day. It was concluded that the Gloucester victims might have died as a result of this. This was not the only outbreak. Plague occurrences are suspected at Wroxeter and London and a *pestilentia* probably reached Britain in AD 443. The army, under constant medical care together with a regime of fitness and exercise, could have expectations of being free from illness, if not wounds in battle, but neither they nor the civilians who would have relied on folk remedies – plants from Silchester included Good King Henry, self-heal, hemlock, deadly nightshade and St John's wort – could escape the inevitable onslaught of an early death.

ROMAN EMPERORS

Augustus	27 BC–AD 14
Tiberius	14–37
Caligula	37–41
Claudius	41–54
Nero	54–68
Galba	68–9
Otho	69
Vitellius	69
Vespasian	69–79
Titus	79–81
Domitian	81–96
Nerva	96–8
Trajan	98–117
Hadrian	117–38
Antoninus Pius	138–61
Marcus Aurelius	161–80 ⎫ Joint reign
Lucius Verus	161–69 ⎭
Commodus	180–92

Pertinax	193 January–March
Didius Julius	193 March–June
Septimius Severus	193–211
Geta	211 February–December } Joint reign
Caracalla	211–17
Macrinus	217–18
Elagabalus	218–22
Alexander Severus	222–35
Maximius	235–8
Gordian I	238 March–April } Joint reign
Gordian II	238 March–April
Pupienus	238 April–July
Gordian III	238–44
Philip	244–9
Decius	249–51
Trebonianus	251–3
Aemilianus	253 August–October
Valerianus	253–60
Gallienus	260–8
Claudius II	268–70
Quintillius	270 August–September
Aurelian	270–75
Tacitus	275–6
Florianus	276 July–September
Probus	276–82
Carus	282–3 } Joint reign
Carinus	283–5
Numerian	283–4
Diocletian	284–305
Maximian	286–305 } Division
Constantius I	305–306 } of
Galerius	305–11 } the
Licinius	311–24 } empire
Constantine I	306–37

Constantine II	337–40	⎫ Civil war
Constans	337–50	⎭
Constantius II	337–61	
Julian	361–3	
Jovian	363–4	
Valentinian I	364–75	⎫ Joint reign
Valens	364–78	⎭
Gratian	375–83	⎫ Joint reign
Valentinian II	375–92	⎭

Eastern Empire

Theodosius I	379–95
Arcadius	395–408
Theodosius II	408–50
Marcian	450–57

Western Empire

Eugenius	392–5
Honorius	395–423
Valentinian III	423–55

SELECT BIBLIOGRAPHY

Books

J. P. Alcock, *Life in Roman Britain* (revised edition, Stroud: Tempus Publications, 2010).

J. P. Alcock, *Food in Roman Britain* (revised edition, Stroud: History Press, 2010).

L. Allason-Jones, *Women in Roman Britain* (London: British Museum Publications, 1989).

L. Allason-Jones, *Roman Jet in the Yorkshire Museum* (York: Yorkshire Museum, 1996).

L. Allason-Jones, *Daily Life in Roman Britain* (Oxford: Greenwood Publications, 2008).

C. J. Arnold, *Roman Britain to Saxon England: An Archaeological Study* (London: Croom Helm, 1984).

G. Askew, *The Coinage of Roman Britain* (London: Seaby, 1980).

B. Barber and D. Bowsher, *The Eastern Cemetery of Roman London: Excavations 1983–1990* (London: Museum of London Archaeological Service, Monograph 4, 2000).

N. Bateman, C. Cowan and R. Wroe-Brown, *London's Roman Amphitheatre, Guildhall Yard, City of London* (London: Museum of London Archaeological Service, Monograph 35, 2008).

G. de la Bédoyère, *Roman Villas and the Countryside* (London: Batsford, 1993).

G. de la Bédoyère, *The Buildings of Roman Britain* (Stroud: Tempus Publications, 2001).

P. T. Bidwell, *The Roman Fort of Vindolanda at Chesterholm, Northumberland* (London: Historic Buildings and Monuments Commission for England, 1985).

P. T. Bidwell, *Roman Exeter: Fortress and Town* (Exeter: University of Exeter Press, 1980).

P. T. Bidwell, *Roman Forts in Britain* (Stroud: Tempus Publications, 2007).

P. T. Bidwell, *Understanding Hadrian's Wall* (South Shields: Arbeia Society, 2008).

P. T. Bidwell and N. Hodgson, *The Roman Army in Northern England* (South Shields: Arbeia Society, 2009).

J. Bird, M. Hassall, M. and H. Sheldon, *Interpreting Roman London* (London: Batsford, 1996).

A. R. Birley, *The People of Roman Britain* (London: Batsford, 1979).

A. R. Birley, *Garrison Life at Vindolanda: A Band of Brothers* (Stroud: Tempus Publications, 2002).

A. R. Birley, *The Roman Government of Britain* (Oxford: Oxford University Press, 2005).

R. Birley, *Vindolanda: Fort and Civilian Settlement on Rome's Northern Frontier* (Carvoran: Vindolanda Trust, 2002).

R. Birley, *Vindolanda: Extraordinary Records of Daily Life on the Northern Frontier* (Greenland: Roman Army Museum Publications, 2005).

R. Birley, *Vindolanda: A Roman Frontier Fort on Hadrian's Wall* (Stroud: Amberley, 2009).

T. F. C. Blagg and A. C. King (eds), *Military and Civilian in Roman Britain: Cultural Relationships in a Frontier Province* (Oxford: British Archaeological Reports 136, 1984).

R. Bland and C. Johns, *The Hoxne Treasure* (London: British Museum, 1993).

G. C. Boon, *Isca: The Roman Legionary Fortress at Caerleon, Monmouthshire* (Cardiff: National Museum of Wales, 1972).

G. C. Boon, *Silchester: The Roman Town of Calleva* (Newton Abbot: David and Charles, 1974).

A. K. Bowman, *Life and Letters on the Roman Frontier: Vindolanda and its People* (revised edition, London: British Museum Press, 2003).

A. K. Bowman and J. D. Thomas, *The Vindolanda Writing Tablets (Tabulae Vindolandenses II)* (London: British Museum Press, 1994).

A. K. Bowman and J. D. Thomas, *The Vindolanda Writing Tablets (Tabulae Vindolandenses III)* (London: British Museum Press, 1994).

K. R. Bradley, *Discovering the Roman Family* (Oxford: Oxford University Press, 1991).

K. R. Bradley, *Slavery and Society at Rome* (Cambridge: Cambridge University Press, 1994).

K. Branigan, *The Catuvellauni* (Gloucester, Alan Sutton, 1985).

K. Branigan (ed.), *The Archaeology of the Chilterns from the Ice Age to the Norman Conquest* (Sheffield: Chess Valley Archaeological and Historical Society, 1994).

K. Branigan and D. Miles (eds), *The Economies of the Romano-British Villas* (Sheffield: Department of Archaeology and Prehistory, University of Sheffield, 1988).

D. J. Breeze, *The Northern Frontiers of Roman Britain* (London: Batsford, 1982).

D. J. Breeze, *The Antonine Wall* (Edinburgh: John Donald, 2006).

D. J. Breeze, *J. Collingwood Bruce's Handbook to the Roman Wall* (14th edition, Newcastle: Society of Antiquities of Newcastle-upon-Tyne, 2006).

D. J. Breeze, *Roman Frontiers in Britain* (London: Bristol Classical Press, Duckworth, 2007).

D. J. Breeze, *Edge of Empire: Rome's Scottish Frontier* (Edinburgh: Birlinn, 2008).

D. J. Breeze and B. Dobson, *Hadrian's Wall* (4th edition, Harmondsworth: Penguin, 2000).

K. W. de Brisay and K. A. Evans (eds), *Salt: The Study of an Ancient Industry* (Colchester: Colchester Archaeological Group, 1975).

A. C. C. Brodribb, A. R. Hands and D. R. Walker, *Excavations at Shakenoak Farm, near Wilcote, Oxfordshire* (Oxford: Privately Printed, 1971).

B. Burnham and J. Wacher, *The Small Towns of Roman Britain* (London: Batsford, 1990).

B. Burnham and H. Burnham, *Dolaucothi-Pumsaint. Survey and Excavation at a Roman Mining Complex 1987–1999* (Oxford: Oxbow Books, 2004).

F. F. Cartwright and M. D. Biddiss, *Disease and History* (Stroud: Alan Sutton, 2004).

P. J. Casey (ed.), *The End of Roman Britain: Papers Arising from a Conference, Durham 1978* (Oxford: British Archaeological Reports 71, 1979).

P. J. Casey, *Carausius and Allectus: The British Usurpers* (London: Batsford, 1994).

P. J. Casey, *Roman Coinage in Britain* (3d edition, Princes Risborough: Shire Archaeology, 1994).

G. Clarke, *The Roman Cemetery at Lankhills* (Oxford: Clarendon Press, 1987).

M. Clauss, *The Roman Cult of Mithras*, translated by R. Gordon (Edinburgh: Edinburgh University Press, 2000).

H. Cleere and D. Crossley, *The Iron Age of the Weald* (Leicester: Leicester University Press, 1985).

R. G. Collingwood and J. N. L. Myers, *Roman Britain and the English Settlements* (Oxford: Clarendon Press, 1936).

R. G. Collingwood and R. P. Wright, *The Roman Inscriptions of Britain* (Oxford: Clarendon Press, 1965).

H. E. M. Cool, *Eating and Drinking in Roman Britain* (Cambridge: Cambridge University Press, 2006).

J. Creighton, *Britannia: The Creation of a Roman Province* (London: Routledge, 2006).

J. Crow, *Housesteads* (London: Batsford/English Heritage, 1995).

B. W. Cunliffe, *The Regni* (London: Duckworth, 1973).

B. W. Cunliffe, *Roman Bath Discovered* (London: Routledge and Kegan Paul, 1984).

B. W. Cunliffe and P. Davenport, *The Temple of Sulis Minerva at Bath: The Site, vol. 1* (Oxford: Oxford University Committee for Archaeology, Monograph 7, 1985).

B. W. Cunliffe and P. Davenport, *The Temple of Sulis Minerva at Bath: Finds from the Sacred Spring, vol. 2* (Oxford: Oxford University Committee for Archaeology, Monograph 16, 1988).

R. I. Curtis, *Garum and Salsamata: Production and Commerce in Materia Medica* (Leiden, Netherlands: Brill, 1991).

K. R. Dark, *Britain and the End of the Roman Empire* (Stroud: Tempus Publications, 2008).

M. J. Darling and D. Gurney, *Caister-on-Sea. Excavations by Charles Green 1951–55* (Dereham: East Anglian Report No. 60, 1993).

J. L. Davies, *Roman and Medieval Wales* (Stroud: Sutton Publishing, 2002).

R. W. Davies, 'The Daily Life of a Roman Soldier in the Principiate', in H. Temporini, *Aufsteig und Niedergang der Römishen Welt* 299–338 (Berlin and New York: de Gruyter, 1974).

R. W. Davies, *Service in the Roman Army*, edited by D. J. Breeze and V. M. Maxwell (Edinburgh: Edinburgh University Press, 1989).

A. Down, *Roman Chichester* (Chichester, Phillamore, 1988).

H. Eckardt and N. Crummy, *Styling the Body in Late iron Age and Roman Britain: A Contextual Approach to Toilet Instruments* (Mantagnac, France: Editions Monique Mergoil, 2008).

P. Ellis (ed.), *The Roman Baths and Macellum at Wroxeter* (London: English Heritage, 2000).

A. S. Esmonde Cleary, *The Ending of Roman Britain* (London: Barnes and Noble, 1989).

J. Fairclough, *Boudica to Raedwald: East Anglia's Relations with Rome* (Ipswich: Malthouse Press, 2010).

D. E. Farwell and T. I. Molleson, *Poundbury Volume II: The Cemeteries* (Dorchester: Dorset Natural History and Archaeological Society, 1993).

N. Faulkner, *The Decline and Fall of Roman Britain* (Stroud: Tempus Publications, 2000).

A. M. Fielding and A. P. Fielding (eds), *Salt: Proceedings of the International Conference on Traditional and Historic Salt Making* (Northwich: Lion Salt Works Trust, Research Report No. 2, 2005).

S. S. Frere, *Britannia* (3rd edition, London: Folio Society, 1987).

S. S. Frere and J. K. S. St Joseph, *Roman Britain from the Air* (Cambridge: Cambridge University Press, 1983).

R. Goodburn and P. Bartholomew, *Aspects of the Notitia Dignatatum* (Oxford: British Archaeological Reports 12, 1976).

K. Green, *The Archaeology of the Roman Economy* (London: Batsford, 1986).

R. Hanley, *Villages in Roman Britain* (Princes Risborough: Shire Publications, 2000).

W. S. Hanson, *Agricola and the Conquest of the North* (London: Barnes and Noble, 1987).

M. Henig, *Religion in Roman Britain* (London: Batsford, 1984).

M. Henig, *The Art of Roman Britain* (London: Batsford, 1995).

M. Henig and A. King (eds), *Pagan Gods and Shrines of the Roman Empire* (Oxford: Oxford University Committee for Archaeology, Monograph No. 8, Oxbow Books, 1986).

P. Hill, *The Construction of Hadrian's Wall* (Stroud: Tempus Publications, 2006).

R. Hingley, *Rural Settlement in Roman Britain* (London: Batsford, 1989).

R. Hingley and C. Unwin, *Boudica: Iron Age Warrior Queen* (London: Hambledon, 2005).

B. Hobson, *Latrinae et Foricae: Toilets in the Roman World* (London: Duckworth, 2009).

P. A. Holder, *The Roman Army in Britain* (London: Batsford, 1982).

H. Hurst (ed.), *The Coloniae of Roman Britain: New Studies and a Review* (Portsmouth, Rhode Island: *Journal of Roman Archaeology* Supplementary Series, 36, 1999).

M. E. Germany, *Excavations at Great Holt Farm, Boreham, Essex, 1992–94* (Chelmsford: East Anglian Archaeological Report, No. 105, Essex County Council, 2003).

A. Goldsworthy, *The Complete Roman Army* (London: Thames and Hudson, 2003).

G. Grainger, *The Roman Invasion of Britain* (Stroud: Tempus Publications 2005).

D. Ireland, *Roman Britain: A Sourcebook* (3rd edition, London: Routledge, 2008).

R. Jackson, *Doctors and Diseases in the Roman Empire* (London: British Museum Press, 1988).

R. P. J. Jackson and T. W. Potter, *Excavations at Stonea, Cambridgeshire 1980–85* (London: British Museum Press, 1991).

M. G. Jarrett, *Early Roman Campaigns in Wales* (Cardiff: National Museum of Wales, 1994).

W. F. Jashemski, *The Gardens of Pompeii, Herculaneum and the Villas Destroyed by Vesuvius* (New Rochelle, New York: Caratzas Bros, 1979).

C. Johns, *The Jewellery of Roman Britain: Celtic and Classical Traditions* (London: University College Press, 1996).

C. Johns and T. W. Potter, *Roman Britain* (London: British Museum Press, 2002).

A. P. Johnson, *Roman Forts of the 1st and 2nd centuries AD in Britain and the German Provinces* (London: A. and C. Black, 1983).

P. Johnson, *Romano-British Mosaics* (Princes Risborough: Shire Archaeology, 1982).

S. Johnson, *The Roman Forts of the Saxon Shore* (London: Elek, 1979).

S. Johnson, *Later Roman Britain* (London: Routledge and Kegan Paul, 1980).

D. E. Johnston (ed.), *The Saxon Shore* (London: Council for British Archaeology Research, Report 18, 1977).

B. Jones and D. Mattingly, *An Atlas of Roman Britain* (Oxford: Blackwell, 1990).

M. E. Jones, *The End of Roman Britain* (Ithaca, New York: Cornell University Press, 1996).

M. J. Jones, *Roman Lincoln* (Stroud: Tempus Publications, 2000).

R. F. J. Jones (ed.), *Roman Britain: Recent Trends* (Sheffield: Department of Archaeology, University of Sheffield, 1991).

R. S. L. Keegan, *Inhumation Rites in Late Roman Britain: The Treatment of the Engendered Body* (Oxford: British Archaeological Reports 333, J. and E. Hedges, 2002).

S. Laycock, *Britannia and the Failed State: Ethnic Conflict and the End of Roman Britain* (Stroud: Tempus Publications, 2008).

M. J. T. Lewis, *Temples in Roman Britain* (Cambridge: Cambridge University Press, 1965).

M. McCarthy, *Roman Carlisle and the Lands of the Solway* (Stroud: Tempus Publications, 2002).

A. McWhirr, *Roman Crafts and Industries* (Princes Risborough: Shire Archaeology, 1982).

A. McWhirr, L. Viner and C. Wells, *Romano-British Cemeteries at Cirencester* (Cirencester: Cirencester Excavation Committee, 1982).

M. Maltby, 'Urban Rural Variation in the Butchering of Cattle in Romano-British Hampshire', in D. Serjeantson and T. Waldron, *Diet and Crafts in Towns in Roman Britain* (Oxford: BAR British Series 199, 1983), 75–106.

M. Maltby, *Feeding a Roman Town: Environmental Evidence from Excavations in Winchester, 1972–1985* (Winchester: Winchester Museums and English Heritage, 2010).

W. H. Manning, *Catalogue of the Romano-British Iron Tools, Fittings and Weapons in the British Museum* (London: Trustees of the British Museum, 1985).

P. Marsdon, *The Roman Forum Site in London: Discoveries Before 1985* (London: HMSO, 1987).

S. Martin-Kicher, '*Mors immatora* in the Roman World: A Mirror of Society in Tradition', in J. Pearce, M. Millett and M. Struck (eds), *Burial, Society and Context in the Roman World* (Oxford: BAR British Series 219, Oxbow Books, 2000), 63–77.

D. J. P. Mason, *Roman Chester: City of the Eagles* (Stroud: Tempus Publications, 2001).

D. Mattingley, *An Imperial Possession: Britain in the Roman Empire, 54 BC–AD 409* (London: Allen Lane, 2006).

G. Maxwell, *A Battle Lost: Romans and Caledonians at Mons Graupius* (Edinburgh: Edinburgh University Press, 1990).

J. May, *Dragonby* (Oxford: Oxbow Books, 1996).

R. Merrifield, *London: City of the Romans* (Berkeley, California: University of California Press, 1987).

D. Miles, (ed.), *The Romano-British Countryside* (Oxford: British Archaeological Reports 103, 1982).

J. I. Miller, *The Spice Trade of the Roman Empire* (Oxford: Clarendon Press, 1969).

M. J. Millett, *The Romanisation of Roman Britain* (Cambridge: Cambridge University Press, 1990).

M. J. Millett, *Roman Britain* (London: Batsford/English Heritage, 1995).

G. Milne, *The Port of Roman London* (London: Batsford, 1993).

G. Milne, *Roman London* (London: Batsford/English Heritage, 1995).

D. Neal, *The Excavation of the Roman Villa in Gadebridge Park, Hemel Hempstead 1963–68* (London: Society of Antiquaries of London, 1974).

D. Neal, A. Wardle and J. Hunn, *Excavation of an Iron Age, Roman and Medieval Site at Gorhambury, St Albans* (London: English Heritage, 1990).

M. Newell and A. P. Fielding, *Brine in Britain: Recent Archaeological Work on the Roman Salt Industry in Cheshire* (Manchester: Council for British Archaeology North West, Lion Salt Works Trust and University of Manchester Archaeological Unit, *Archaeology North West* Vol. 7, 2005).

R. Niblett, *Verulamium: The Roman City of St Albans* (Stroud: Tempus Publications, 2001).

K. S. Painter, *The Mildenhall Treasure* (London: British Museum Press, 1977).

M. P. Parker, *The Archaeology of Death and Burial* (Stroud: Alan Sutton, 1999).

C. Partridge, *Skeleton Green: A Late Iron Age and Romano British Site* (London: Society for the Promotion of Roman Studies, 1981).

J. Pearce, M. Millett and M. Struck (eds), *Burial, Society and Context in the Roman World* (Oxford: BAR British Series 219, Oxbow Books, 2000).

A. Pearson, *The Roman Shore Forts: Coastal Defences of Southern Britain* (Stroud: Tempus Publications, 2002).

J. Peddie, *Conquest: The Roman Invasion of Britain* (Stroud: Sutton, 2005).

J. Percival, *The Roman Villa: An Historical Introduction* (London: Batsford, 1976).

D. Perring, *The Roman House in Britain* (London: Routledge, 2002).

D. Petts, *Christianity in Roman Britain* (Stroud: Tempus Publications, 2003).

R. Philpott, *Burial Practices in Roman Britain* (Oxford: British Archaeological Reports 219, 1991).

L. F. Pitts and J. K. St Joseph, *Inchtuthil: The Roman Legionary Fortress* (London: Britannia Monographs, No. 6., Society for the Promotion of Roman Studies, 1985).

C. Price and H. E. M. Cool, 'The Evidence for Glass Produced in Roman Britain', in D. Foy and G. Sennequrer (eds), *À Travers la Verre* (Rouen:, France: Museé Departmental des Antiquités, 1989).

E. Price, *Frocester, Volume I: The Site* (Stonehouse: Gloucester and District Archaeological Research Group, 2000).

A. Rainey, *Mosaics in Roman Britain* (Newton Abbott: David and Charles, 1973).

R. Reece, *The Coinage of Roman Britain* (Stroud: Tempus Publications, 2003).

A. L. F. Rivet, *Town and Country in Roman Britain* (London: Hutchinson, 1958).

A. L. F. Rivet and C. Smith, *The Place-Names of Roman Britain* (London: Batsford, 1979).

W. Rodwell (ed.), *Temples, Churches and Religion in Roman Britain* (Oxford: BAR British Series 77, 1980).

J. P. Roth, *The Logistics of the Roman Army at War, 264 BC–AD 235* (Leiden, Netherlands: Brill, 1999).

D. Rudling (ed.), *Ritual Landscapes of Roman South-East England* (Oxford: Heritage Marketing and Publications, Oxbow Books, 2008).

P. Salway, *The Oxford Illustrated History of Roman Britain* (3rd edition, Oxford: Oxford University Press, 1993).

E. Scott, *A Gazetteer of Roman Villas in Britain* (Leicester: Leicester University Press, 1993).

S. Scott, *Art and Society in Fourth-century Britain: Villa Mosaics in Context* (Oxford: Oxford University School of Archaeology, Monograph No. 53, Oxbow Books, 2000).

P. R. Sealey, *The Boudican Revolt against Rome* (Princes Risborough: Shire Publications, 2004).

D. Serjeantson and T. Waldron, *Diet and Crafts in Towns in Roman Britain* (Oxford: BAR British Series 199, 1983).

J. Shepherd, *The Temple of Mithras London* (London: English Heritage, 1998).

E. Shirley, *Building a Roman Legionary Fortress* (Stroud: Tempus Publications, 2001).

A. Simmonds, N. Márquez-Grant and L. Loe, *Life and Death in a Roman City: Excavation of a Roman Cemetery with a Mass Grave, 120–122 London Road, Gloucester* (Oxford: Oxford Archaeological Monograph No. 6, Oxford Archaeological Unit, 2008).

J. T. Smith, *Roman Villas: A Study in Social Structure* (London: Routledge, 1977).

J. T. Smith, 'Villas as a Key to Social Structure', in M. Todd (ed.), *Studies in the Romano-British Villa* (Leicester: Leicester University Press, 1978), 149–86.

S. Stallibrass and R. Thomas (eds), *Feeding the Roman Army: The Archaeology of Production and Supply in N. W. Europe* (Oxford: Oxbow Books, 2008).

A. Taylor, *Burial Practice in Early England* (Stroud: Tempus Publications, 2001).

J. Taylor, *An Atlas of Roman Rural Settlement in England* (York: Council for British Archaeology Research, Report 151, 2008).

M. Todd (ed.), *Studies in the Romano-British Villa* (Leicester: Leicester University Press, 1978).

M. Todd (ed.), *Research on Roman Britain* (London: Society for the Promotion of Roman Studies, 1989).

M. Todd, *Roman Britain* (Oxford: Blackwell, 1999).

M. Todd, *A Companion to Roman Britain* (Oxford: Blackwell, 2004).

M. Todd, *Roman Mining in Somerset: Excavations at Charterhouse on Mendip, 1993–1995* (Exeter: Mint Press, 2007).

J. M. C. Toynbee, *Art in Roman Britain* (London: Phaidon, 1962).

J. M. C. Toynbee, *Art in Britain under the Romans* (Oxford: Clarendon Press, 1964).

J. M. C. Toynbee, *Death and Burial in the Roman World* (London: Thames and Hudson, 1996).

J. R. Travis, *Coal in Roman Britain* (Oxford: British Archaeological Reports 468, J. and E. Hedges, 2008).

P. Tyres, *Roman Pottery in London* (London: Routledge, 1996).

J. Wacher, *The Towns of Roman Britain* (2nd edition, London: Batsford, 1995).

T. Waldron, *Counting the Dead: The Epidemiology of Skeletal Populations* (Chichester: Wiley, 1994).

G. R. Watson, *The Roman Soldier* (London: Thames and Hudson, 1969).

G. R. Webster, *The Roman Imperial Army of the 1st and 2nd centuries A.D.* (London: A. and C. Black, 1969).

G. R. Webster, *The Cornovii* (Phoenix Mill: Alan Sutton, 1975).

G. R. Webster, *The Roman Invasion of Britain* (London: Batsford, 1980).

G. R. Webster (ed.), *Fortress into City: The Consolidation of Roman Britain First Century AD* (London: Batsford, 1986).

G. R. Webster, *The Roman Legionary Fortress at Wroxeter* (London: English Heritage, 2002).

L. P. Wenham, *The Romano-British Cemetery at Trentholme Drive, York* (London: HMSO Ministry of Public Building and Works. Archaeological Reports, No. 5, 1968).

S. E. West, *West Stow, Suffolk: The Prehistoric and Roman Occupation* (Ipswich: East Anglian Archaeological Report No. 48, Suffolk County Planning Department, 1990).

R. White, *Britannia Prima: Britain's Last Roman Province* (Stroud: Tempus Publications, 2007).

R. White and P. Barker, *Wroxeter: Life and Death of a Roman City* (Stroud: Tempus Publications, 1990).

J. Wilkins, D. Harvey and M. Dobson, *Food in Antiquity* (Exeter: University of Exeter Press, 1995).

T. Wilmott, *Birdoswald Roman Fort* (Stroud: Tempus Publications, 2001).

T. Wilmott, *The Roman Amphitheatre in Britain* (Stroud: Tempus Publications, 2008).

T. Wilmott (ed.), *Hadrian's Wall: Archaeological Research by English Heritage (1976–2000)* (London: English Heritage, 2009).

P. Wilson and J. Price (eds), *Aspects of Industry in Roman Yorkshire and the North* (Oxford: Oxbow Books, 2002).

R. J. A. Wilson, *A Guide to the Roman Remains in Britain* (4th edition, London: Constable, 2002).

P. Witts, *Mosaics in Roman Britain* (Stroud: Tempus Publications, 2005).

A. Woodward and P. Leach, *The Uley Shrines: Excavation of a Ritual Complex on West Hill, Uley, Gloucestershire, 1977–9* (London: English Heritage, 1993).

P. J. Woodward, S. M. Davies and A. H. Graham, *Excavations at the Old Methodist Chapel and Greyhound Yard, Dorchester 1981–4* (Dorchester: Dorchester Natural History and Archaeological Society, Monograph Series No. 12, 1993).

G. Woolf, *Becoming Roman* (Cambridge: Cambridge University Press, 1998).

D. Zienkiewicz, *The Legionary Fortress Baths at Caerleon: II The Finds* (Cardiff: National Museum of Wales, 1986).

Articles

J. P. Alcock, 'Classical religious belief and burial practices in Roman Britain', *Archaeological Journal*, 137 (1980), 50–85.

R. G. Austen, 'Roman board-games', *Greece and Rome*, 4 (1934), 24–34, 76–82.

C. J. Bailey, 'An early Iron Age/Roman-British site at Pins Knoll, Litton Cheney: Final Report', *Proceedings of the Dorset Natural History and Archaeological Society*, 89 (1967), 147–59.

S. Barnard, 'The Matres of Roman Britain', *Archaeological Journal*, 142 (1985), 237–45.

A. M. Barratt, 'Saint Germanus and the British missions', *Britannia*, 40 (2009), 197–217.

N. Bateman and A. Locker, 'The sauce of the Thames', *The London Archaeologist*, 4: 8 (1982), 204–207.

S. Bates, 'Excavations at Quidney Farm, Saham Tovey, Norfolk', *Britannia*, 31 (2000), 201–37.

N. Beagrie, 'The Romano-British Pewter Industry', *Britannia*, 20 (1989), 169–91.

P. Beaumont, 'Water supply at Housesteads Roman Fort, Hadrian's Wall: the case for rainfall harvesting', *Britannia*, 39 (2008), 59–84.

D. G. Bird, 'The Claudian invasion campaign reconsidered', *Oxford Journal of Archaeology*, 19 1 (2000), 91–104.

E. W. Black, 'Romano-British burial customs and religious beliefs in Roman Britain in south west England', *Archaeological Journal*, 193 (1986), 201–39.

E. W. Black, 'How many rivers to cross?', *Britannia*, 29 (1998), 308–307.

I. Blair, R. Spain, D. Swift, T. Taylor and D. Goodburn, 'Wells and bucket-chains: unforeseen elements of water supply in early Roman London', *Britannia*, 37 (2006), 1–52.

G. C. Boon, 'Potters, oculists and eye troubles', *Britannia*, 14 (1983), 1–12.

A. G. Brown, and I. Meadows, 'Roman vineyards in Britain: finds from the Nene Valley and new research', *Antiquity*, 74 (2000), 491–92.

J. B. Calkin, 'Kimmeridge coal money', *Proceedings of the Dorset Archaeological and Natural History Society*, 75 (1955), 45–71.

S. A. Castle, 'Amphorae from Brockley Hill 1975', *Britannia*, 9 (1978), 383–92.

D. Charlesworth, 'The Hospital, Housesteads', *Archaeologia Aeliana*, 5 (1976), 17–30.

D. Charlesworth and J. H. Thornton, 'Leather found at Mediobogdum, the Roman fort of Hardknott', *Britannia*, 3 (1973), 141–52.

G. Clarke, 'The Roman villa at Woodchester', *Britannia*, 13 (1982), 197–228.

T. H. Corcoran, 'Roman fish sauces', *The Classical Journal*, 58 (1962), 204–210.

H. Cleere, 'The Roman iron industry of the Weald and its connexions with the *Classis Britannica*', *Archaeological Journal*, 131 (1974), 171–99.

A. T. Croom, 'Experiments in Roman military cooking methods', *The Arbeia Journal*, 6–7 (1997–8), 34–7.

N. Crummy, 'Bears and coins: the iconography of protection in Late Roman infant burials', *Britannia*, 41 (2010), 37–93.

P. Crummy, 'The Roman circus at Colchester', *Britannia*, 39 (2008), 15–31.

R. W. Davies, 'The Roman military diet', *Britannia*, 2 (1971), 122–42.

M. J. Dearne and K. Branigan, 'The use of coal in Roman Britain', *Antiquaries Journal*, 75 (1995), 71–105.

B. Dobson and J. C. Mann, 'The Roman army in Britain and Britons in the Roman army', *Britannia*, 4 (1973), 191–205.

A. Fox, and W. Ravenhall, 'The Roman fort at Nantstallon, Cornwall', *Britannia*, 3 (1972), 56–111.

J. Gerrard, 'The Drapers' Garden's hoard: a preliminary account', *Britannia*, 40 (2009), 163–83.

S. J. Greep, 'Lead sling-shot from Windridge Farm, St Albans and the use of the sling by the Roman army in Britain', *Britannia*, 18 (1987), 182–200.

J. Grieg, 'Garderobes, sewers, cesspits and latrines', *Current Archaeology*, 85 (1982), 63–84.

R. T. Günther, 'The oyster culture of the ancient Romans', *Journal of the Marine Biological Association*, 4 (1897), 360–65.

M. Isenberg, 'The sale of sacrificial meat', *Classical Philology*, 70 (1975), 271–3.

R. Jackson, 'Cosmetic sets from Late Iron Age and Roman Britain', *Britannia*, 16 (1985), 165–92.

R. Jackson, 'An ancient British medical kit from Stanway, Essex', *Lancet*, 350 (1997), 1471–3.

C. M. Johns, 'The Roman silver cups from Hockwold, Norfolk', *Archaeologia*, 108 (1986), 1–13.

C. Johns and R. Bland, 'The Hoxne Late Roman treasure', *Britannia*, 25 (1994), 165–73.

G. D. B. Jones, and P. R. Lewis, 'The Dolaucothi gold mines', *Bonner Jahrbucher*, 171 (1971), 188–300.

G. D. Keevil, 'A frying pan from Great Lea, Binfield, Berkshire', *Britannia*, 22 (1992), 231–3.

A. King, 'Animal remains from temples in Roman Britain', *Britannia*, 36 (2005), 329–69.

B. A. Knight, C. A. Dickson, J. H. Dickson and D. J. Breeze, 'Evidence concerning the Roman military diet at Bearsden, Scotland in the 2nd century AD', *Journal of Archaeological Science*, 10 (1997), 139–52.

J. Liversidge, D. J. Smith and I. Stead, 'Brantingham Roman villa: discoveries in 1962', *Britannia*, 4 (1973), 84–106.

R. McIver, R. I. Brooks and G. A. Reineccius, 'The flavours of fermented fish sauce', *Journal of Agriculture and Food Chemistry*, 30 (1982), 1017–20.

R. MacMullen, 'Market days in the Roman Empire', *Phoenix*, 24 (1970), 191–328.

J. Mann, 'The Housesteads latrine', *Archaeologia Aeliana*, 5: 17 (1989), 1–4.

I. Meadows, 'Wollaston: the Nene Valley, a British Moselle?', *Current Archaeology*, 150 (1996), 212–15.

V. Nutton, 'Roman oculists', *Epigraphica*, 34 (1972), 16–29.

A. J. Parker, 'Birds in Roman Britain', *Oxford Journal of Archaeology*, 7 (1988), 197–226.

S. Penney and D. C. Shotter, 'Further inscribed lead pans from Shavington, Cheshire', *Journal of the Cheshire Archaeological Society*, 76 (2002), 53–61.

B. Rawes, 'The Romano-British villa at Brockworth, Gloucestershire', *Britannia*, 12 (1981), 45–78.

I. A. Richmond and J. P. Gillam, 'The Temple of Mithras at Carrawburgh', *Archaeologica Aeliana*, 4: 29 (1951), 1–92.

S. E. Rigold, 'The Roman haven of Dover', *Archaeological Journal*, 126 (1969), 78–100.

A. Ross, 'The horned god of the Brigantes', *Archaeologia Aeliana*, 4: 39 (1961), 59–85.

D. Rutling, C. Butler and R. Wallace, 'Barcombe Roman villa', *British Archaeology* (March–April 2010), 22–7.

P. R. Sealey and P. A. Tyera, 'Olives from Roman Spain: a unique amphora found in British waters', *Antiquaries Journal*, 69: 1 (1989), 53–72.

E. A. M. Shirley, 'The building of the legionary fortress at Inchtuthil', *Britannia*, 27 (1996), 111–28.

G. R. Stephens, 'Aqueduct delivery and water consumption in Roman Britain', *Bulletin of the Institute of Archaeology, University of London*, 1 (1984–5), 21–22, 111–17.

G. R. Stephens, 'Civic aqueducts in Roman Britain', *Britannia*, 16 (1985), 197–208.

A. Stirland and T. Waldron, 'The earliest cases of tuberculosis in Britain', *Journal of Archaeological Science*, 17 (1990), 221–30.

V. G. Swan, 'Legio VI and its men: African legionaries in Britain', *Journal of Roman Pottery Studies*, 5: 11 (1992), 1–33.

D. J. A. Taylor, 'A note on the building of the legionary fort at Inchtuthil', *Britannia*, 30 (1999), 297–99.

E. A. Thompson, 'Britain, AD 404–410', *Britannia*, 8 (1977), 303–18.

R. C. Turner, M. Rhodes and J. P. Wild, 'The Roman body found on Grewelthorpe Moor in 1859: a reappraisal', *Britannia*, 22 (1991), 191–328.

R. S. O. Tomlin, 'The date of the "Barbarian Conspiracy"', *Britannia*, 5 (1974), 303–309.

R. S. O. Tomlin, 'The girl in question: a new text from Roman London', *Britannia*, 34 (2003), 41–51.

C. V. Walthew, 'The town house and the villa house in Roman Britain', *Britannia*, 1 (1970), 114–30.

J. P. Wild, 'Clothing in the north-west Provinces of the Roman Empire', *Bonner Jahrbucher*, 168 (1968), 166–240.

J. P. Wild, 'The textile industries of Roman Britain', *Britannia*, 33 (2002), 1–32.

D. Williams, 'Viticulture in Roman Britain', *Britannia*, 8 (1977), 114–30.

R. P. Wright, 'Official tile-stamps from London which cite the province of Britain', *Britannia*, 16 (1985), 193–6.

ACKNOWLEDGEMENTS

I am grateful as usual for help from the librarians of the Institute of Classical Studies/Joint Library Hellenic and Roman Societies, and to Helga Pihlakas and Stephen and Barbara Kern for checking the text. Mark Hassall gave valuable advice on the army chapter. I am indebted to David E. Johnston for permission to reproduce the map of the Saxon Shore forts. My editor Leo Hollis has showed patience and understanding in the delivery of this book.

The aerial photographs of Maiden Castle, Dorset, Richborough Roman fort and Housesteads Roman fort are reproduced by kind permission of the Cambridge University Collection of Aerial Photography. All other photographs are from my own collection.

APPENDIX
A GLOSSARY OF CLASSICAL WRITERS

Ammianus Marcellinus (c. AD 330–395). A Roman historian, who was a Greek native of Antioch, became an officer to the Roman general Ursicinus in AD 354. He joined the Emperor Julian's invasion of Persia in 363 and later visited Egypt and Greece. In the late AD 380s he wrote a history of Rome continuing the history of Tacitus from AD 69 to his own day. The first thirteen books have been lost; the remainder cover the years AD 354–378.

Arrian (c. AD 85– after 145). Flavian Arrianus, a Greek historian and philosopher, born at Nicomedia in Bythinia, followed a successful career in the Roman army probably serving in Gaul and on the Danube frontier. He wrote books on military and civil customs and philosophy.

Aristotle (384–322 BC). A Greek philosopher who taught in Athens at the Academy. His works cover every branch of philosophy and science known to his day and had a great influence on late antiquity and subsequent eras.

Caesar (100–44 BC). A Roman statesman, general and dictator. He subdued Gaul between 61 and 56 BC and invaded Britain twice in 55 and 54 BC. His *De Bello Gallico* (*Commentaries on the Gallic Wars*) is written in the third person to indicate his belief that this is an objective, truthful record of events.

Cato (234–149 BC). A Roman statesman and moralist. His literary works included *Origines*, a history of the origins of Rome and the Italian cities, together with the more recent Punic wars. His *De Re Rustica*, also known as

De Agri Cultura, is concerned mainly with the cultivation of fruits, olives and vines. He writes from his own experience and is mainly concerned with the practical necessities of running an estate.

Cicero (106–43 BC). A Roman statesman and orator, whose prolific writing include poems, letters and prosecution and defence speeches. His numerous letters include many to his friend Atticus. His political career includes the governorship of Cilicia.

Claudian (died AD 404). A Roman poet, one of the last to write in the classical tradition. He was a native Greek speaker who composed in Latin as a court poet to the Emperor Honorius. He wrote a eulogy of the emperor and a three-book panegyric of the general and regent, Stilicho.

Columella (active AD 60–65). A Spaniard, who served in the Roman army, he composed a treatise on farming, *De Re Rustica*. This covers all aspects of running an estate including livestock, cultivation, gardens and the duties of a bailiff and his wife.

Dio Cassius (c. AD 150–235). Also known as Cassius Dio. A Roman historian, born in Bithynia, and governor of Dalmatia and Africa. He wrote a history of the civil war, AD 193–97 (now lost) and a history of Rome in eighty books. This begins with the coming of Aeneas to Italy after the Sack of Troy and ends in AD 229. Much of the part after AD 9 has been lost, but what remains is useful, especially his contemporary comments on the third century.

Diodorus Siculus (active c.60–39 BC). A Greek historian who wrote a world history in forty books centred on Rome. These are based on ancient sources and are a useful, but uncritical, compilation of legends, social history and mythology. He was the first to write an herbal on the medical use of plants.

Dioscorides (First century AD). He was a Greek physician who served in the Roman army and was the author of *Materia Medica*, five books in which he described the medicinal properties of plants and drugs produced from minerals. In spite of its irrationalities, it remained the standard textbook on pharmacy for many centuries.

Frontinus (c. AD 30–c. AD 104). After serving as consul in AD 73 or 74, he was Governor of Britain 74–78. He wrote *Strategemata*, a manual on war strategies for the use of officers and *De Aquis Urbis Romae*, dealing with the history, technicalities and the regulation of the aqueducts of Rome.

Herodian (active c. AD 230). An historian, born in Syria, who wrote the *Historia Augusta,* a history in eight books from the death of Marcus Aurelius (AD 180) to the accession of Gordian III (AD 238).

Horace (65–8 BC). A Roman poet all of whose published work survives. The *Epodes* and the *Satires* were written about 30 BC and the *Odes* in 23 BC. He also wrote the *Epistles* and *Carmen Saeculare,* the latter dealing with the Secular Games of 17 BC.

Josephus (AD 37–after 93). A Jewish historian who wrote a history of the Jewish Revolt against Rome, which began in AD 66. The work contains one of the best descriptions of the Roman army.

Juvenal (active second century AD). He was probably the greatest of the Roman satirical poets, writing sixteen bitter, humorous *Satires* portraying life in second century Rome.

Livy (59 BC–AD 17). He was born in Padua and is the author of numerous dialogues and of a monumental history of Rome, *Ab Urbe Condita Libri* (*From the Beginning of the City*) in 142 books, the last 22 of which dealt with events in his own time. He was welcomed at the court of Augustus and is said to have advised the future emperor Claudius in history.

Lucan (AD 39–65) A Latin poet born at Cordoba in Spain, educated in Rome, who continued his studies at Athens. He was admitted to the circle of Nero who later, either because of Lucan's literary success or because he satirised the emperor, forced him to commit suicide. His sole surviving work is *Pharsalia.*

Martial (c. AD 40–103). A Spaniard who worked in Rome after AD 64 and relied on his poetry for a living. Between AD 86 and 98 he wrote eleven books of *Epigrams*, short poems, each of which pithily expressing a concept with the subject matter ranging across the whole spectrum of Roman life.

Ovid (43 BC– AD 14). He was born in the valley of the Apennines, east of Rome and travelled round the Mediterranean. His poetry aroused the displeasure of the Imperial court and he was banished to Tomis on the Black Sea. His main poems are the *Ars Amatoria, Tristia, Fasti* and *Metamorphoses.*

Petronius (died c. AD 69). A Roman satirical writer and author of the *Satyricon*, a novel of which the most well known part is Trimalchio's feast, an ostentatious dinner party to which a motley crowd gain admittance.

Pliny the Elder (AD 23/24–79). Born in Como, he was a naval and army commander and a personal friend of Vespasian. A prolific writer on natural history, his thirty-seven books cover most aspects of natural history, ranging through natural phenomena, medicine, botany, zoology, geography and minerals. His nephew records his death during the eruption of Vesuvius.

Pliny the Younger (AD 61–112). He was adopted by his maternal uncle, Pliny the Elder, and became an administrator, holding several offices of state, including that of Governor of Bithynia-Pontus on the Black Sea, where he died. He wrote a large number of letters, which cover a wide variety of subjects, personal and official.

Plutarch (c. AD 50–129). Mestrius Plutarchus of Chaeronea visited Athens, Egypt and Italy and eventually lectured at Rome. For thirty years he was a priest at Delphi. He wrote over 200 books including a group of rhetorical works, a series of dialogues, Roman questions and Greek questions dealing with religious antiquities. He also wrote *Parallel Lives* exemplifying the virtues and vices of famous men.

Pomponius Mela (First century AD). Born at Tingentera in Spain, he was the author of *De situ orbis* in three books, which describes national characteristics, scenery and natural phenomena in countries round the Mediterranean. His work is especially useful for describing the customs of a variety of tribes and organisations such as the Druids, which are not known elsewhere in literature.

Procopius (AD 500–after 562). A Byzantine-Greek historian and secretary to Belisarius, general to Justinian. His *History of the Wars of Justinian*, AD 527–553 is a clear and reliable account of these years and the main source of the first part of Justinian's reign.

Ptolemy (c. AD 90–c. AD 168). A Roman citizen, born in Egypt who was the author of seceral scientific, mathematical and astrological treatises. His *Geographica* is a compilation and detailed description of what was then known of the ancient world.

Seneca the Younger (c. 4 BC – AD 65). Roman politician, philosopher and dramatist, who was born at Corduba in Spain and came to Rome to study rhetoric and philosophy before setting out on a political career. He was chief advisor to Nero but in AD 65 was implicated in the conspiracy of Piso and forced to commit suicide. He wrote voluminously on many subjects including rhetoric and philosophy. His *Naturales Quaestiones* deal with natural phenomena. He also wrote twenty books of *Epistulae Morales ad Lucilium* , an artificial correspondence.

Scriptores Historia Augusta. A collection of biographies of later Roman emperors from Hadrian to Numerianus compiled by Casaubon, a Swiss scholar in the early seventeenth century, which are attributed to six authors including Aelius Lampridius. These may have been written at the end of the fourth century AD and their historical value is doubtful. Nevertheless they give details of the lives of the emperors, which would otherwise have been unknown.

Solinus (either mid-third century or mid-fourth century AD). A Roman compiler and author of *De Mirabilius Mundi* which described the ancient world and its curiosities. Much of it is based on the writings of Pliny the Elder and the first century AD Roman Geographer, Pomponius Mela.

Strabo (64–after 24 BC). A Greek geographer who came to Rome several times after in 44 BC and travelled widely round the Mediterranean. His seventeen books, the *Geography*, covers the chief provinces of the Roman world and other inhabited regions round the Mediterranean.

Suetonius (born c. 69 BC). He was a friend of Pliny who helped him to gain secretarial positions with Trajan and Hadrian. He wrote widely on antiquities and natural sciences, but the work that survives is his *Lives of the Caesars*, an account of Julius Caesar and the eleven subsequent emperors.

Tacitus (AD 56–c.117). Born in Gaul, he eventually became a Roman senator and Governor of Asia. He married Agricola's daughter and wrote a life of his father-in-law, published in AD 98, which gives a much-quoted description of Britain. In the same year he wrote the *Germania* dealing with the history and customs of the German tribes, north of the Rhine and the Danube. His major works, the *Histories,* dealing with the period AD 69–96, and the *Annals,* covering the period AD 14–68, are invaluable for the events in the first century AD.

Tertullian (c. AD 160–220). A Latin Christian writer who was born in Carthage and trained as a lawyer. He converted to Christianity about AD 195 and then devoted himself to Christian writings, including defending the Church against charges of atheism and magic.

Valerius Maximus (early first century AD). A Roman historian who accompanied Sextus Pomponius, the younger son of Pompey, to Asia in AD 27. On his return he wrote nine books of historical examples illustrating moral and philosophical points mainly drawn from Cicero and Livy.

Varro (116–27 BC). A prolific writer who is said to have written over 600 books. Of these, probably the most important were *De Lingua Latina,* a treatise on Latin grammar, and *De Re Rustica*, in three books, which was intended as a practical manual of running a farm for the benefit of his wife, Fundania.

Vegetius (active c. AD 379–395). A military writer who wrote a manual, *Epitoma Rei Militaris,* on military training and the organisation of the Roman Legion. He also wrote a book on veterinary medicine.

Vergil (70–19 BC). A Roman poet born in Cisalpine Gaul, who studied philosophy in Rome. About 42 BC he began the composition of the *Eclogues* while he was living in the Campania. This was followed by the *Georgics* and the *Aeneid*. After his death he was regarded as one of the greatest of the Latin poets and his works and his tomb, outside Naples, became the objects of a cult.

Vitruvius (first century BC). A Roman engineer and architect who saw military service under Julius Caesar. His treatise in ten books, *De Architectura* (*On Architecture*) covering civil, military and domestic architecture, building materials, interior decoration, water supplies and the qualifications for architects was compiled from his own experience and from works of other architects. It achieved immense importance during the Renaissance.

Zosimus (late fifth century AD). A Greek historian who wrote a history of the Roman Empire from Augustus to AD 410). He is an important source for the years AD 395–410.

INDEX

Page numbers in *italic* refer to maps and illustrations